Maps to the Other Side

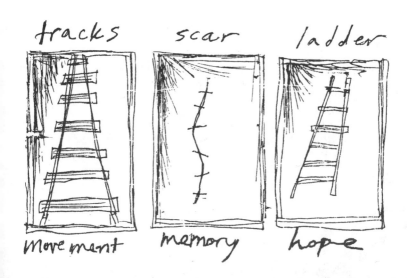

tracks   scar   ladder

movement   memory   hope

Maps to the Other Side
The Adventures of a Bipolar Cartographer
Sascha Altman DuBrul

First published March 31, 2013
First printing of 3,000 copies

Distributed by IPG (Chicago) and Turnaround (UK)

Microcosm Publishing
636 SE 11th Ave.
Portland, OR 97214
www.microcosmpublishing.com

ISBN 978-0-9788665-0-1
This is Microcosm #76141

Developmental Editing by Joe Biel, Adam Gnade, Nicole Lynch, and Lauren Hage
Designed by Joe Biel
Cover by David Nishizaki

The images in this book are owned by the original artists:
Dalia Shevin (title page)   Sascha Altman DuBrul (P.91)
David Nishizaki (P.10)   Fly (P.106)
Jacks McNamara (P.11)   Text by China Martins, Design by Jonah Ellis (P.112)
Eric Drooker (P.12)   Sophie Crumb (P.114)
Cristy Road (P.25)   Becky Cloonan (P.133)
Direct Action Network (P.42)   Sarah Quinter (P.162)
Trish Tripp BASIL Logo (P.4)   Tatiana Makovkin (P.177)
Sarah Quinter (P.60)   Kevin Capliki (P.189)
Becky Cloonan (P.62)

Interview on page 169 by Al Burian

Maps to the Other Side

Sascha Altman DuBrul

INTRODUCTION
Making Maps to the Other Side

Look into my eyes and I'll tell you a story about this kid who got lost wandering the train tracks in outer space, made his way back by leaving a trail of candy wrappers and love letters and one day he woke up and was right back where he started. "I had the strangest dream, Auntie Em. I was wandering the streets mad and kissed beautiful women and walked through warzones and swam in waterfalls and created a new language with my friends and felt the entire city breathing in my fucked up lungs. I wrote a book about it in the future so I could go back and change the past and then I met myself in the mirror and only recognized what was happening when he looked me square in the eyes and told me it was my responsibility to write the next chapter."

Welcome to the inside of my mind

The stories in this book are the personal maps through my jagged lands of brilliance and madness. They're mostly adventure stories—unapologetically wild and free and full of love for the underdogs, the marginalized and mad ones. They are personal stories—about the things that I love: traveling free, growing food, saving seeds and being a part of radical social and political movements. They are also stories about madness and manic-depression—visionary and grandiose and sometimes messy. I was 18 years old the first time I got locked up in the psych ward. Once I got out and put the pieces back together I was determined to live my dreams loud and proud. After I ended up in the psych system a couple more times I had the vision and inspiration to find others like me and build community to change the whole culture of mental health and illness.

Those of us who've been through the rough times and almost not made it out—whether through failed suicides, near-death accidents, or psychotic breakdowns that land us in white padded rooms—we come out the other side with knowledge that can only be learned from living close to death. We understand things that other people don't about the tenuousness and preciousness of life, and we have the choice to make meaning from the horror we carry around with us. We find strands of wisdom waiting for us in the depths of our nightmares. We come out the other side with scars that stay with us through our lifetimes. And the scars become part of the maps we use to guide us along our paths.

If I want to get through this mad life I've realized I have to make tangible maps for myself. I make them in my journals, I write them in the stories I share with friends, I use words and metaphors and parables, and sometimes very concrete reminders that help me stay on the path. *Remember to breath into your belly. Remember to sleep for 8 hours tonight. Remember you are part of a movement much larger than yourself.* Over the years I've learned to chart my dips and peaks, learned to cultivate the grounding I need to come back to center, learned to pick myself up out of the depths and rope myself back in when I'm flying too high. I leave clues for myself in the darkness. Some of them are obvious and clear as day and some of them are written in code, only decipherable when I'm in the head states that need to hear them.

The contours of my internal terrain are complex and serrated, carved from a life of adventure and pain and deep determination to make sense of it all. To build bridges with others like me so we feel less alienated and alone. I have scars from climbing over barbed wire fences between the borders of depression and mania and getting my heart broken and patching it back together with pieces from the sea and the land and the sky. My inner landscape is full of canyons and rivers and makeshift dams. Pleasure and trauma cut grooves into my soil like new streams during flashfloods. I build stone walls to control my emotions and inevitably they grow old and obsolete, like monuments to old fears, leaving me with puzzles of how to dismantle them. My internal landscape is sometimes like an unstable government with shifting borders—young, nervous men with guns waiting along chain-link fences and bandits waiting to rob me in the shadows. I wait till nightfall to make the long journey through the desert of my mind. In this story I'm telling you I'm the illegal aliens *and* the border patrol. I police myself the way I was taught.

•   •   •

Let's get this clear—even though I use the word "bipolar" in the title of this book, I don't believe in the biomedical model of mental illness. I don't think I have a "disease" or a "disorder." I think bio-psychiatry is just one of many stories we can choose to tell ourselves and there is nothing sacred or solid about it. The modern psychiatric labels locate the problem within individuals, and in trying to fix us can be more about maintaining the current economic system than about helping us understand ourselves. The disease model is the story that currently dominates and erases so many other important stories. I believe in the power of people's stories, and in the power of language, metaphor, and collective narratives. I have come to believe that one of the keys to our larger political struggles lies in our ability to own and rewrite our personal stories.

So with that in mind, here's what I want you to know before we go on this journey together:

I was born a sensitive kid and raised by parents who hated each other and fought over me like two superpowers would fight over a tiny island in the ocean. By the time I was three and my mom left my dad, everything about my life was split in half, like separate worlds with a huge border in between. Growing up I was shuttled back and forth between them but I never had a place that felt like home or a place inside myself that I could trust.

One of my earliest memories involves screaming at the top of my lungs and slamming my head against a wall over and over again till I collapsed in pain on the floor in the hallway outside my dad's apartment. I was probably 3 years old. I was so full of rage and I had no idea how to channel it. It was like I had a war inside of my little body and I would periodically erupt into volcanic tantrums.

From about age 8 until 13, I watched my father die slowly and painfully in front of my eyes, hooked up to machines and withering away in physical and emotional agony. My father was a visionary man, and I loved him deeply. The trauma of watching him die like that left me with an incredibly broken heart and a kind of psychic pain so great it could cut holes in the fabric of the reality around me. No one taught me how to mourn in any way that made sense. I carried his angry ghost, along with the parental cold war I inherited, everywhere I went.

When I was a teenager I was so grateful to find the punks and the anarchists because I don't know who else would have been able to understand me or hold my rage and frustration at all the injustices I felt underneath my skin. I was raised by people with a leftist political consciousness who taught me it was my responsibility to fight oppression and work for peace, so my anger got directed at people in power and big corporations, not at everyone else around me. I was lucky to find a community of freaks and rebels like me, people who weren't afraid to share their strong emotions and channel their intensity into creativity and visions of a new world.

I poured my 20s into creative political projects and living as full of a life as possible. I had a hard time in school, and despite all the social and familial pressure, dropping out of college was the best decision I ever could have made at 19. I rode freight trains and hitchhiked across the country multiple times. I lived in Mexico and Central America with rebel communities fighting the takeover of their lands and cultures. I learned how to work with my body and I learned how to grow food on community farms. I built seed libraries and urban gardens with my friends. I fought in the streets with tens of thousands of others to protect the global commons. And I kept a detailed journal of my travels and adventures. My coping mechanism in those years was that I'd pretend that everyone I knew was reading my words as I wrote them—that my life was important—and I was a character in an epic love story about the fate of the world.

This was a few years before the internet existed as a popular tool of communication, before the rise of social networking sites and blogs. Back in those days I wrote zines (short for maga*zines* and pronounced the same way)—self-published, photocopied stories that were circulated by other travelers through our underground community. Most of the stories at the beginning of this book were originally written for my friends. Like collective love letters, they were my way of figuring out what I cared about and why, and were my desperate attempt to not feel alone and despondent in a world run by bandits and bullies. Knowing there were others out there who could relate to my thoughts was the most precious of lifelines. It was also a way of leaving a trail for myself, a record of my journey so I could go back and make some sense of it later on, have some witnesses to the inside of my thoughts and the wild sights seen through my eyes.

•   •   •

When I dramatically ended up in the psych ward a couple times again in my mid-20s, and then my lover and travel partner Sera committed suicide by jumping off a bridge, I started writing stories about it. I had a quarterly column in a punk magazine called *Slug and Lettuce*. Printed on cheap newsprint and laid out in tiny 8pt font, *Slug and Lettuce* was distributed to punks as far away as Romania, the Philippines, and Brazil. It also went all over the prisons in the U.S. It was an institution in my community and it was an honor to be one of the regular featured voices. My column was supposed to be a "gardening column," but as it happened, I started writing about madness and mental health. I started getting a lot of mail. There were so many people in the punk community struggling with mental health issues and not having comfortable language to describe what they were going through. Then I wrote a cover story for the *San Francisco Bay Guardian Lit Magazine* called *The Bipolar World* and I really got a lot of mail. I also learned an important lesson which has served me well over the years—when you are brave—or crazy—enough to bare your soul to strangers, inevitably a bunch of them will feel compelled to bare their souls back to you. One of those strangers was Jacks Ashley McNamara, a 22 year old queer art student whose personal stories of madness rivaled mine in intensity and outlandishness. The night we met in person we stayed up till the sun was rising, sharing everything about our lives and manically decided to start a website called The Icarus Project. Named after the boy in Greek mythology who is given wings and flies too close to the sun, we saw the myth of Icarus as capturing the vision we had of our own experiences; rather than seeing ourselves as "mentally ill," we saw ourselves as having "dangerous gifts," like having wings made out of wax and feathers, that could get us into a lot of trouble but allowed us to fly! We decided to create a place for people like us who had been in the psych system or just didn't fit into society and wanted to create a new one.

Quickly, my maps started to change. The internet, and the Icarus Project discussion forums in particular, ended up having a big impact on my conception of myself in relation to community. Suddenly a lot more people were reading and responding to my writings than I could have imagined. Jacks and I were crossing paths with so many others with similar ideas, and ours became two in a chorus of voices calling for change in the mental health system—we wanted to rewrite the whole story of how we talked about ourselves and how others talked about us. Jacks and I self-published *Navigating the Space Between Brilliance and Madness: A Reader and Roadmap of Bipolar Worlds*. It was filled with beautiful art and the voices of people in our growing community.

As the Icarus Project expanded its scope, more folks began gathering face to face, and sharing the ideas with ever-larger numbers of people. We facilitated workshops all over the country. We got a decent-sized grant and partnered with a well-respected organization that gave us an office in Manhattan. Jacks and I started a collective farm with a crew of our friends in the Hudson Valley of New York and raised goats and grew vegetables. I would come into the city every week and work on the Icarus Project from our office. We discovered a model that some wise people had created for making personal and practical maps to share with friends and loved ones in the event of crisis, and the Icarus online community started embracing the vision of creating "Wellness Maps" or "Mad Maps." We started writing and experimenting with these personal maps, documents of how to take better care of one another, how to identify when one of us was having a hard time, and being clear about the tangible steps for what to do in the event of a crisis. We had a vision of creating a new model of community where those who struggle with extreme states of consciousness could be embraced. Through developing our skills and reckoning with our shared experiences we could create vibrant community support networks.

All the beautifully written maps and visions of resilient community didn't keep me from ending up back in the story I tried to leave behind. When I was 33, I dramatically ended up in a psych hospital after years of thinking I would never again be in a locked ward as a patient. It was so ironic—a month earlier I had been lecturing to a room full of psychiatrists at the same hospital. When the police brought me there in hand cuffs, the same psychiatrists filled out my paperwork and ran the daily meetings for my unit. Once again my world came crashing down around me. It became clear that my internal heroic narrative, the story that helped me climb depression's walls and escape through holes in psychic fences, the one that had made me feel like I was living in a grand love story about the fate of the world…it wasn't going to help anymore. It had outlived its usefulness in the current incarnation. I needed a new relationship with it.

So I dropped everything—all my projects and responsibilities and a bunch of my relationships (many of which had been falling apart anyway in the months leading up to my breakdown), and I went to live in a yoga ashram. It was an unlikely move for an old punk and anarchist—but probably the best decision I could have made. I developed a regular meditation practice for the first time in my life. I had the experience of living in a spiritual community that taught me important lessons about the power of group practice and worship. I learned how to talk about God and grace and spirit—things left out of my secular upbringing, but not unfamiliar considering my many brushes with altered states of consciousness over the years. I got my yoga teacher's certification and a lot of experience teaching yoga classes. And then, by the time I was healthy and strong, I grew so sick of being around people who weren't using their critical thinking skills that I decided to go back to college.

After the ashram I moved back to the Bay Area and got work as a gardener. At 37 I finished my bachelor's degree. In the course of my studies I thought about and articulated the lessons I'd learned from my years traveling and organizing. I studied the history of political and social movements that came before us and the healing modalities that nearly died out in the 80s, buried under the rise of bio-psychiatry and neo-liberalism. I got wrapped up in the rise of the Occupy movement and realized the importance of having mentors and being a mentor myself. The Icarus Project celebrated its 10th anniversary and I reveled in living so long, watching a bunch of my friends die, grow up and have kids, and do totally amazing things with their lives. I got inspired to develop a vision for collective map making that I'm still working on which involves popular education, spiritual practice, and social justice.

•   •   •

So these are stories and essays I wrote for my friends and community over almost two decades. I write these stories for myself as much as anybody else. Sometimes they are my escape hatches. Sometimes they are safety nets. Sometimes they are reminders of promises to myself or trails I left to pass on or pick up later. I think of these words like the golden thread of Theseus, the guy in Greek mythology that had to make his way through the labyrinth and left a trail so he could find his way in the darkness. These stories are my golden thread through epically crazy times. They hold ghosts of dead friends to keep them alive in our collective memory. They hold metaphors and maps we can bring with us into the future. They are my outlandishly flaming, heroic narrative that spectacularly crashes into itself and has to come up with a better, more self-aware and mature story.

I wove these words together to reach into the void and touch you, dear reader, in the hopes that they will wake up something inside of you that feels familiar and old and in need of companionship and inspiration. I want more of us to be empowered to tell our personal stories of brilliance and madness and reweave the cultural fabric of what gets labeled mental health and mental illness. My greatest wish is that these maps will inspire you to make maps of your own, and that you share them with the ones you hold dear. May our collective stories rethread the tired, old, lonely narratives and build a better future for us and the ones after us.

Mad love in mad times
Sascha Altman DuBrul

Part I - Golden Thread

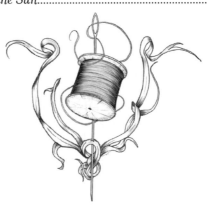

PART II - Wax and Feathers

PART III - Bipolar Cartography

PART

Golden Thread

JUAN CARLOS' GRANDFATHER

Juan Carlos' grandfather had fought in the Mexican Revolution, and as our boxcar swayed back and forth, the rumbling sound of the train grinding along track like the ocean or the rain coming down hard, Juan Carlos told me stories his grandfather had told him of Emiliano Zapata's soldiers riding from town to town on the same freight lines, gathering troops, spreading the word and supplies. He spoke of the peasant uprisings and fought against the *Federales* with the battle cry of land and liberty, the re-appropriation of land from the wealthy *haciendas* by the poor armies, the traditional indigenous *ejido* system of communal land ownership, and visionaries like Ricardo Flores Magón[1] who dreamed of a future free from the tyranny of corrupt leaders and brutal authority.

It was nearly a century later, in post-NAFTA[2] Mexico that the two of us rode on a north-bound freight train filled with desperate men fleeing the poverty of their hometowns, risking their lives to make the long journey to the border of the U.S. As the creaky old train carried us through small *pueblos* with thatched roof houses and corn fields, we stared into the hot sun and made a pact of eternal friendship, swearing that we'd spend the rest of our lives fighting for justice and breaking down walls put up by our governments and the societies that had raised us.

Juan Carlos was from the state of Aguascalientes and was a fiery young anarchist punk on his way north to find work in a hotel and send money to his seven brothers and sisters. I was a gringo from New York City, traveling alone and slowly making my way back after working as a human rights observer in the Lacandon Jungle in Chiapas with the *Zapatistas*. We'd met at the anarchist library in Mexico City and traded good stories and the T-shirts off each others' backs. After half a year of traveling and working volunteer jobs down in rural areas, I was suddenly back in the city, the fast paced slang-filled *chilango* Spanish much more akin to my native urban tongue, full of swears and cuss words. There was a whole crew of punks from Guadalajara that Juan Carlos had hooked up with, and they were leaving that night to head home after a weekend of playing a big show with their band. We traveled together up north on passenger trains as Juan Carlos and his friend rode freight, and we all met up in a punk house on the outskirts of Guadalajara a couple days later.

Just like most of my anarchist friends back home, I'd ridden a few freight trains in the U.S. I knew how to dodge a bull and read a train map and use a crew-change guide. I knew how to get on and off a moving hopper car or

---

1   Magón's ideas, which united into one creed the ideas of anarchism and indigenous communalism, had great influence among workers and peasants who heard of them through the *Magónista* periodical *RegeneracoXn* published during the Mexican Revolution. Magón died in Leavenworth Prison in Kansas in 1920 after being sentenced to twenty years under the U.S. espionage act.

2   When the North American Free Trade Agreement (NAFTA) was passed in 1994 the *Zapatista* army called it a death sentence for Indians, a gift to the rich that would deepen the divide between narrowly concentrated wealth and mass misery. As with most international trade agreements, the idea was that corporate capital could move freely across the border while workers, communities, and the environment would suffer the consequences of unchecked free trade.

48 well, hoist myself onto an open boxcar, hide between strings of track and tell which trains to ride by the number of units and what cargo they carried. I'd heard a few stories about the freight trains in Mexico and how dangerous they were, how they were full of bandits and thieves ready to knife you for a dollar and leave you dying in the desert sun. When Juan Carlos offered to take me on the freight lines in Mexico, I had no idea what I was getting myself into and how the short trip would change the course of my life forever.

It was a magical ride. After a loud and beautiful farewell party from the crew of punks, the two of us caught a train of empty boxcars out of the yard in Guadalajara and rode it up the coast to Mázatlan. By the time we had passed through all the yards. The train was full of people; it took us two nights and a day. The car we rode was full of corn scraps and as the train sped along the track, Juan Carlos and I threw handfuls of the grain off the sides on to the earth around us, laughing and singing to each other about sowing the seeds of the revolution. It was the middle of spring, and when our train sided amidst acres of mango orchards, hundreds of us jumped off the train and filled our pockets with handfuls of the huge red and green fruits. At night we watched shooting stars from the door of the boxcar and during the day we watched the huge jagged mountains fly by in the distance.

Unlike the trains back home, where the sight of another tramp was rare if ever, the freights in Mexico were literally covered in riders. Our boxcar was filled with people, all men, all full of stories of hardship and suffering. Some had made the journey before. For some it was their first time. All of them carried few or no possessions and all of them had dreams of life on the other side of the border. They called themselves *las trampas* and when they spoke of the U.S., they always called it *El Otro Lado*, literally, The Other Side. The men on the boxcar next to us were from Tegucigalpa, Honduras, and each of them had money saved to pay to the men who were known as *coyotes* to guide them across the border. There was a Salvadorian family two cars down, a thick-mustached man, his wife, and two little children who would smile at me when I passed. Everyone was friendly to me, the only gringo on the train. They asked lots of questions about the Zapatistas and my travels and treated me like a brother.

After a day and a half on the train, I started to have an intense realization—riding freight trains south of the U.S. border was like the accounts I'd read of riding during the Great Depression in the U.S. It was straight out of a John Steinbeck novel except it was Mexico in the 1990s. After a day and a half on the train, listening to people's stories, having time to reflect on the months I'd spent in Guatemala and Chiapas, as the mountains and towns blew by the door of the boxcar, I started thinking about the inevitability of revolution. I started to think about how so many of the people who have been fucked over by the U.S. and their own nationals in league with American business, left without recourse, slowly but surely make the journey across the border solely for survival. I started to realize that the men I was traveling with were refugees fleeing the wasteland that had been created by the economic equivalent of a scorched earth policy throughout Mexico and Central America. Everyone waiting at the militarized border were desperately trying to get a tiny piece of the riches horded in the U.S. If these people couldn't be confined to urban slums, they'd surely end up in prison or dead. A geographical divide cannot sustain the wealth disparity for long. I shivered in the warm, tropical air.

I crossed the border in Tijuana a few weeks later, scruffy and broke. My Zapatista literature and photos had been confiscated back in Mázatlan by the *Federales*, but all I had to do was flash my passport and I didn't get a second look by the immigration police.

When I returned to the Bay Area, I rode freight trains with a crew of friends to Active Resistance, the anarchist gathering in Chicago. During those summer travels, waiting in the hobo jungles and on the edge of yards and in the towns along the train line, I began to notice that most people I came across on freight trains were from Mexico and Central America. I recognized Spanish graffiti under train bridges and on the trains, calling out hometowns and Central American countries with scrawled grease sticks.

I became obsessed. Back in New York, after a friend taught me to use the internet, I began to look up articles and press releases from the U.S. rail companies. I found news articles on labor websites about modern day Mexican train robbers, poor peasants who would put rocks on the tracks and rob the trains for corn and sugar as they passed through their towns. And it wasn't an isolated incident I read about—it was happening all over Mexico, from Durango to Veracruz to Gómez Palacio.

At the same time, along with everything else in Mexico in the post-NAFTA economy, the Mexican railway was being privatized and sold to U.S. corporations. I started to see a pattern. As rail lines in Mexico were consolidated into U.S. conglomerates, and the country became evermore impoverished, the people lost respect for the system. The railroads in Mexico had been an icon of nationalism since the revolution. It interconnected the different rural areas. It was the way that low-income people got around. The freight lines were thought of as fourth-class travel, a necessary social service for the poor and destitute. The global economy was robbing them of their only means of transportation.

After living in Oakland for the winter, I spent spring and summer riding trains up and down the West Coast, working in the day-labor spots with immigrants and sleeping in missions and hobo camps, writing stories about the men I met and the life and struggle on the road. I had a plan to write exciting travel stories to educate people about the global economy and give voice to this population. My plan was to cross to the other side of the border and ride freight to Tapachula, the industrial city in Chiapas on the border of Guatemala, where the train line ends and the journey to the U.S. for so many begins. I never made it.

I ended up in jail in Texas for stealing food. I ended up in love in California. I ended up living on a farm on a tiny island in British Columbia with my girlfriend. I was determined to learn how to grow my own food so I wouldn't be reliant on the agribusiness death machine for the rest of my life. I grew weary of carrying all my stuff in a backpack and dreaming of having a room of my own somewhere.

One of my struggles, as I traveled and wrote, was that I didn't know why I was doing it. Who was I writing to? Why was I writing at all? After writing zines for my friends and dreaming of being a writer like my father, I thought this was going to be my first big story that would launch me on my career as an up-and-coming journalist. But my days along the Texas-Mexican border convinced me that the world was too fucked up for another gabacho travel writer trying to pass through Mexican people's lives and pitch self-indulgent stories to U.S. leftist weeklies. I was sick of being an outsider and I was sick of being so lonely.

The traditional path for someone from my economic class and culture would have been to go to college and get a job with the Peace Corps or a non-governmental organization working for justice. To use my white skin privilege and education to make the world a better place in a socially conventional way, to have a comfortable and stable life. But I just never fit into the place that I came from. Some part of me carried around the feeling of a perpetual underdog. Something about my temperament led me to the world of the anarchists, who taught me about the difference between charity and mutual aid, about finding my allegiance with people's movements rather than the governments or big organizations that claim to represent them.

Underground Tradition

Once upon a time I had this cool girlfriend who taught me how to ride freight trains. We practiced getting on and off boxcars and grainer ladders together in a switch yard in West Philadelphia. We had met in the summer under the big Texas sky and traveled with friends to the West Coast, packed into a van full of carnival dreams of revolution. We caught a hotshot out of Roseville, California, in the middle of the summer and rode it up through the Cascade Mountain range through the thick, lush forest land of Southern Oregon. I was hooked. Something alchemical happened to me during those summer travels. I got a taste of freedom and never wanted to turn back.

The railroads were the first corporations in the U.S. who monopolized transportation and transit. Before highways and cars outnumbered people 11 to 1, trains were a way of traveling the country and moving goods. Now trains are a relic from a period of history; a reminder of how things once were, with lessons to teach us—if we listen to their stories.

We can learn so much about this country by looking at the rise and the fall of railroads, reading the stories in the names of the old rail companies painted on the sides of cars and the years on the steel bridges spanning across rivers. The trains can be read like memoirs and unbiased history texts; robber barons who ransacked the public good to make their fortunes, pillaging of Indian lands, the boom and bust of train towns, sweat and blood of thousands of immigrant workers who died laying track, migration west in search of fortune and the acquisition of new territory after the Mexican war, industrialization and growth of cities, the appearance of national rather than regional markets, and the development of the modern interdependent American economy and culture.

But like the Chinese rail laborers excluded from the photos of white men in suits celebrating the opening of the Union Pacific's transcontinental railroad in 1869, there is a social and economic history that is not taught in school or documented in our history texts. While luxurious passenger trains brought the wealthy from one side of the country to the other there was a hidden class of passengers whose story is rarely told. While wealthy speculators and small businessmen rode on seats with room to stretch their legs, relax their arms, and were fed culinary delicacies by waiters in uniform, hordes of poor and displaced people rode freight trains. They were hobos and tramps, economic outcasts of society who lived on the social fringe in the jungle camps at the edge of train yards. These two stories transpired simultaneously, but only the first was widely narrated.

The common thread of war and work throughout history is the story of the poor doing the work of the rich. The first hobos were lost armies of Civil War veterans looking for work, traveling on the newly completed iron network of tracks built during the wartime economic boom. No one seems to know for sure, but the term *hoe boy* is reputed to be the name given to guys who would travel with their possessions tied up on the stick of their hoes, riding trains looking for farm work on the plantations of the wealthy.

The hobo's ranks grew as the U.S. began industrializing on a mass scale in the middle of the 19th century. New machines displaced workers from iron, coal, printing, glass, shoe factories, and flour-mills. The economy needed a growing workforce that could follow the new industries created at greater distances. They found work at the railroad construction sites, in the mines, in the timberlands, on the sheep and cattle ranches, in the grain belt, and in the orchards. The wandering mass of homeless men traveling by railroad was an important source of labor that fueled industrial expansion. The drive of American industry westward opened these new kinds of jobs—jobs remote from family and communal life. The labor was irregular, in scattered and often isolated areas, and the men who answered the call to work had to be mobile and adaptable.

When the Great Depression hit in the 1930s, hobos swelled into the millions as the search for work sent men and women out onto the rails. A thriving subculture emerged throughout the country with its own slang and symbols written on walls. Hobo colleges were setup by visionaries who dreamt of empowering and educating homeless travelers. The Industrial Workers of the World, an anarchist labor union, sent men all over the country on the trains in an attempt to organize itinerant workers with their dream of creating the "One Big Union."

But that was a long time ago. After World War II, massive public subsidy into the highways and airlines took a toll on the railroad industry. In the early 1970s, many lines went bankrupt and were saved by the federal government. The 1990s saw a huge consolidation in the railroad industry as corporate giants ate each other and tightened security. When I tell people that I ride freight trains, they laugh or get wide-eyed incredulous. They didn't realize people did that anymore.

When you travel the rails it's possible to get a different grasp of what's going on around the country. You see forest clear cuts, factories spewing towers of chemicals, barbed-wire lots of rusted-out cars—the backyard of capitalism away from highway rest stops. When you travel on the trains, you can talk to guys at the missions, the labor pools, and the hobo camps—the ones trying to float up to the thin layer of wealth like a thin layer of oil on water. The very thing that once had the power to unite the disenfranchised masses is a purgatory, straddling dreams of the past and a grave, impenetrable present.

And then, of course, there's me and my friends—the anarchists and the activists, the crusties and punks, riding to gatherings and radical communities and Earth First! camps. We do it because it's a free ride on The Man. We do it because it's pure adventure and adrenaline, sweet like sex, and as dirty and beautiful. My friends and I have this whole other map we read when we travel across the country—grainy and faded, it's a forgotten path, blazed long before those we are familiar with today. We have our underground networks of friends that pass information about catch out spots to each other, the crumpled crew-change sheets at the bottom of all our backpacks and the rail maps drawn in each others' journals.

Back when freight trains carried the major farming and mining products from big cities to work sites, hobos would ride the rods underneath the freight cars, in or on top of boxcars, on flatbeds and the big rectangular buckets called gondolas, or behind the cow catchers on the front of old steam engines. These days, the majority of the heavy stuff that is moved on train lines is coal, stone, gravel, sand, chemicals, corn syrup, grains, big industrial equipment, scrap metal, rebar, lumber, and new fresh cars from the factories. These days we still ride in boxcars, but have other tricks. We sneak into hopper cars, or what we call *grainers,* equipped with good hiding spots on either side. When it is cold out, or there are no other viable cars, we ride in the engines, or, "units," at the front of the trains. We hide in the tiny bathrooms when the engineers come through. Then, of course, there are the piggybacks or TOFC (Trailor on Flat Car) trains which haul containers that will be transferred from the rails to the ships or trucks. Those are the 48's and pig-trains that we call "hotshots"—fast trains with important cargo that speed their containers from port to port. They carry everything from television sets to boxes of green bananas to bottles of alcohol to computers. They also carry us in container wells or under the axles of truck wheels on flatbeds.

Other things have changed as well. Whereas the hobos of the old days would ride from town to town looking for work and begging for meals, making their way to big urban centers like Chicago to bum on the street, today we ride hotshots straight across the country—a result of the 1970 "land bridge" service that connects the east and the West Coasts to make trade easier between Europe and Asia. Those are the transcontinental trains from New Jersey to California or Seattle to Chicago, a product of the global economy. Whereas the hobos of yesteryear rode in the hundreds of thousands, today our ranks are fewer every year as stricter rules and corporate consolidation drive us onto the highways.

Riding trains isn't for most people. As my friend Okra once said. "Hopping on freight trains is a great way to get somewhere, especially if you don't mind getting there late or going somewhere else completely." You need time on your hands and good company or good books. I can't count the number of times I've been sitting in a train yard while 100 airplanes flew over me. But I'll be doing it as long as my legs can run. I love sneaking around train yards and hiding from the train police or, "bulls," piecing the situation together like a puzzle that needs solving, and with perpetually rising stakes.

Riding trains, there are no signs to tell you where you are. You have to seek out the clues on a license plate or billboard, a water tower or a famous monument. I like the blithe freedom, my head full of places and faces. I feel alive eating cans of beans by the moonlight. It keeps me sane in a world spinning out of control. The train humbles us and teaches us patience.

I share these stories with the hope that they will open your eyes and make you feel strong emotions, that they might project a moving image for you, and that they make you feel connected to my soul and the eyes I have seen through. I pass these stories along to you as a gift of friendship and in the hope that you will be sharing stories with me someday.

La Esquina

Ricardo is the first one who invites me to sit down. He's wearing a red, white, and green cap with the name of his home state *Michoacán* proudly emblazoned on the front in gold letters. He motions with his hand and makes room for me on the sidewalk. "There's work here every day. You just have to be patient. It'll come. Wait with us." There are five guys looking bleary eyed, staring out into the morning traffic, waiting patiently. We're on the corner of South Van Ness and Cesar Chavez; it's 8:30 in the morning in San Francisco. There are small groups of Latino men on every corner all down the avenue, waiting for work. The commuter traffic is speeding by, every pick-up truck that drives past loaded with construction supplies is longingly stared at by a long line of dark brown eyes.

Luis from Guanajuato says, "This is your first time? The church down the street has free coffee and bread every morning."

Just as he tells me this, a big old guy with the white beard and dark sunglasses comes bounding down the street, cursing loudly. "*La pinche iglesia!* The fucking' church! I slept there last night and now I got bugs! Look! Look at my arm! It's all red! I'm getting out of this country, I've had enough already! I'm going to Cuba! *Soy un socialista!* I'm a socialist!"

Everyone's staring at him, the first spectacle of the day. "You're crazy, man." Luis says matter of fact. "There's no food in Cuba. You'll starve."

The old man straightens his posture and says to Luis, "I don't care what you say. I'm going to Cuba. Cuba has *juevones* like this," He motions to his crotch and makes a big circular motion. "Castro is the only one to say *'Chinga a su madre'* to the U.S. Tell me—if the U.S. is so rich, then how come all these people are out here every day with nothing to do, waiting for work? If the U.S. is so rich, then how come I've been living out here for eight months and I'm dressed in rags and I have bugs and I'm out on the street? I'm going to Cuba! At least their government takes care of them. Every child can read and write—everyone has free medical care."

The old man has everyone's attention now. They're all staring at him in disbelief, not saying a word. Finally Luis retorts, " This *carbron* is loco, don't listen to him. You see those Cubanos around here, lazy bastards. None of them want to work. My friend went to Cuba and said the women stand out on the street corners and sell themselves for a pair of Levis. Stupid people. Listen to this guy talk about Cuba like it's the promised land!"

The old man takes off his dark sunglasses. And looks Luis right in the eyes. *"Hermano,* at least give me the benefit of the doubt. Look at my white hair, I'm a few years older than you. Listen to me, we need to unite." He clasps his fists together for emphasis. "The only way things will change is if we all get together and throw off the shackles of *capitalismo*—organize and take over the economy. You heed my words. *Ya me voy.* I'm going to the library." And with that dramatic exit, he disappeared down the block.

"That guy's been out on the street too long—he's gone mad." Says Hector from Mexico City. "Castro'll throw you in jail just as quick as here. It's no different over in Cuba." I just nod, trying to take this whole crazy scene in. I'm only two blocks away from my girlfriend's apartment in the Mission district but I already feel like I've stepped into another world. My excuse to myself and my friends is that I'm working on an article about the "underground economy" of Latino laborers in the U.S., but really I'm just curious and don't have a job. I see these guys out on the street every day and I always wonder what they're thinking about. What their take is on life from the bottom of the economy, waiting to get picked up in the labor pool. It's the middle of the summer and I've been doing this all over the West Coast for a couple months now—hanging out on the street corners with the guys and getting picked up for work, making $7 or $8 dollars an hour doing demolition or roofing, sometimes garden work up in the hills, or moving furniture. It's always a gamble where I'm going to end up but we always get paid in cash off the books and I've been having pretty good luck. Considering my white skin and slick English and citizenship papers, I could probably be working some well paying job in an office somewhere, but I can't stomach the idea. Besides, I don't mind being broke half the time and I always meet the most incredible people while I'm waiting on *la esquina*.

The guys I meet are from all over Mexico: Jalisco, Sinaloa, Oaxaca, Durango, Guanajuato, Michoacán, Zacatecas, sometimes even Central American countries like Guatemala, Honduras, and El Salvador. They're from places that aren't so far geographically but feel like they're on the other side of the planet. Places where the average daily wage usually comes out to about $5 a day. They're here in the pioneering tradition of people coming from poorer countries searching for a better life in our land of resources and prosperity. Unfortunately, while corporations from our country have free reign to exploit the cheap labor on the other side of the border, these men without papers don't have any rights at all—they're constantly risking deportation and exploitation everywhere they turn. Every one of these guys is carrying around a story about risking his life by sneaking over the border and making his way up the coast to find work, evading the immigration police, and trying to stay out of trouble— learning to survive in a country with a whole new language and culture. While we can travel freely in their land, spending our dollars, when they come here they're "illegal aliens." If I was on the other side of the border I have a feeling I'd be doing the same thing these guys are doing. You might too.

"Where's your family from anyway?" Hector asks me after I've been asking a bunch of questions and scribbling down notes in my journal. "My folks? New York City. But their families were from Greece and Ireland and Canadians from France." I'm a bunch of different stuff." I tell him. He laughs, "See, you're not really from here either. We're all immigrants around these parts. We're all *mestizos*. We're all mixed up. You're a *mestizo, también*. The only ones who are really from here are the *indios. Los Yaquis del desierto.*" He motions a mohawk with his hands. "We're all foreigners around here. But we're all equal, in God's eyes at least." I agree. "Some guys, they don't like the Blacks. But what they don't remember is that their families were brought here as slaves from Africa. Now we're the slaves, us guys out here on the streets—la Raza. We do all the work no one else wants to do. We're the ones building the houses and working in the gardens. The Blacks all get welfare, but look at us; out on the streets. *Pero todo somos iguales en los ojos del Dios.*"

Marcod from Tijuana was checking out the tattoo of a barcode on my arm. "What's that for?" he wanted to know.

It's kind of a *broma*, a joke." I said. "It's dark humor, like we're all products. Like in the supermarket."

He smiled but looked serious. "Oh, I see. They say all you Gringos are gonna have your social security numbers tattooed on your hands sometime in the future. I believe it. I'm not stupid. I know what's going on."

"*Hijo de la chingada!*" They want us all to carry papers or they'll take us to jail." Ricardo piped in. "I was walking down the street one day and this cop asked me, "You got papers?" And you know what I told him? "Yeah, I got papers. *Tengo un chingo.*" And I pulled a bunch of napkins out of my back pocket. Everyone cracked up laughing.

"We don't go up to Oakland to work because they say *la migra* busts guys out on the street there." Mario from Zacatecas told me. "Here in the Mission they leave us alone. This is my seventh time staying here—*my barrio*—*El Mission*. People take care of each other out here."

Ricardo leaned in next to me and confided, "Yeah, it's alright here, but I've been here four months already. I'm gonna catch a train up to Seattle soon and find my friends. I gotta lotta friends in Seattle. I head up to Washington to work in the fields every year. I pick apples. It's hard work but you can work all day—not like here where we're waiting around for some guy in a truck. You can work seven days if you want, 15-16 hour days, maybe make six hundred bucks. It's alright out there in the fields. There's women there too, working right next to you." I looked up and down the street and realized there were no women anywhere.

"Where I'm from in Tijuana there's a lot of factories where they make electronics. All the women work there, but they only make 40 bucks a week." Marcos said. "You can't do that factory work for more than a couple years without your eyes going bad. Those companies don't care at all. They're all from here and Japan. My sister worked in one of those factories. That's shitty work, man. You make more in one day here than they make in a week. They work like *esclavos*, like fucking slaves.

After not seeing a woman for what seemed like hours, finally a middle-aged woman wearing hoop earrings and an old flower patterned dress appeared from down the street and approached us on the corner. She handed us all little scraps of torn paper with a number and an address on each one. "$350 a month for a room in our house, it's just up the street." She said, hands on her hips. "If any of you fellows are interested."

Mario looked at her and said, "*Gracias Señora*, but that's way too expensive."

She frowned. "Oh, but it's a nice room, large enough for a couple. We give you a key. You can use the bathroom and the kitchen. It's a good price… these days." We all took the notes graciously and stuffed them in our pockets. She continued walking towards the next group of guys on the next corner.

"Man, times have changed in El Mission" said Ricardo shaking his head. "It never cost so much to live around here." He spit out into the street. "Lemme see the tattoo on your arm, man. The black cat? Nice. Check out mine." Ricardo rolled up his sleeve. "*The Haché*. It's a street in Los Angeles where I used to hang with my friends. And this here on my other arm, the three dots."

"What's that mean?" I asked

"That's the three dots, man. It stands for *mi vida loca*."

"*Mi vida loca*? What's that all about?" "*Mi vida loca*? That's life man. That's everything. That's all those trains you ride and your girl that lives down the street." He motioned to the oncoming traffic and the buildings. "That's all this shit out here, man. It's all the times I've been caught crossing the border and all the times I've been to jail. It's all my dead friends everywhere. It means I don't give a fuck and I'm crazy. That's *mi vida loca*."

Luis shook his head. "Don't listen to this guy. It just means he smokes too much of *la mota* and drinks too much of *la cerveza*. Ricardo grinned widely.

Sergio from Sinaloa came across the street and introduced himself to me. He was older than the rest of us, taller and stocky with a light brown goatee sticking out of his chin. "Yeah, I used to work up in el campo in Oregon. You know, picking cherries and apples. You used to be able to make good money up there. Sometimes I'd put in $900 a week, usually more like $700. But not anymore. Shit, that was a long time ago. Times have changed. It seems like since Cesar Chavez died things have gotten bad. The big companies run the show now even more and you have to bust your ass for half of what you made before. Now I have to come to the city and work construction to make any kind of money."

It seemed like a pretty bad day for work. I only saw two men get picked up for jobs the whole time, the rest of us just sat there talking shit and staring into traffic. I stuck around till the church bells started ringing at noon and then I said goodbye to everyone and started making my way back home. So many guys waiting for work all over the streets, old baseball caps shielding their eyes from the mid-day sun.

What's going to happen to these guys, I wondered? Everyone knows their cheap labor makes up a huge part of the economy and the government needs them to keep the system running smoothly. But if wealth is getting more consolidated and the border is getting tighter, they're building more prisons and making it harder to live in the city, what is this street going to look like in five years? Where will all these guys be?

Back on Folsom St., a huge CAT machine is knocking down the old Army Street housing projects, the sound of snapping plywood reverberating throughout the neighborhood. Out of the corner of my eye I glimpse a sink and a wall of cupboards up on the third floor, the exterior wall pulled clean off the foundation, the old kitchen uncovered like the room of a doll house, revealed just for a second before it's bathed in a sea of rubble and disappears from sight.

Sellout Story

I wrote this story when I was 22 years old and published it in a zine called The Secret Life of White People. *The title was an ironic poke at myself after spending a lot of time being a white guy writing stories about Mexicans. I decided to turn my gaze back on my own community and write about the experience coming of age in the punk scene in New York City. "Selling Out" was the first story I wrote that inspired a lot of interesting, self-reflective discussion. The act of writing it informed and nuanced the way I've chosen to live my life and hold my own identity in relationship to things like subculture and outsiderness. It was also my attempt to define the parameters of my community as everything was beginning to shift with the rise of the internet.*

When the Conquistadors invaded the shores of what was to become Latin America in 1504, the Roman Catholic Church, which controlled the majority of Spanish society, came along for the ride. They brought the fanaticism and patriarchy of Old World Europe and waged war against all the native civilizations that had walked the land previously, like the Aztecs and Mayans. In their ignorance, the foreigners declared war upon the old religions and burned thousands of ancient temples and books of spiritual knowledge. They forced the people to bow down to a new god and instituted a new class structure and semi-feudal society revolving around skin color and property ownership that we're still seeing miserable after-effects of five hundred years later. Incredibly, after an attempt at brutal and bloody genocide, the descendents of the Mayans still inhabit a good chunk of the area from the Yucatan Peninsula through almost all of what is today know as Guatemala and Belize. In the face of a rapidly homogenizing world, run by transnational corporations who do the best they can to export the vapid culture of their strip mall homeland to the furthest reaches of the planet, Mayans still speak their own languages and carry on the traditions and customs they've followed since before the Spaniards arrived on their shores. Although seemingly subjugated long ago, the Maya were smart enough to figure out ways to work within the system and give the appearance of total capitulation while holding on to pieces of their culture, adopting aspects of the new while holding on to what was important. If you visit their churches you'll see that they worship the white man's God. But everyone knows that their statues of Jesus have old Mayan idols hidden inside.

Selling Out

It was autumn and I'd been riding trains and hitchhiking through the Southeast. I was travel weary and I ended up at a friend's parent's house in Louisiana. One night I stayed up late writing and listening to the radio, flipping across the channels. There was this catchy song I kept hearing. It was all over the dial, one of those songs you inadvertently start humming days after you've heard it and only then realize it's been stuck in your head for the past week. The voices sounded familiar and I could have sworn it was this cool band I used to listen to a long time ago but I couldn't imagine why the big commercial stations would be playing their song next to all the other fluffy pop dance hits I'd been hearing in the background since the summertime. I was scribbling away, not paying much attention, when the radio announcer came on and said, "...and that was the latest smash hit from the U.K. pop combo Chumbawamba!"

I dropped my pen.

Do you remember 1985 when all those icons of rock got together and had that Live Aid concert to send money to the starving children of Ethiopia? It was a huge extravaganza with the big names of the time like Michael Jackson, Cindy Lauper, Sting, Boy George, Phil Collins, and Bono. It was in the same era as those videos for We Are the World. Do you remember that shit? Coked-out superstars holding hands in some music studio and singing about giving money to the poor? It's not just some figment of your twisted imagination. That happened. We all watched it on TV.

Or at least I watched it. I was in elementary school and after school we would go home and sit in front of our TV sets and watch this new and exciting thing called MTV—three minute, fast-speed, cut-up rock advertisements blended with watered-down images of sex and violence for the Pepsi generation. Like most kids my age, I'd stopped watching *Sesame Street* a couple years back, but this was basically the same—colorful puppets and bouncing alphabets replaced by supermodels and flashy guitars. I was your typical pre-teen. I sucked up all the garbage in front of me, from Def Leppard videos to Clearasil commercials. I ate up pop culture because it was what everyone did. I felt connected to the rest of the world.

I don't remember having many friends when I was growing up. I was awkward and I couldn't run fast, and all the cool boys in my school played softball. I got picked last when they were dividing up the teams. I remember the hot shame on my face, wishing I could disappear through the floorboards. I hated sports and competition. I was daydreaming in the back of the classroom. I got made fun of because it took me longer than the other kids in my class to learn how to spell and do basic math. Everything seemed so much harder for me than the people around me. There was something about me that never fit in, and I carried it around with me like a dark cloud.

But my imaginary playmates were TV show stars like Gary Coleman from *Diff'rent Strokes* and Ricky Schroeder from *Silver Spoons*, Mr. T from *The A-Team*. I'd come home after school and start watching TV and not turn it off until I went to sleep, the glow from the screen keeping me company from the 12th story of the apartment complex where we lived. It was the electronic babysitter standing in for my parents who were working late, my faithful playmate and pop culture tutor. My models for the relationships in my life came straight out of the relationships on TV. TV had this way of tugging on my insecurities and pre-adolescent, needful emotions. I developed big crushes on movie actresses and was lonely and depressed when I realized that I had no chance of knowing them in real life, and that they didn't exist anyway.

So, like I was saying, I remember when Live Aid happened because I was super excited. All the big pop stars were going to be together in the same place at the same time, and that meant more to me than anything that was happening in my real life. It'd been promoted for weeks in little clips in between music videos that warned viewers to be ready to watch it on TV all day. Of course when it happened it was a let down.

By junior high I'd gone to a few rock concerts. I'd win free tickets by calling up the local radio station until I was the lucky 95th caller and pledge my soul as a dedicated listener. But I'd always end up feeling distanced from the performers, like they were super human beings and I was just one of a million souls watching something that I'd had nothing to do with. It was this strange mix of contempt and admiration that would leave me feeling empty and sad. I looked up to the people on the stage but once again it was that feeling of them being so far away from my life that I wasn't sure they really existed. Not too long after that I became disillusioned with the pop culture I'd fed on all my life.

So many childhood memories have been glossed over with this thick layer of sitcoms and action show episodes, like so many memories aren't even my own, they're just some script someone wrote somewhere in Hollywood. I have trouble untangling what was real and what I watched on TV, the apartment I grew up in from all those cardboard living room sets, the nightly news and the war movies. I wonder how many of us have this bond with people our age because we grew up with the same dumb shit.

A couple years later I had a lot of friends because there were a lot of alienated, fucked up kids. There was one neighborhood we'd hang out in, and kids from all over the country would run away from home and come live in the abandoned buildings and hang out on the street. A lot of my friends had been through worse than I could have even thought up, their step-fathers had beaten or raped them, they'd been locked up and escaped from juvie or psych wards, they came from trailer parks and ghettos in middle America, and their families were drug addicts and psycho military people. My dad had just died, and my early teenage years were full of my own family trauma. But for the first time in my life I felt like I was accepted. I related to the punks. I learned what it was like to have a community who looked after each other.

So I stopped going to school and started hanging out in this place called Tompkins Square Park. The scene was a real mix of kids coming from out of town who were out on their own surviving, and kids like me who were still in high school and living at home but had fucked up or complicated lives to get away from. We were a tight knit group, us punks; we created a family together and built community out of the scraps and fragments of all our life experiences as alienated teenagers. It was us against the world.

I started to unlearn programming I'd been fed about social interaction and started to learn how to relate to people authentically. We had our own culture that strived to have nothing to do with the larger popular culture. Music was a big part of the scene we created. We'd put on our own shows and had our own spaces to play music. We had our own underground networks for distributing our demo tapes and little magazines with stories that poured out our souls to each other. There was a real emphasis, in those days, on creating a self-sufficient culture. Do It Yourself was the rallying cry for so many of us fed up with the over-processed, blood-soaked consumer culture and the vapid corporate madness we'd been raised with as children. Independent record labels popped up all over the place. Selling out the scene was a big part of the dialogue in those days. There was an album that came out in Europe called *Only Stupid Bastards Help EMI*. Major record labels were corporate conglomerates affiliated with arms contractors so there was a consciousness in keeping the music within the scene, not letting the profit slip into someone's pocket. Making money off your art was selling out to us. Our defiance of societal norms kept us feeling like a big family.

Everything was informal and down to earth. There were no managers or big labels. If there was a band from out of town that I liked I could write them a letter, and they would write me back inviting me to come sleep on their couch and give me a personal tour of their town. When I saw bands play at the squat shows and I danced in the pit with my friends, I felt like I was part of something, something that I'd helped to create that had nothing to do with mainstream society.

We eventually grew out of our alienation from society through a hyper-awareness of injustice in the world. Even if you were white, the cops treated you just as bad as the black kids if you were on the street, if you were dirty and punk.[3]

Everything looked ugly at fifteen, life was short and we were gonna die young. It was the tail end of the Cold War, and we'd been raised with the threat of nuclear annihilation present in the back of our minds. We hated society. And along with our hatred of society, we felt affinity with animals stronger than our feelings for humans—it was easier to feel emotions for imprisoned veal calves and cats with their heads cut open in vivisection laboratories than the people that were fighting wars against each other all over the planet. A lot of us didn't eat any animal products at all, and it can be pretty alienating to be a vegan in a meat culture—people become threatened. They think you're crazy.

My friends and I got tighter as we slipped outside the norms of society. We built our world underground with our codes of ethics that most people wouldn't be able to begin to understand, unless they hung out with us for a long time. Our fashion statements were for each other, the obscure band names on our T-shirts or the cryptic symbols on our canvas patches we used to hold our clothes together. We had community. We'd smash TVs and cook food in big groups, we'd hang out on the streets and play music and drink a lot. Some of us became more overtly political.

We hooked into older activist networks and started organizing in our schools and on the street. We got our inspiration from the Young Lords, who had a squatted community center on 9th street, a couple of old Black Panthers, and the aging Yippies, who would sit around smoking pot and telling stories about the good old days of guerrilla theater pranks. We'd have meetings in an old pacifist resource center in the neighborhood full of anti-nuclear activists. There were older housing activists and squatters floating around who'd opened the abandoned buildings in the late 70s and had years of experience building radical community and fighting the city.

In the late 80s New York City was a trip—for the first time since the 1930s there were homeless people everywhere, shanty towns in the middle of Manhattan island—the after effects of a housing crisis and Reagan cutting mental hospital funding and social services. The Lower East Side, our beautiful

---

3   Although it felt like I was being oppressed as bad as kids of color, I've come to realize that not only was I not, but that it's important to be real about the layers of white privilege I was carrying around that made me unaware of just how much oppression was going on around me. I was choosing the role of the oppressed in that dirty, spiked jacket. For many white kids, punk was an attempt at creating an ethnicity, a rejection of straight white culture, and embracing the otherness that our immigrant forbearers had faced, before their children "made it" as white people. There's a riddle in the way oppression brings people together, and as an alienated teenager from the dominant culture, I wanted a part of that togetherness. It was the only way I felt like I belonged. The problem with white kids trying to give up skin privilege is that we can't own up to how different the experience is for folks who have to deal with racism on a daily basis. I grew up in a multicultural New York City, and had a middle-class public school education where I was taught to be "color blind," leaving me with lots of privilege blind spots. Despite punk's creation of a space where kids from diverse backgrounds could come together, for many of us it was a way of not thinking about where we came from, and the ways our experiences were different.

         Punk, in it's rejection of history and tradition, both created a space where kids from diverse backgrounds could come together, but it also was a way of not having to think about where we came from, and the ways our life experiences were very different.

neighborhood, was going through a huge and complicated economic battle against the forces of gentrification. Everyone from the old Puerto Ricans and Ukrainians to the young artists and the anarchists were mixed up in it. There were riots in Tompkins Park over the tent city constructed by a small army of homeless people and their supporters. I watched friends get beat bloody over nothing in the middle of police riots. I threw my first brick at a cop and set my first barricade on fire in the middle of the street. I'd get arrested all the time in skirmishes with the police and my mom would freak out and think I was going to end up in Juvenile Hall. So much of our politics were reactionary—channeled adolescent anger fueling direct actions of our rage against society. But there truly was love and inspiration behind all that rage and anger. We had a vision of society where everyone was free and equal and had autonomy from the government.

Admittedly, as a young teenager in the middle of the city, it was hard to articulate sustainable models for alternative futures and practical ways to live cooperatively on large scales. But more important than our far off visions for a new society, we had community that stretched across the world—scenes of punks all over the country with similar ideas and styles, comrades we'd hear of in Europe who were battling Thatcher's reactionary government, the Poll Tax Riots, the thriving West German *Autonomen* scene with their romantic black blocs and whole occupied neighborhoods. We listened to old punk records that told our history, all shrouded in legends and mysteries but still more accessible and less alienating than whatever pop star crap that was playing on the radio.

Meanwhile, we had more fun than everyone else. We dyed our hair all different colors and wrote our opinions about the world on the backs of our jackets in spikes for everyone to see in crude slogans. We pulled off a subtle yet appealing mix of not giving a fuck but caring a whole lot at the same time. We didn't subscribe to the gender rules that everyone else seemed forced into about dating or the male/female binary concept of sex roles. For teenagers we were aware and conscious of sexism in our scene. For the first time in my life I started to meet girls I could relate to, girls who would school me in feminist theory and teach me how to make stencils, girls who didn't shave their legs and would throw bottles at cops when they were angry.

There was this great album we listened to, *Pictures of Starving Children Sell Records: Charity, Starvation, and Rock & Roll* by this cool U.K. punk band Chumbawamba. We used to hang out at Michelle and Isa Moskowitz's house and dance to it and cook big vegan feasts. It was this incredible critique of the corporate rock structure and the hypocrisy of the stars that profited off the image of caring about the poor. But it was so much more. It beautifully and simply articulated the destructive relationship between the rich nations and the developing world, the history of imperialism, the evils of apartheid, the corporate media and the rich families who perpetuated it all. It was like a punk rock opera.

From the first lines:
I'm the boss of the company—and I've got hunger working for me. Listen, and you'll begin to understand: I build my profits from stolen land. It's the economics of supply and demand. And I make the demands around here.

To the last lines of the album:
And the cycle of hungry children will keep on going round. Till we burn the multinationals to the ground.

I still get chills when I think about it. It wasn't like any other punk album—the distorted guitars, chaotic drum beats, and screaming vocals had been replaced by keyboards, drum machines, and melodic, intelligible lyrics. But it was obviously a punk album. We loved it and knew all the words. We joked that if we wanted anarchists to infiltrate mainstream society we'd get broadcasting Chumbawamba on the radio.

Eight years later my friends are scattered all over. We're doing a wide spectrum of things. There's a lot of us doing radical activism on one front or another—organizing protests and collectives, working with pirate radio and alternative media projects, traveling through the network of infoshops and radical houses around the country, cooking Food Not Bombs and bridging connections. Some are off doing eco-activism in the forests of the Pacific Northwest and Northern California, keeping the last of the old growth trees from getting clear-cut. Some of my friends do jail support with Prisoners Literature Project and send books and letters to incarcerated inmates all over the country. Some of my friends are in the jungle in Mexico working with the Zapatistas or doing solidarity work with Third World rebel movements back in our home towns. Some work in bicycle shops and teach kids how to build bikes or help organize Critical Mass rides that protest car culture. Some work in food co-ops and have studied herbal medicine and natural healing to help provide alternatives to the medical industry drug culture. The ones that stayed squatting the tenement buildings on the Lower East Side are now master carpenters, total alcoholics, or some twisted combination. My friends are the most creative people I've met and I'm lucky to know them. If you ask any of us about growing up on the Lower East Side we'll all talk about how influential and inspiring it was.

As for me, I stuck around the anarchist scene, nixed the punk thing with disgust in the mid-90s when things got ugly and Green Day ended up on the cover of Rolling Stone, but I've kept my roots and my friends and I still feel like I have a big community all over the place.

•　　　•　　　•

When I showed up in New Orleans, I had a crumpled up piece of paper with an address in my pocket for one of the local squats I'd gotten from a kid who'd drawn a map of how to find his house. We'd met in the summertime on a piece of land in Southern Oregon. I found a nice squatted shotgun with pirated water and a wood stove and a sculpture of twisted copper coils hooked up to a bathtub in the backyard, which created a makeshift hot water shower. There was a small tight-knit crew living there who shared a love for books and radical history and a hatred of authority. There were familiar art and maps and flyers for protests and shows all over the walls. I felt at home.

The Crescent Wrench bookstore was a couple blocks away and I got the grand tour. The Emma Goldman books and *Spectacular Times* Situationist pamphlets, the *Slingshots* and *Shadows* and *Blasts* and *Love & Rages*, all the national rags. There were racks of good zines, lonely kids pouring out their souls from all over the country captured in time on little folded pieces of paper. There was a whole library with everything from carpentry do-it-yourself books to cheesy sex guides to Howard Zinn history. Every night there was a different activity going on at the Crescent Wrench—from watching Noam Chomsky movies to book binding workshops to a room full of people polka dancing. It was a cool little scene I'd stumbled into made up almost entirely of people from other parts of the country who'd come together to create an enclave of radical culture.

That first day at the Crescent Wrench I was talking to the punk guy behind the counter and I was happy to be back around my own kind before I headed back to small town life across the water. I asked, "hey, didja hear that old band *Chumbawamba* made it to the top of the charts? I keep hearing them on the radio. Isn't that crazy, who would have thought, huh?"

He looked at me and I realized I'd struck a chord. His face got all red and he managed to sputter out, "Man, those fucking sellouts! They're such hypocrites! I can't believe they're doing exactly what they preached against all those years ago! Fucking rock star bastards selling out our culture! Walking by Tower Records I saw they had the album in the window! Can you believe that? Fucking rich rock star sellout fucking bastards making money for EMI…"

I could relate to his gripes. The truth is that I'm just as sick of watching the music and art I care about get co-opted and bought out by big business. I freaked out when I turned the TV on one day to see that the Nike corporation had bought the rights to the Gil-Scott Heron song, "The Revolution Will Not Be Televised" and was using it to sell their fucking sneakers. It was like whitey using his own anti-manifesto with the meaning sucked out and spit back evil. It was some sick voodoo shit, insidious exploitation of black kids in the ghetto who were too young to remember that the song had originally been a call to smash the consumer culture of the early 70s. Even more, the whole "punk explosion" in the media a couple years ago was enough to make any self-respecting older punk kid slip into an identity crisis. It was like everything you thought had meant something had had the meaning drained out when those videos with the guys with mohawks started playing on MTV.

It's strange when the stuff that you and your friends used to treasure like secrets is suddenly in the public domain. The music that got you through adolescence with its caustic critiques of pop culture is suddenly sold as the same pop culture you were rebelling against in the first place. It's stranger when you start seeing all these kids walking around who look like you and your friends did and you want to be able to relate to them, but they're nothing like how you and your friends were. To you, they feel like the hippies in the 80s—shallow retro fashion victims with so little political consciousness you could rub the contradictions in their face and they'd pay you to do it some more. I grew cynical. Hopeless.

Back at the Crescent Wrench I found myself struck with how much I could relate to this guy's angry ramblings. A couple days later, back at my friends' place across the water, I couldn't get this stuff off of my mind. By chance, I'd been listening to the radio and heard an announcement that if I was the 104th caller I'd win tickets to see Chumbawamba live in concert. It was too surreal, too close to home. I suddenly felt betrayed. I kept getting visions of drunk frat boys singing along to poppy, vapid feel-good songs and record executives sitting in some office cashing in with big grins. It tore at the painful wounds of my alienated youth. The thing was, I was positive Chumbawamba knew exactly what they were doing. They talked about it years ago. They were the ones who articulated it to me in the first place. Shit.

Something didn't seem right. Drastic action made it seem appropriate to go buy their CD at the mall. Standing in line at Circuit City in the big Louisiana Shopping Center with my friend Kaia the weekend after Thanksgiving, everyone was rushing around doing their Christmas shopping. It was a total fucking nightmare. A wall with 40 television screens played the same droning images of war and sex—explosions and scantily clad bodies on beaches. There were kids transfixed before the flickering images and running around begging their parents to buy them the new super-hype video games and CD-ROMs. I stood in line with the glossy shrink-wrapped CD in my sweaty hand and studied it for a signifier that the contents were more radical than they appeared in their slick green and pink neon packaging. The only promise was a little note in the bottom right hand corner—www.chumba.com, an invitation to check out their website.

Times have changed, and now everyone and their mom has a website on the internet. My neo-luddite forest friends still think its a conspiracy to suck our brains out of our skulls for The Man, but the more I learn about the potential communication capabilities of the internet and the longer its around the more open minded I become. Unlike television, which injects straight blasts of commercial garbage into our brains, the net is full of radical information that is easy to access and sift through. Given that it's getting cheaper to use and the medium is inherently interactive, I'm convinced that it's going to be a positive tool for large sections of the population. Not like there aren't 40 online reactionary business web pages for every cool online lefty labor journal or radical bulletin board, but the more people that get on there, the more the scales tip.

We got back to the house and I walked straight to the computer, turned on the modem, and logged online. I typed in the web page address, and the screen flickered for a second and came up full of text. Chumbawamba had links to all of the most cutting edge, radical websites: Mumia-Abu Jamal, The Noam Chomsky Archive, The Liverpool Dockworkers, Anti-Fascist Action, AK Press, Billboard Altering Sites—and tons of stuff I'd never heard of. The 12 character address I found on the back of the CD and punched into a computer terminal gave me access to a wealth of information; all I had to do was click on what I wanted to know about and the screen would fill with text and photos. There was a section full of ongoing debates about current political issues and dialogues from people all over the world asking questions to the band. They featured a list of corporate shops where they recommended stealing their new album from, "If you get caught, just tell the store detective that you have full support of the band," they encouraged.

I was relieved and happy. I don't care that EMI is a weapons contractor. If selling out means using resources to proliferate valuable information into the mainstream, then I'm ready to sign up.

Myself and my friends never had an easy time imagining a large scale social revolution. Most of us were too alienated from mainstream culture to begin thinking on such levels. We are covered in emotional scars and retreated to safe enclaves in big cities or rural communities. Our political organizing ends up only reaching each other because we only know how to talk to a certain kind of people. But there are too many battle-fronts to spend our time hanging out with one another. I want people to rise up and take the power from big corporations. I want a social revolution on a mass scale in my lifetime. I commend anyone for trying.

I scoff at popular culture and often retreat to the familiar world of my friends, who opt out of the system and live in the middle of the woods or scam their way through life in the city. I'm inspired by the freedom of the radical environments that can be created out of the clutches of the law.

But the older I get the more I realize that I don't want to surround myself with people who think like me. That's too easy. If we want to change the world and make things better for people other than our network of friends, it takes a way more challenging type of organizing; thinking about things on a mass scale.

If we want to be effective we must negotiate a balance with the system. We have to dance with our enemies because we know its for the best in the long run. We have to be that statue of Jesus with the Mayan idols hidden inside, and to be proud of it too. My culture's not getting robbed. My friends and I can find more secret stuff to enjoy that's not for public consumption. If they figure out some way to make money off of it then we'll just think up something new. I don't give a fuck about an old code of the underground scene. I'm interested in change.

Waiting in line at Circuit City, I thought of the kids who weren't born in cultural centers like New York City, relying on popular culture to inform them of what's going on in the world. I think of those kids buying the new hit from Chumbawamba and discovering a world they never had access to before. I think about people from my community making it into the mainstream and having an impact on larger culture. And I smile thinking about strange twists of fate and the unknown future in store for all of us.

"Revolution will be built on the spread of ideas and information, on reaching people, rather than on our habit of creating ghettoes within which to stagnate. It's no use standing outside shouting. We have to start kicking down the doors!"

—Sleeve notes to first Chumbawamba single, 1985

Can't Hang with the Monocult/Lessons in the Forest

At 23 I dropped everything and followed my girlfriend to a tiny organic farm school on an island between the mainland of British Columbia and Vancouver Island, seven hours north of a big city. I lived there with her for a full growing season, learned how to grow a garden, how to work in the fields, and how to repair trails in the woods. We had weekly classes like solar mapping, greenhouse design, soil science, and compost building. My back got strong digging ditches, shoveling manure and wood chips, and hoeing fields of weeds. The forest surrounding the farm was so wild, and became my university, infinitely complex in all its multi-layered relations. I thought about applying the ecology lessons to my life in the city. My teachers used the language of Permaculture, which began to drastically remap my understanding of what was going on around me. I started writing a gardening column for the punk newspaper *Slug and Lettuce,* as my attempt to share the wisdom of the forest with folks back home.

•　　　•　　　•

Sitting under a huge cedar on a thick cushion of moss, needles, and decomposing wood, I'm in the middle of the forest on Saturday afternoon. I've been clearing trails for hours, cutting sollal roots and pulling ferns. While I rest in the shade, I watch squirrels run across the upper story of the trees. I listen to my breath, birds chirping, and wind blowing. The soil under the cedar needles is thick and black, held together with decomposing organic matter, in flux and full of life. A carpet of the tree's energy is breaking down, building up, and breaking down again. It holds the energy in and lets it go little by little. The old growth fir stumps were hand-logged in the 1920s and have giant new hemlocks growing out of them; taking advantage of the old root systems carved through the soil and rock.   Everything is connected—from the smallest microbe fixing nitrogen in the soil to the cougar catching a deer on the edge of the bluff.

My friends are in the city cultivating their stress, balancing activism and computer temp jobs, or scamming train lines and supermarket dumpsters. This urban kid has been learning to grow food near the edge of the forest for the past half a year.

I wake up with the sun and write down my crazy dreams, slip out of the house and feed the pigs, water the greenhouse full of tomatoes and peppers, and tend to my little broccoli transplants, which are just starting to make heads for fall. If it's not too chilly, I'll jump in the lake. After breakfast, we harvest corn, beans, squash, carrots, eggplants, leeks, beets, lettuce, tomatoes, zucchini, and basil. We build compost or fences. We slow erosion in the creek that feeds into the lake. We may have a discussion class on soil chemistry or composting toilets or land trusting. Some of us are building a seed bank and networking with local farmers, seed companies, and exchanges. My housemates are canning tomatoes, cooking jam, drying plums, threshing amaranth and quinoa and beans, making pesto, and tending to the berry wine. Our eight month sustainable agriculture program ends in six weeks, and we're all planning our futures, taking on the world with this knowledge. My days are full and revolve around food. I've been t-bud grafting fruit trees and rooting semi-hardwood cuttings of shrubs and trees in tins of wet sand, saving different vegetable, flower, and herb seeds, staying up late reading drip irrigation, bio-fertilizer, and plant propagation textbooks. It's like casting spells—getting the timing down and mixing up the right amounts of soil and seeds and water and sun and—poof—it starts growing.

People aren't learning these skills anymore; food cultivation and land stewardship are lost arts. Generations back our families were providing their own food. Our grandmothers had fruit trees, our grandpas caught fish, people would save seed and grow the same tomatoes their grandparents had grown. We lived in tighter communities with more localized economies and had a closer connection to the land. Now multinational chemical companies own most of the crop seeds and genetically alter our food to be dependent on their fertilizers and herbicides. We grow food on huge tracks of mono-cropped land and transport it in monster trucks to buy it wrapped up in plastic. We've covered our best agricultural soil with suburban development and industrial parks. Our economy is based on an infinite growth model that doesn't factor in our limited natural resources or peoples' livelihoods and happiness. There's a law against growing fruit trees in my hometown because the fruit might fall on cars.

When I listen to the news about the latest war, I take comfort that the skills I'm learning will never become outdated. I'll spend the rest of my life cleaning the shortsighted mess the corporations created.

Permaculture and Energy Cycling

Everything on this farm mimics things that happen in nature. Instead of acres of tractor-tilled pesticide mono-crops, we have organic vegetable gardens and happy animals. There are little patches of sustainability and ecological regeneration—small models of how we might rebuild our world in a way that actually works for a healthy future for the planet and its people.

In the forest, water falls from the sky, soaks and moves through the soil, rises in the trees, and returns to the atmosphere. We flow energy through the farm in the same way. Our pipe runs from a spring, up in the hills, and intercepts the flow before it runs down the creek and into our lake. It collects in a ferrocement tank at the top of a bluff, which connects to a number of pipes carrying water to our houses and fields. Recycling kitchen waste into compost, channeling household greywater into the garden, raking leaves up around trees as mulch—these are all energy cycling. We keep the trade—and the economy— flowing in a circle.

Accelerated Succession—Pioneers and Climax Species.

The forest develops, giving rise to a new succession of different species. Each stage creates the conditions for the next stage. When the trees get cut down on this land, the alders grow. Alder is a pioneer species. Their roots fix nitrogen in the ground and build up the soil for the next generation. As flora and fauna develop around them, cedar and fir slowly begin growing again. Eventually the alder break down into soil, shaded out by the cedar and fir. The same thing happens in abandoned lots and anywhere where the land has been disturbed.

Blackberry bushes with big thorns will invade and keep everything away while the land heals itself. Eventually, trees grow through the blackberry vines and shade them out. We do the same thing by building up the soil and substituting our own herb, pioneer, and climax species.

Depending upon the soil, it's possible to introduce plants that will survive and be more useful than existing vegetation. We grow cover crops of clover, alfalfa, peas, or beans to fix nitrogen in the soil and then turn them in to the ground to build up fertility. We grow buckwheat, a phosphorus accumulator, or winter rye, which suppresses weed growth. We can introduce animals into a system and have them do our work. If we play our cards right, in 20 years we can end up with forests of hazelnuts, peaches, and blueberries.

Plant Stacking and Time Stacking

Instead of planting a flat field of one crop which needs attention and water, we intercrop taller and shorter species, climbing plants and herbs and different kinds of trees—everything placed according to their shade tolerance, heights, and water requirements. In one site there is a sequence of long level excavations dug to store water in the underlying soils. They are connected to a small pond that carries nutrients to the bottom of the slope. Instead of diverting water so it can drain somewhere else, swales intercept the water flow, hold it for a few hours or days, and let it slowly infiltrate the ground water, recharging soils and tree root systems. At the bottom of the slope, there's raised beds of sticks and mud where all the garlic is planted. The site was a big swamp full of alder trees a couple years ago and, slowly, the permaculture crew has been rerouting the water to make the wet areas nicer and the surrounding areas more fertile for growing ground crops.

Rather than thinking about organisms individually, it's useful to think of them in clusters or groups. When the individuals are clustered around a central element, we call these groups guilds. There are a couple of fruit orchards spread around the farm, mostly apple and plum trees. There's a herd of sheep whose grazing keeps the grass down in the orchards. They also eat up any fruit that falls and rots on the ground, preventing diseases in the trees.

The quintessential crop guild is the traditional Native American planting of corn, beans, and squash. As the runner beans trellis their way up the corn stalks, they fix the nitrogen that's being lost to the soil from the corn, which needs a lot of nutrients to grow. As the squash plant provides an understory which keeps away weeds and helps to keep the soil moist, their big spiny leaves also keep the animals from trying to climb up and steal the corn ears as they ripen.

Edge

Ecological productivity increases at the boundary between two ecologies because the resources from both systems can be used. This is true for land/water, forest/grassland, estuary/ocean, sidewalk/street—wherever. Energies and materials always accumulate at the edges—soil and debris are blown by the wind against fences or walls. Increased edge makes for a more productive landscape, which creates more surface area, more patches of microclimates.

We built an herb spiral next to our house out of smashed up concrete from an old building foundation. The raised spirals condense space, create a bunch of little microclimates for shade and sun tolerant herbs, increase the surface area, and look cool. Edges define areas and break them into manageable sections.

Urban Guerrilla Gardening—Growing Food in the City

We can't keep importing and trucking food all over the globe, letting big corporations control the most basic aspect of our lives. There is so much potential for growing food in the cities and suburbs—taking over abandoned rubble lots and rooftops and lawns and starting community gardens, building compost with all the organic wastes from supermarkets and restaurants and our kitchens, catching water before it runs into the sewers, building ponds and attracting birds and insects, creating urban woodlots of fire and timber wood grown around industrial zones that can filter pollution from the air, produce oxygen, create habitat for birds and small animals, and not make all the buildings so damn oppressive. There's more edge and vertical growing space than you can shake a stick at in the city. Like sculpture and art, it's about dealing with living systems that change over time. Everyone around here knows me as the aggressive city kid, the one who's sometimes too impatient and loud and talks faster than everyone else and goes out smashing up concrete slabs with a sledgehammer and builds raised vegetable beds out of sticks and blackberries just to prove we can grow food even in really crappy soil. As I've lived on this farm for almost an entire growing season, I've learned a little bit of patience and calm and a whole bunch of skills that I'm looking forward to bringing home.

Back on the Road

As an adult I've cultivated my ability to reach out to others who can help guide me. Not having much biological family, I had to create my own family and find older mentor figures to teach me the lessons I needed to learn. I've cultivated friendships with a lot of different people who have taught me lessons and skills, filled in the little pieces of my navigation map, helped me figure out both how I want to live my life and how I don't want to live my life.

•   •   •

I opened my eyes this morning in Portland at 6 AM. A friend drove me to interstate 5 on her way to work. After a few hours, my frozen fingers continued to clutch my cardboard "Corvallis" sign, jumping around to stay warm. I was all smiles and hopes, until the rain started coming down, and then I was screaming at the cars, motioning to the sky and then my sign. "Please pick me up—it's raining." My pleading mantra quickly turned to exasperated screams of, "*What the fuck is wrong with you people?!*" till I couldn't see straight.

Finally a young agricultural student researching pesticide evaporation in fields picked me up. After studying agriculture for four years and he'd never grown a carrot or a row of peas. He was fascinated by the farm work I'd been doing. I gave him lists of internships and apprenticeships and by the time I stepped out of his car he told me I'd changed his life. Suddenly, all that time soaking wet on the highway was worth it.

Dr. Alan Kapuler, a famous renegade plant breeder, who I'd come all this way to find, greeted me with a warm smile and a big hug. He motioned to the greenhouse and told me to go meet his assistants and put down my pack inside. A long-dreadlocked woman named Hope was winnowing and cleaning seed with an electric fan as I entered. Her daughter, Tibet, was threshing a whole bunch of other seed, jumping up and down on a sheet and laughing. In the background was a huge banana tree framed by a jungle of vining and trellising tropical plants from all over the world—ginger with its beautiful red and yellow flowers, gigantic spiny forests of yucca and aloes, a patch of perennial teosinte, the distant relative to corn standing ten feet by the door. There were tree frogs hanging out in the pepper plants and racks of drying red corn and rows of cactus in the back.

"The garden is laid out evolutionarily," Hope explained. "We start at the beginning with early relatives like teosinte and work our way forward. We're learning as we go, laying plants out according to kinship and seeing what happens." Alan soon joined us and we toured the entire farm. He was brilliant and animated, his dark eyes twinkling behind wise wrinkles and a scraggly long white beard. The Latin names were pouring off his tongue as he motioned with his hands and picked leaves for me to taste and flowers to smell and seeds to examine. While answering the numerous questions I had about the origin and connection of specific species and families and tribes, he kept bringing up that it was diversity we should be striving for at all costs, the missing element we'd lost amidst our industrial agriculture of mono-crops and profit. His passion felt like an energy field surrounding him. We walked together through the garden for hours. He explained all about the work he's been carrying out for years breaking down hybrid seed back into open pollinated varieties, the work I was the most interested in. He referred to it as "putting the plants back in the public domain." "See this broccoli?" he asked. "It's a Packman variety that I broke back down to an open pollinated.[4] The tricky thing is that a lot of times the parent strains they use for hybrids don't have big heads. You grow out the F2 generation and get a bed of broccoli with huge roots and leaves. Maybe there'll be two large headed ones growing among them, and those are the ones you save for seed and start again." I helped him transplant a row of brassicas he was leaving to overwinter—another hybrid broccoli he was breaking back down to a stable OP. As we worked, he spelled it out for me, "These fuckers trying to patent life and genetically alter our seed crops into sterility—they're fascists, total fascists! Why would anyone knowingly attempt to prevent the cycle of life from taking place and deprive farmers all over the world of the right to save their own seed? We've been doing it for 12,000 years—the crops we eat are our collective human heritage."

I followed Alan around the garden and watched him as he worked. He dug up four cabbage plants from a large bed and wheel-barrowed them over to another spot nearby, next to a small patch of carrots left for seed. With a shovel he dug the trenches and transplanted each one carefully in. We needed one more so we walked back to the bed and found the one with the biggest leaves and dug it up.

I asked him how two plants from the same family evolved to be poisonous or full of vitamins and he shrugged his shoulders, "One pill makes you larger and one pill makes you small..." Then he grinned widely, "and the ones that mother gives you don't do anything at all!" He leant me his magnifying glass and I explored all over the greenhouse checking out as many flowers and seeds as I could. It felt like the first time I took acid and hallucinated my head off as a teenager or the first time I hit the road and realized that my destiny was to be a traveler. The world is an incredible playground and infinitely full of potential, screaming out its beauty like the energy between atoms.

Dr. Kapuler asked me how long I was planning to stick around, and I told them I was planning to be in Eugene by nightfall. He told Hope to take the afternoon off and drive me exactly where I needed to go. I bid farewell to the doctor and continued on my way, feeling so blessed that our paths had crossed.

---

4   See Breaking Down the Fancy Seed Talk in *The Wild Garden Waits to Grow* on P.XX

The Battle in Seattle

This is an important part of the map—a moment where my story crossed paths with many others. The protest against The World Trade Organization in Seattle, Washington at the end of November of 1999—"the WTO protests," "N30," or "the Battle of Seattle"—was a fight against arguably the most powerful organization on earth, and against the WTO's central operating principal—that commercial interests should supersede all others.

Falling just before the millennium, the protests were an important marker for social change makers in North America, culminating years of organizing and sparking the imagination of a generation of young rebels and dreamers. They brought together activists from environmental movements, labor unions, student groups, nonprofits, and community organizers of many stripes. The Independent Media Center network, which exploded all over the world in the years that followed, started that month in Seattle. New communication technologies gave us the ability to organize and outsmart the law; friends got their first cell phones and a new era of internet journalism began.

I hitchhiked from New York City with my friend Sera Bilizekian and arrived two weeks before the protests. Our friends rented a giant warehouse and there was an enormous, festive reunion of folks from around the world. The People's Global Action caravan bus made stops from New York to Seattle, doing outreach and media as they went.

Sera and I stayed in an apartment packed full of people, sleeping bags on the floor like sardines. It felt like precious family, including people I'd known since I was a teenager. My old communist union organizer grandpa—who had always given me shit for my anti-authoritarian politics and countercultural lifestyle (e.g not joining a trade union)—showed up at the warehouse while I was co-facilitating a spokes council meeting of 200 people. It was incredibly gratifying to feel the power of our numbers and the energy of a growing movement.

The Direct Action Network (DAN) was initiated by a network of activists who were coordinating activities that month. The DAN agreed that the main blockades would be nonviolent and not include property destruction. Thousands of people received non-violent direct action training. We formed thirteen "pie slices," dividing downtown Seattle into shutdown zones come the morning of the protests. Small, self-reliant affinity groups of five to twenty-five people were the basic planning and decision-making bodies of the action. It was anarchist organizing, inspired by tradition going back to the *grupos de affinidad* of the Iberian Anarchist Federation of Spain from the Spanish Civil War.

Meanwhile, the "black bloc," folks from my travels and years in the punk scene, were having their own meetings. They remained autonomous from the DAN structure. One of my activist mentors, David Solnit, asked Sera and I, the token young dirty traveler kids, to be liaisons to the black bloc. We went back and forth, communicating between conflicting factions.

Tens of thousands encircled the WTO conference site, keeping the most powerful institution on earth shut down from dawn till dusk, despite an army of federal, state, and local police driving armored vehicles and shooting tear gas, pepper spray, rubber plastic, wooden bullets, and concussion grenades. Thousands of activists engaged in direct action throughout the week, despite a clampdown of nearly 600 arrests, continued tear gassing and police rioting, the declaration of a "state of emergency," and suspension of the basic rights of free speech and assembly in downtown Seattle. It was a moment in history when it felt like the media veils were lifted and we were actually winning the story. When we chanted "*The Whole World is Watching*," it was actually true.

The confrontations in the street were a surreal blur; the storm troopers shelling us with tear gas and all kinds of bullets. Our coordinated affinity groups shut down the meetings on the first day and we declared victory. The black bloc, wearing masks and carrying crowbars and rocks, created a lasting spectacle smashing corporate windows all over downtown. Despite a heated disagreements about tactics, especially after the media focused so heavily on the sexy spectacle of black masked young people smashing things, there was solidarity in those streets; a tangible sense of people power.

Because it happened right before the millennium, everything felt more dramatic. The following year, the Global Justice Movement erupted in mass protests on the streets of Washington DC, Los Angeles, Genoa, Italy, and Quebec City, Canada, and it kept going, with protests erupting at the next WTO meeting in Cancún, Mexico, at the World Economic Forum meeting in Davos, Switzerland, at the meeting of the Free Trade Area of the Americas in Miami. For awhile it seemed like these protests were happening everywhere, all the time. There was a rise in the popularity of anarchist organizing—consensus-based decision-making, spokes council meetings, direct action, and affinity groups. There was a resurgence of interest about the history and philosophies of anarchism. The obscure traditions that my friends and I had been carrying around in our zines and punk records were all over the internet and on college syllabi. All of this is taken for granted now, but before 2000, the word anarchist was virtually unheard outside our circles.

The protests kept going—and keep going still—but the World Trade Center attack on September 11, 2001 marked a major shift, when the stakes of mass protest got a lot higher. Liberals withdrew from vocally protesting U.S. policies at a time when the U.S. was supposedly under attack, and our movements became quickly marginalized again. The "War on Terror" targeted our friends and put many in the radical environmental movement in prison, scaring others from public dissent. Regardless, our experiences in the streets of Seattle made us never again doubt that we were part of an international movement—and it made people around the world aware that there were people in the U.S. who were able to bring an entire city to its knees in the name of social and economic justice.

In aftermath of the Seattle Protests, some friends and I started the Bay Area Seed Interchange Library (BASIL) in the same spirit. Inspired by Vandana Shiva and the Navdanya network of farmers in India, we decided that even without much farmland we could start a community seed project. The seed library was my excuse to make friends in my North Oakland neighborhood. We had a network of activist houses, but gardening was a way to build alliances with our neighbors who weren't part of an anarchist culture. We went door to door, talking to folks who had front yard gardens about saving their own seeds and what it would look like to have an agriculture system where the people had local control. We taught free permaculture workshops. We put in greywater systems that fed the gardens. We propagated and gave away plants.

All these years later, there's a "food justice" movement spreading around the country, the BASIL library still stands, and there are dozens of urban seed libraries in North America, inspired by our work at the turn of the millennium.

•　　　•　　　•

The BASIL mission was:

The Bay Area Seed Interchange Library (BASIL) is part of a growing network of concerned farmers and community gardeners dedicated to conserving the remaining genetic diversity of our planet's seed stock. We have created a library of healthy vegetable, herb, and flower seeds that are being made available free to the public.

Why be concerned with seed saving?

Monsanto and Novartis, who now own the majority of seed companies, are not interested in creating sustainable food systems and communities. They are replacing carefully bred strains of vegetables and flowers with hybrids and patented varieties. Hybrids don't produce viable seed, and the seed from patented varieties cannot legally be collected and used. Instead, the seeds must be bought fresh each year, forcing farmers to purchase from corporate seed sources annually.

Genetic engineering enables "life science" corporations to control plant traits by "programming" the seeds. Monsanto's infamous implementation of trait-control technology is often referred to as the "Terminator" seed. "Terminator" seed plants produce no viable seeds. Trait-controlled plants that breed with traditional varieties may pass on engineered traits to the offspring. If non-evolved plant varieties are permitted to squeeze out natural and/or carefully cultivated varieties, seed saving is made much more difficult. Nourishment could depend on chemically dependent or infertile trait-controlled plants.

In order to create a positive ecological future for the planet, we need to begin teaching each other the skills necessary to save our own seeds. BASIL allows local gardeners to "check out" seeds with the agreement that they attempt to grow them out and return seeds of the next generation. BASIL encourages good growing techniques through classes, literature, and one-to-one help from experienced seed savers.

Excerpt from *Sowing Revolution: Seed Libraries Offer Hope for Freedom of Food* by Bill McDorman & Stephen Thomas (2012):

The seed library story begins, appropriately, with a rebellion. In late November 1999, thousands of anti-globalization activists descended on Seattle to protest a meeting of the World Trade Organization. The massive demonstrations shut down the city for days. Sascha DuBrul, a 24-year-old activist and New York native living in Berkeley, took part in the protests and returned to California charged with excitement. "It was a really vibrant time," he recalls. "Here in the Bay Area, there were all these amazing projects starting up that are still around."

Seeds were DuBrul's newly discovered passion. While interning at a CSA farm in British Colombia the previous year, he became fascinated by the invigorating genetic relationships that arose when domestic crops intermingled with their wild relatives. Diversity was the key to the health of a community, he realized, be it plant or human. This idea had great relevance to urban spaces where people live in close quarters but thrive on cultural differences. "I had this vision of articulating the relationship between biological and cultural diversity, and bringing that idea to kids in the city," says DuBrul.

That opportunity soon came following a Faustian deal between the University of California at Berkeley and the Swiss agribusiness giant Novartis. One of the first decrees under the alliance was for the eviction of an on-campus CSA farm to make way for trials of genetically modified corn. "There were all these seeds left over in a cabinet and nothing was going on," recalls DuBrul. "So I thought, 'Hey, why don't we start a seed library?' We could have a collection of seeds that people can take out, and then have regular seed saving workshops where gardeners can come and learn the basic techniques." He started brainstorming with his friend Christopher Shein, who had been running the Berkeley campus CSA. Their vision quickly blossomed into the first seed lending library.

DuBrul counts an unlikely pair of inspirations behind the BASIL project: Gary Paul Nabhan, co-founder of Native Seeds/SEARCH and father of the local food movement, and the Black Panthers. "Reading [Nabhan's] book *Enduring Seeds* rocked my world," he says, "and the Panthers had this history of community-controlled movements where people took over their communities for their own." Over the next nine months BASIL flourished out of the nonprofit Ecology Center as a grassroots hub for seed saving and self-reliance in the Berkeley community.

GUERRILLA GARDENING IN NORTH OAKLAND

Ruth Ozeki's novel All Over Creation *immortalized these experiences by writing a fictionalized account of what BASIL's activities in North Oakland. But this is how the events played out in reality.*

It was dark when we left the house, all of us wearing black with a shovel and a couple of fruit trees under each arm. Our destination was three blocks away—an irrigated median strip. We scoped the area for signs of trouble from the Man and then planted six trees: pear, orange, persimmon, lemon, poplar, and maple. The guys at the liquor store across the street just stood and stared. We made the final touches and mulched each tree with straw. Moments later the irrigation system came on to welcome the trees into their new home. A couple weeks later the trees had taken—the city workers mow the grass around them like they planted them themselves. A couple years from now they'll be huge and full of fruit for the neighborhood.

Back in the early spring we tore up our lawn and planted a vegetable garden. We pulled up the grass, hoed out the roots, and double dug a spiral shape. Two local community gardens were being evicted—one for a new parking lot and one for a crop of genetically engineered Novartis corn on the Berkeley University property. We planted a huge artichoke in the center with a web of broccoli and lettuce seedlings all around. Neighbors we didn't know came to stop by and compliment us on our work. We invited them in to check out our backyard and gave them the tour.

I live in a house full of badass people who know how to do incredible things. We dumpster and salvage everything from our furniture to our food. The place is constantly in flux. This so called 'three bedroom' house sleeps seven to nine people paying rent and usually a couple transient folks camping out in our living room keeping things interesting. There are extra rooms built in wherever there's space—from the front room to the attic to the back shed. Every Monday morning a crew of rad older women take over our kitchen with crates of organic produce and cook Food Not Bombs to serve in People's Park. Just as you can't separate the individual trees from the greater forest, neither can we isolate our house from a greater network stretching around the neighborhood that make up part of the East Bay activist community. Bekey showed up at our door last night with a crate full of dumpstered tofu she got in the city. The house down the street that used to broadcast the pirate radio station gave us a swarm of bees for our backyard. Our older next door neighbor Tom let us sheet mulch part of his garden and plant a bunch of food for him and his mom. Our neighbors down the street put on puppet shows for kids and sometimes invite us to come paint murals with them at the train yard. We go down to Emeryville in bike posses to dumpster dive and paint the town.

When another group of activists started our house about five years ago, there was no backyard garden, only a concrete floor and a beaten up garage. They tore up concrete blocks with pick-axes and sledgehammers to plant their vegetables. They turned the garage into a bicycle library full of frames, parts, and a good set of tools. Now all the kids in our neighborhood come over to visit and fix their bikes. There are usually a couple folks working on their bikes in the backyard whenever I get home. But the garden was small until a couple months ago.

Then Mark showed up from North Carolina with her fiddle and boxes of tools and inspiration. She and a tight crew of folks organized the DIY Skillshare Gathering out of our house—four days of workshops from Seed Saving to Making Your Own Biodiesel to Stilt Walking to Anti-Racist Organizing to Auto Mechanics. People came out of the woodwork to participate. A month later all kinds of projects were sprouting up all over the neighborhood. Our friends setup the graywater from their shower to channel out the window to three staggered bathtubs filled with gravel and reeds that purify it like natural wetlands and then send it off through a hose to water the garden. We're setting up a similar system in our backyard with their help. Some houses in the neighborhood already have basic graywater systems in their bathrooms, the water from the sink drains into a bucket used to flush the toilet. We're setting up a solar hot water system, water is diverted from our furnace and pumped to the solar heater on the roof where it snakes through pipes heated by the sun's rays and dumped into the low-flow shower head. We have a food dehydrator where we dry tons of dumpstered apples and bananas and strawberries and papayas. We have drying racks built high up near the ceilings that dry our herbs and spices.

Then Tim showed up, back from Austin, all emotionally mangled and garden-obsessed, and we started our therapeutic late night dumpster runs for containers and missions to the racetrack for straw bale. The city is full of trash that can be used for growing containers—barrels, stacked railroad ties, tires for growing potatoes, (fill them with straw and stack them as the plants get higher—they'll send off potatoes on the sides and you can harvest by pulling the tires off), bathtubs, wire baskets for hanging, milk crates filled with garbage bags, refrigerators—use your imagination. A bunch of us including me and Tim work at a composting collective called Berkeley Worms that picks up the organic waste from the university and turns it into black, rich, beautiful compost. The red wriggler worms make the compost—they eat half their weight a day in "garbage," sleep, and reproduce. We started sheet mulching boxes with a layer of food, then straw, then worm compost. Suddenly our tiny backyard started blooming huge tomato plants full of flowers started from seed. Now, scarlet runner beans trellis up the ladder to the roof and boxes full of chard and mustard greens and squash.

In nature, animals have coexisted and co-evolved with plants for millions of years. In urban areas, there's a severe lack of animals because so little habitat exists for them. So it's important for us to create habitat. The wild creatures we're left with are the ones that can fly—birds and insects. Birds are incredible—they eat insects and process them into phosphorus, they eat berries and etch the seeds in their stomachs, so that they germinate, and then shit them out in a fertile puddle. Fences are usually really fertile places, full of interesting plants because that's where the birds like to kick it and shit out their seeds! So Tim has been making nest boxes and bat boxes. He built some mason bee houses that are wooden blocks with 3/8" holes three inches deep, which solitary bees use to hatch their young. We've left our thorny blackberries to vine and flower so we can collect the fruit and let all the bees pollinate. Life is sweet.

From coast to coast, I've been watching my friends learning more skills and teaching one another how to do things. As we get older we learn more about everything, we get wiser and find our places in this crazy world, and we start putting our words and dreams into action.

Portrait of a Protest

When the next big global protest in Washington DC—targeting the International Monetary Fund and World Bank—was gearing up, a group of us from both coasts put out a press release saying that we were "Urban gardeners in solidarity with the farmers of the developing world whose livelihoods were being destroyed by the skewed development policies of the World Bank and the IMF." This was an interview I did with the *Village Voice* at the time.

Taking globalization personally: Nine New Yorkers say what moved them to march on the IMF
Sascha Scatter Age 25 *Resides* Oakland, California *Occupation* landscaper

> *"I was raised by democratic socialists who believed in electoral politics,"* says Sascha Scatter, *"but my political education happened amidst the Tompkins Square riots of the late '80s."* . . . Scatter organized *"tactical communications"* in Seattle for two weeks prior to the protests. He was tear-gassed seven times. His mission in D.C.: Guerrilla gardening—activists planted trees, vegetables, and flowers on abandoned lots and lawns. His point: self-sufficiency. As Scatter sees it, there's plenty of food—it just doesn't get to the people who need it. *"If you look at the history of agriculture and the World Bank, they continually try to give technological solutions to problems fundamentally political and sociological,"* Scatter says. *"In this day and age, growing your own food and saving your own seeds has become a revolutionary act."*

TOO CLOSE TO THE SUN

I was at my house in Oakland when the phone call came. A mutual friend in the Midwest heard from her friend in Oregon about a girl on the East Coast who jumped off a bridge. She thought it might be a rumor—a crazy story that sometimes happens in our travelers' community—a big game of international telephone. I didn't believe it.

"Naw, man, I just talked to Sera a week ago. She was going traveling and had a ticket to Europe in February. She said she had been a little down but she didn't sound so bad. She always goes through her waves of depression like the rest of us."

But my heart was beating fast and my fingers were starting to shake.

So I called her house in West Philly. The voicemail picked up and when it said press two for Sera I was greeted by her cheery voice, "Hi, this is Sera. Leave me a message and I'll get back to you when I can." BEEP.

"Hello…Sera? Uh…[long pause]…I, I just heard this rumor that you, you killed yourself. I really hope it's just a rumor. I'm going to be pissed at you if you killed yourself, hear me? Uh…so, uh…call me when you get this message, alright? I love you…[long pause]…Bye."

I hung up the phone.

For the first couple months after my dad's death I had this reoccurring dream where he and I were talking on the telephone. It wasn't always the same backdrop, sometimes it was from a payphone on the street, sometimes from the kitchen at my mom's house, sometimes from school, but the same thing would always happen. We'd say goodbye, hang up the phone, and then I'd suddenly remember he was dead. Confused, I'd pick up the phone and dial the number—222-5046—and the mechanical operator would come on and say the number had been disconnected. I'd wake up with my heart beating really fast and wish that I had my dad back.

I met Sera in the summer of 1999. I was recovering from being locked up in the psych ward, working on an organic farm north of New York City. She had been working at the Victory Gardens Project in Maine and wrote me a letter about one of my zines. I wrote back and she boldly invited herself to visit me at the farm. She impressed me, she was intimidating smart, quoting Baldwin and Faulkner from memory, eloquently articulating her revolutionary critiques of global capitalism, teaching me about the horrors of 20th Century Eastern European history, and knowing the lyrics to all my favorite CRASS songs. She was also strikingly beautiful, she had this amazing smile and this olive Armenian skin that was dark from working in the fields, dreadlocks that hung down to her shoulders, and these deep brown eyes that would constantly study my facial expressions and try to read me, searching for the meaning in everything I said.

She was passionate about everything she did, which was a whole lot. She threw herself into the middle of the struggle wherever she went, and she went to a lot of places. As we got to know each other she took off to rural Nicaragua to work on a construction project with a group of women in a Sandinista village. Her traveler's energy was infectious and helped inspire me to remember the parts I liked about myself, hidden under my layers of self-doubt and depression.

It was obvious from the first time we hung out that Sera wasn't afraid to feel strong emotions and dream big dreams. Underneath tattoos and attitude, Sera was insecure—struggling with her identity and feeling out of place. But she had this brilliance that shined. She'd tell me with a smile that she was going to be a famous writer one day. She took herself too seriously, but knew how to make fun of herself at the same time. She had a sarcastic, biting, punk rock sense of humor and didn't take my shit without dishing it back twice as hard. I fell for her for sure.

"Its true man, she's dead. I'm sorry to have to be the one to tell you. Things have been strange around here the last couple days," said Spam in West Philadelphia. I called his house after talking to Sera's voicemail. "Everyone around here is freaking out. You two were really close, huh? I'm really sorry." Shock. Disbelief. As the tears started down my face I could feel this unfamiliar emotion rising up inside of me the way that you feel unfamiliar muscles in your body the day after doing a new exercise. It really hurt.

Sera and I had a lot in common. We were hopeless romantics who suffered from wanderlust. We waxed poetic over freight trains and the call of the open road. She was a great traveling partner. We loved gathering stories in our travels and were obsessed with recording history as it unfolded, but also making our own and illuminating the meaning of our experiences as young traveling anarchists at the end of the millennium. We loved punk rock, the music of course, but the cultural scene that had nurtured us as teenagers and made us feel somewhere that we belonged. Sera was a couple years younger than me, a few generations in punk rock years, and she'd make tapes for me of bands she loved that had come around after my time like (Young) Pioneers and Anti-Product. I'd tell her stories about going to Nausea and Missing Foundation shows in the old squats on the Lower East Side.

We spoke a similar language. We loved words and communicating. Her letters were a crafty mix of English, Spanish, and broken French, with a periodic smattering of Armenian from her childhood. We shared intense common ground because we had a lot of the same neurosis and insecurities. In our own ways we both tried to shirk our sheltered, educated, upper middle-class backgrounds by dropping out of school to hang out on the streets and learn lessons the hard way. We both had a lot to prove to ourselves and the people around us. We were never satisfied with our work, no matter how much we were doing. We threw ourselves into crazy situations to feel alive, to feel things intensely. We were running from the ghosts of our childhoods and found peace on the open road, in the excitement of the new, the stories of strangers, and in the struggle for justice. We were both manic depressive.

Mike Antipathy called from Maryland, his voice breaking up on the message. He and Greg Wells and Ammi Keller had gone to the bridge Sera had jumped from on their way back to Richmond from the funeral in New York. Greg said, "It was beautiful, man. That's the crazy part. You could almost see the ocean from the bridge. It was so peaceful."

He was crying just a little, and I could picture the expression on his somber face as we talked and bonded in the intense way that mutual friends do when their connecting link is suddenly gone. When we hung up I found the bridge on the road atlas. North of Baltimore on the I-95. The Susquehanna River feeding into Chesapeake Bay feeding into the Atlantic Ocean. Death by water. Painful. All that time in the air to think about what you've just done. The finality. *And I am not scared, looking at myself, if anything, I'll recognize the real truth of who I am.* Sera's cryptic words in her last piece for *Slug and Lettuce*, the newspaper we both had a column in. How long had she been planning it? How long did she torture herself with the thought before she finally got the nerve to do it? I shuddered, and took a deep breath.

When the depression comes it's like having lead weights on all your limbs and thoughts and feelings and emotions. Its not just being really sad. I'm sad because Sera's dead, but I'm not depressed. Imagine for a second that all of your deepest and worst insecurities have risen to the surface and are present with you wherever you go—every conversation you have is accompanied by a second internal dialogue telling you in real time that everything coming out of your mouth is full of shit, and that you're a liar and a hypocrite and a coward and you better kill yourself as soon as you can before everyone finds out how fucked up you really are. And then imagine that the pain and shame of hating yourself is so great that the thoughts of ending your life are constant, like a broken record, throwing yourself in front of moving cars, jumping out of windows, gun in the back of the head, carbon monoxide in the garage, a handful of pills—it's both exhausting and horrible. And it feels like it's never going to end.

The couple times it has happened to me, I've stopped being able to take care of myself. I get cuts on my hands and don't tend to them, even after they get infected and nasty. I get confused and scattered, lose sense of direction and get lost in neighborhoods I know like the back of my hand. I shut down. I stop being able to go to work and buy groceries. I stop being able to communicate with anyone because I can't formulate sentences between the black noise and records skipping in my brain. Everything seems pointless and irrelevant because I know I'm going to be dead soon. The only thing I seem to remember is to eat, and that's what I do, I eat until I'm sick because I'm craving something that I'm not getting. And then I feel like shit because I'm not even paying attention to what my body wants or needs. I stop being able to get out of bed. I curl up in a ball and wish someone would put me out of my misery. My life is one big mistake. And no matter how many times I've come out of it, each new time it never feels like it's ever going to end.

I can't really get mad at her. Sera wasn't in control of herself when she jumped off that bridge. She just wanted the pain to end. She felt so uncomfortable in her skin that she couldn't take it anymore. Suicide is not a malicious act. The year before, I spent four months suicidal and psychotic, stuck in a miserable halfway house for people with severe psychiatric disabilities. Manic-depression is a sickness, a disease. But it's more complicated because it's the most brilliant and talented people who are cursed with it. Its a blessing and a curse—an imbalance of chemicals that torments but lets them see and feel things other people can't, allows them to create art and music and words that grab people by the heart and soul, allows them to kiss the sky and come back down to tell the tale.

There just aren't words in our vocabularies to talk about it. I don't like *disease* at all. It doesn't capture what's going on because it's so two-sided; on the flip side of all that horror lies so much beauty. But the fact is that although there's so much we still don't know about manic-depression, we do know it's genetic—passed down through the generations, through blood. It's brought out by environmental factors like a fucked up childhood, but only for those who are genetically predisposed to it. You can't get it by watching too much television and eating too many Pop Tarts as a youth.

Sera was sensitive to the pain of others because she truly knew what pain felt like. She had an incredible head on her shoulders that raced with a fury and drew connections in seconds; the structure of her written sentences reflect a mind that could juggle multiple subjects with ease. She was a brilliant thinker and had a haunting way with words. She knew how to paint a picture in text and relay it to you like a priceless gift. She had an extraordinary memory, she talked about going to school for environmental law and we knew she could do it. But she was tormented by the demons inside her. She struggled for justice and peace wherever she went, but she didn't know how to treat herself justly or what it was like to be at peace.

•　　　•　　　•

My friend Matt is a seaweed farmer. He lives with his partner Kehben on a piece of land on the coast of Maine. They're both dedicated activists I've known for years who left the city to create sustainable revolutionary community. Kehben swears she sees a change in Matt since he started spending so much time in the ocean. "It's just become a part of him," she says, "the sea, the salt in the water, the waves. He's out there all day. You can see it in the look in his eyes," she tells me, "he's calmer, more stable, more at peace."

I take a drug called Lithium Carbonate—600mg, twice a day, every day. You can find Lithium on the periodic table; it's an element. The pills I take are synthesized in a laboratory somewhere, but the material they're synthesized from comes from the ocean. It's a sea salt. Even after using it for more than half a century the doctors don't know how it works but it has something to do with altering the ion exchange in the brain. It keeps me stable. It's still mysterious, but Lithium creates a homeostasis in the brain, some type of equilibrium that theoretically keeps one from jumping off bridges or walking down subway tracks thinking the world is about to end. It keeps you from getting too manic or too depressed. They give it to people diagnosed with Bipolar Disorder.

Bipolar Disorder is a fancy word for manic depression. Some officials decided that the word depression in manic depression was too much of a stigma and they wanted something more clinical for their medical reports. The polar thing refers to the fact that some folks are depressed all the time (unipolar) and some folks switch back and forth between mania and depression (bipolar). Some bipolar folks—like me—have huge dips and peaks over long periods, while folks like Sera go up and down quickly. In the psych jargon, they call what Sera had rapid cycling. These words get thrown around and become quite ambiguous and confusing. Doesn't everybody have mood swings? At what point does it become something that gets labeled a disease? At what point, if any, does it make sense to start taking the drugs? The majority of my friends would probably be diagnosed with some form of crazy label by mainstream psychiatrists because a lot of mainstream psychiatrists are just the pawns of the big drug companies, which want to doll out as much product as they can to get you hooked, so you'll be coming back for the fix. As a subculture we don't usually take the whole *crazy* thing too seriously. It's a word that me and my people throw around with ease. In a world so obviously insane, it's a complement to be considered crazy by the mainstream, right? I recall Sera saying that to me on more than one occasion.

But a lot of us struggle with our madness and don't always find ways of coping that work, and we deal in different ways. There is a point where you have to come to some kind of conclusion about the nature of your problems. This time last year I was sitting in a tiny cell in the psych unit of Los Angeles County Jail talking to the flickering light bulbs, thinking that they were listening. I was picked up by the LAPD because I was running down the streets putting my fists through car windows and hopping over fences and running through traffic screaming the lyrics to early 80s pop songs and laughing hysterically. I was very happy that the world as we had known it had just ended and we were all living on in dreamtime and that everyone I saw was just a reflection of me so it didn't matter what I did. I thought that the helicopters flying above had fancy cameras and were recording all my actions and broadcasting them live to members of the secret illuminati all across the world. I was convinced that I was the center of the universe and it was all so crystal clear, it all made so much sense that it was a wonder that everyone else couldn't see it. By all measurements, I was stark-raving loony toons.

I'd been building up to it for months. What happened wasn't inevitable. I'd stopped taking my psych drugs a few month earlier because it seemed obvious that I didn't need them anymore and I was just being my usual hectic self—working on too many projects, leaving piles of paper everywhere, riding around on my bike and being super busy. I'd actually convinced a foundation to give a grant to an organization I'd started—a regional seed library for community gardeners. I was happy to have some focus in my life. I'd been out of town for a couple months interviewing farmers and I was back—making a million phone calls and setting up meetings between people who I didn't know and didn't know each other. I had all these exciting ideas about building alliances between small seed companies and organic farmers. I was going to raise a ton of money and get jobs for my friends and the kids in my hood hanging out on the street and smoking weed all day.

We were going to have a little revolution on our block. I was having these amazing conversations with my neighbors who remembered when the Black Panthers, who had formed as an organization a couple blocks from our house in the late 60s, had their free breakfast program and community patrols going. I was talking on the radio and giving speeches in front of local community groups and making appearances on the local public access TV station, articulating a vision of taking power out of the hands of petrol-chemical corporations and putting it back in the hands of the people through localized community controlled agriculture. I was charming and eloquent and articulate and full of passion. And I seemed to inspire people wherever I went. I was on fire. It felt historic. I was loving it.

Then things began to get out of control. I stopped sleeping well because my head was bursting with amazing ideas. I would draw complex diagrams in my journal, fleshing out the importance of edge space between wild and cultivated systems and how one was dependent on the other. I'd take detailed notes on a curriculum I wanted to teach to high school students about the relationships between cultural and biological diversity. I was reading twenty books at the same time and writing twenty-five essays. My mind would race, moving micro and then scaling out to macro and then right back to micro within a matter of seconds. I could feel the presence of old friends with me, as things they had said to me in the past would surface in my mind. I would have conversations with them and write them down. I was channeling spirits or something.

Then, my thoughts started to get more desperate. Everything started to seem relevant. I mean everything. My mind took any two things and drew connections between them. The projects I was working on suddenly seemed very urgent. I had discovered *the* secret that was going to bring everyone together— unite everyone in the world against the global power structure. I was reading *Revolutionary Suicide* by Huey P. Newton and books about COINTELPRO, the program the FBI used to destabilize activist groups in the '70s. I started getting paranoid. I started to have the very disconcerting feeling that I was about to die, that there were important people that wanted me dead.

I started getting short with my friends, cutting them off in mid-sentence because I knew how important it was that I get my thoughts out before it was too late. I knew that I wouldn't live to see the day, but I wanted to make sure I did as much as I could before *they* got me. I needed to leave behind instructions for everyone so they'd know what to do without me around. I'd wake up in the morning from a couple hours of restless sleep and pour out pages and pages of ideas for what life should look like after the revolution. My housemates, my girlfriend, and everyone else was getting sick of this and telling me to chill the fuck out. I had great ideas, they said, but no one was going to listen if I was talking this fast.

They'd understand later. I stopped hanging out with anyone who knew me well and started hanging out with people I'd just met and didn't find it so disturbing that I had slipped totally off my rocker. I started walking up to total strangers on the street and having amazing conversations. I'd walk to the community garden down the street and just hang with the plants. I was so in tune with the universe that I could feel every last blade of grass as if they were breathing with me. Each plant had an incredibly different personality and I would spend hours just listening to them talk to me. It was so incredible. Meanwhile, I began to get more and more estranged. My housemates were scared of me. Everyone was talking about me behind my back, but no one had the courage to confront me.

My mom came to visit and in her typical fashion, proceeded to organize my friends to take some direct action. One night they sat me down and pleaded with me to start taking my drugs again. I was furious.

Were they fucking blind? Hadn't they been reading the news? Didn't they realize that the pharmaceutical companies and the agri-chemical companies had merged into the *Life Science Industry* and these people wanted nothing less than enslavement of the human race and control of the entire planet? These were the same people who were trying to genetically engineer the world's crops to be dependent on their herbicides, the same ones who created the technology that can make seed crops reproduce sterile. It's so fucking American to think that you can fix everything with a pill or feed people with chemicals. Hadn't they read Huxley's *Brave New World*? How could they not see what was going on when it was so obviously right in front of their eyes? You want me to trust these people's medicine? You gotta be kidding me. These people peddle pesticides to farmers in the developing world and graft human ears to lab mice. They are evil motherfuckers. I'm not going to put those drugs in my body—they're just going to kill the parts of my brain that are working so well! You just want me to be a robot like the rest of you. Fuck that shit and fuck all of you!

So off to Los Angeles I went to get myself locked up in jail. It's very hard to argue with someone who is not only manic and delusional but also not that far off the mark. For brevity's sake, I'll spare all the details, but let me just say that I'm lucky I didn't end up with an LAPD bullet in my chest. While mourning Sera, the whole thing hit me on another level because I was conscious that it could have been me dying in some fucked up and dramatic way, and the same people would have been freaking out and trying to figure out what they could have done to stop it if only they had known.

A big conflict while traveling with Sera was that she'd always try to get me to stop taking my psych drugs. She said that they slowed me down. The whole idea of them just made her uncomfortable. Sera didn't believe in a life without extremes and she didn't want her experiences mediated by some drug made by The Man. "They just want you to think that you can't take care of yourself without those drugs," she'd say. She'd taken Prozac for a while when she was a teenager and had hated it. It made her numb. It killed her sex drive. She said she just couldn't feel anything real when she was on it. She got off it quick and didn't look back.

For many of our friends, psych drugs symbolized defeat. Like having to spend your last money on a greyhound after getting kicked out of the train yard. But worse. Taking psych meds means adopting a different lifestyle. It means having health insurance, so it means having a job. It means staying in one place, so it means being stable. The pills are a constant reminder that you're dependent on the system that you hate to keep you alive and healthy, that you're tied right into the death machine.

They say that most manic-depressives go off their drugs a bunch of times before they either kill themselves or realize that they need them. That's a hard one to hear, and I still don't really believe it, but mania is alluring. They say that we get addicted to the intensity like a drug. But the intensity is a pendulum swing—if you swing too far over to one side, you're inevitably going to swing in the other direction. I can plot the last eight years of my life on a graph and it would look like a big sine wave. Huge peaks and dips. And the upswings have been responsible for everything cool I've done in my life. But the downs are fucking miserable, and anyone who knows will tell you that delusions of grandeur are masking great insecurity deep down.

So in the interest of sticking around the planet for a while, I'm learning new dances with the enemy. I've made my choice to take the drugs and deal with all the sacrifice that go along with that choice; not being able to stay up all night, slowing down, staying in one place, holding down a job for more than a couple months at a time, going to a bunch of therapy, all things I've always been scared of. But I want to live and grapple with my demons and it's going to take a long time. I was worried the drugs were going to turn me into a zombie, but trust me, I feel strong emotions everyday and I need to keep that shit in check. Reading her letters, looking at her smiling face in the dozens of photographs I have of her, listening to the mix tapes she lovingly made me, thinking about the impact she's had on my life, its so hard to believe Sera's dead. She had such wide-open, traveler eyes. I remember when we were on the road and we'd wake up and tell each other our dreams. She taught me this word once in Armenian, *yavroos* which translates to something like *one who knows your soul.* I loved that woman something real. She bared her soul to me. She still feels so alive. And that's the strange paradox about the whole thing, it's because she was more alive than most of us. She felt things more. She took more risks. She refused to play by society's rules. She lived with an intensity that most people only dream of. And she lived her life like someone who always felt like she didn't have enough time.

But it's really fucking sad, and I can't stop thinking of that ancient Greek myth of Icarus and his wings of wax. In the old story Icarus' father Daedalus builds a pair of wings out of wax and feathers for his son so that they can escape from the island they've been imprisoned on. Despite his father's warnings, as the myth goes, Icarus flies too close to the sun, melts his beautiful wings, and falls into the ocean to his death. The moral of the story is that Icarus was fortunate enough to have been given wings, but he wasn't patient enough to learn how to use them safely—he couldn't see to anything but soaring as high as he could, so he ended up in the sea.

•   •   •

About a month ago, me and my people were having a party at the house in Oakland. My friend Matt was visiting from Maine, and we were sitting by the fireplace catching up. Matt said to me, "You know, Sascha, you should really come harvest seaweed with me back East next summer. I think you'd really love it. He smiled warmly." "It sounds great man," I replied. "But I don't think I'm going to be able to make it really. I'm trying hard to settle down for a little while and Maine is about as far as you can get from here without leaving the country." He smiled again. "That's alright, man. We'll be there for the next thirty to forty years. You have plenty of time." I looked at his face and suddenly imagined it full of wrinkles, the two of us in our sixties living by the ocean with a bunch of our crazy friends and growing old together. It didn't seem that outlandish.

I wanted to get old with Sera Bilizikian in my life. I figured that's the way it would be. Sera had a beautiful pair of wings that carried her to faraway places and on amazing journeys. She burned bright in her short twenty-three years, did a lot of good for the world while she was here, and will be missed by many people. I hope that as a community we can learn the lessons from this fucked up tragedy, and that it inspires us to learn how to understand and take better care of each other.

PART

2

Wax and Feathers

The next five years of my life were full of wild adventures and epic lessons, far beyond what I could have imagined riding freight trains and all my travels down south and up north. The publication of The Bipolar World in the San Francisco Bay Guardian was like casting a powerful magic spell, suddenly all of these doors began opening and people came out of the woodwork to join me and share their stories and mad visions. There were a lot of brilliant and creative people who had been waiting for an excuse to start talking about their complicated and painful relationships to the psychiatric system. That article was the first time my written voice reached ears outside of the anarchist cultural ghetto that had been my home for so long, and it felt good to be heard and understood by people from different lifestyles and cultural backgrounds. I began to feel like a pioneer species in a permaculture model, like a dandelion with deep taproots, pulling up underground ideas and culture and letting them filter into the waters of the mainstream. Even if it was just a small beginning, a whisper in a sea of bio-psychiatric noise, I was using the power of my subcultural voice to shift old narratives about "mental illness" and "madness." After so many years of struggling with my identity and feeling like an outsider in other people's movements, I was carving a place where I could be myself; use my experience to build bridges between worlds and help other people who had struggled in similar ways. Because it was so personal and raw, my writing felt much more powerful, something that was breaking down barriers, and creating spaces for new possibilities. Below is the more punk rock edit of that original article:

WALKING THE EDGE OF INSANITY
I.

I was 18 years old the first time they locked me up in a psych ward. The police found me walking on the subway tracks in New York City and I was convinced the world was about to end and I was being broadcast live on prime time

TV on all the channels. After I'd been walking along the tracks through three stations, the cops wrestled me to the ground, arrested me, and brought me to an underground jail cell and then the emergency room of Bellevue psychiatric hospital where they strapped me to a bed. Once they managed to track down my terrified mother, she signed some papers, a nurse shot me up with some hardcore anti-psychotic drugs, and I woke up two weeks later in the "Quiet Room" of a public mental hospital upstate. I spent the next two and a half months there, another couple months in this strange private "behavior modification" program/halfway house that my mom put me in, and the following years trying to figure out how to set my life up in such a way that that shit would never happen again.

Before the big dramatic crash back in New York, I'd gone off to college and had been living on the other side of the country in Portland, Oregon. I'd lost contact with my old friends and spent the school year studying in the library, immersed in academic books and ignoring the outside world. Around finals' time, I got sick and went to the heath clinic. The nurse gave me a prescription for penicillin and I had an allergic reaction to it and almost died. To counteract the effects of the penicillin, the hospital gave me a hardcore steroid called Prednizone, which fucked up my sleeping schedule and, along with the bit of mescaline and lots of pot and coffee I'd been indulging in earlier that year, sent me off the deep end.

It seemed innocent at first, if not a little strange. Somehow I managed to have this infinite amount of energy—I'd ride my bike fast everywhere and do tons of sit-ups and push-ups after sleeping badly for two hours. I slipped into a perpetually manic state, and by the summertime had this idea to start a food co-op at our school, which somehow mushroomed into this grandiose plot to destabilize the U.S. economy by printing our own currency. That was just the tip of the iceberg. I had a new idea every couple hours, all involving connecting different people and projects, and I managed to convince people that my ideas were good. We started stockpiling food, putting flyers around town, and building our little empire.

Then it got crazier. I started to think the radio was talking to me and I was seeing intense meanings in billboards that no one else was seeing. There were subliminal messages everywhere trying to tell a small amount of people that the world was about to go through drastic changes and we needed to be ready. I'd been studying anthro-linguistics and was fascinated by language, how the words we use shape our perception of reality. I started reading too much meaning into everything. People would talk to me, and I was convinced there was another language underneath what we thought we were saying that everyone was using without even realizing it. I kept having visions that the world was going to end, but we were all going to live on in something that looked liked television and was going to connect us all. We were living in a big computer program someone had written, or an ancient riddle, or some cosmic joke. Whatever was going on, it was obvious I was the only one who could see it because no one knew what the hell I was talking about! I couldn't finish a sentence without starting another because everything was so fucking urgent. There was so much to say I couldn't get the words out without more that needed said appearing on my tongue.

The thing that made the situation so complicated and inevitably tragic, was that no one knew me enough to know that I'd lost my shit and was about to crash really hard. In 1992, Portland was not the cool anarcho-mecca it is today. The folks around me thought, "Oh, that's Sascha—the guy doing the food co-op thing. He's just a little crazy." No one seemed able to see that I was having a psychotic breakdown and if they did, they were too scared to get near me for fear I was going to bite them or something.

Thankfully, I took a "quick" trip to Berkeley, and my old friends realized immediately that something was wrong. They called my mom, she bought me a plane ticket, and they managed to get me on a plane back East. When I arrived at the airport my mom brought me back to her apartment. She told me that she was going to take me to see "a man that could help me" in the morning. I didn't like the sound of that, and it was obvious that *they'd* brainwashed her memory so she wouldn't remember the role she was playing in the *grand scheme.*

After I'd been in the psych ward for awhile they diagnosed me with bipolar disorder (or manic-depression) and, along with a pile of pills they were shoving down my throat, gave me a mood stabilizing drug called Depacote. They told my mom to get used to the idea that her son would be grappling with a serious mental disorder for the rest of his life.

I didn't realize it at the time, but I, like millions of other Americans, would spend years wrestling with the implications of that diagnosis. Manic-depression kills tens of thousands of mostly young people every year. One out of five diagnosed ends up doing themselves in. But I wasn't convinced that gulping down a handful of pills everyday would make me sane. At the time I thought it was a bunch of bullshit. Their treatment of me in the ward didn't give me much faith in the medical establishment.

The mental ward was some twisted circus where the psychiatrists would visit everyday and write our scripts with these huge, expensive gold and silver Cross pens, emblazoned on the side with "Prozac" and "Xanax," while we all sat there, shaking and drooling on ourselves, staring off into space and pacing white hallways. It was a nightmare.

I'm not sure why, but the bipolar diagnosis didn't last long. By the time I got out of the halfway house five months later, the doctors were blaming the incident on bad drug interactions—the high levels of Prednizone at the hospital mixed with coffee and hallucinogens. It had been too much for my fragile system. It was going to take a while to recover, but I'd be able to lead a normal, healthy life like the rest of the population.

For years, I shelved this period into a corner of my brain—I never knew what to make of it. Somehow it didn't fit together. It became another crazy story that I'd share with new friends. "Yeah, ha, ha, I'm kinda loony toons, for real man, check out what happened to me when I was a teenager…" But in the back of my mind was this fear that I was going to end up getting locked up again.

For someone diagnosed with a *serious mental illness*, the next six years were amazing. I had adventures all over the place. The company I kept didn't stigmatize people who were eccentric or weird; we reveled in it, wore it on our sleeves. It seemed obvious that my crazy behavior as a teenager had been a natural reaction to being raised in a crazy environment.

I was raised by leftist parents who taught me to question everything and be skeptical of big business and capitalism. I spent my teenage years growing up in the punk scene, which glorified craziness and disrespect for authority. From the time I was little, people noted that I was very sensitive to the world around me and the suffering of others, maybe too sensitive. My world-view didn't leave room for the possibility that my instability and volatility might have something to do with inherent biology. So I went on with my life.

A year after I'd gotten out of being institutionalized, my mom was freaking out that I'd dropped out of college to travel and then show up at her apartment talking about this big freak circus we were organizing. She was convinced I was going crazy and getting delusional and grandiose again.

I was one of two "organizers" of the festival but everyone kept making fun of me because I was always leaving my shit everywhere and juggling a dozen projects and periodically dropping all the pins. So people started calling me "Scatter."

That fall and winter I wrote a big zine about the experience and it ended up published as a book by this anarchist press, Autonomedia. I used the name "Sascha Scatter" because it sounded cooler to me than "Sascha Altman DuBrul"—although, comically, at the last minute my mom called up the Autonomedia warehouse in Brooklyn and convinced them to put "Sascha Altman DuBrul" on the spine! My mom can be pretty pushy. I kept using "Sascha Scatter" and sometimes still do, depending on who I'm writing for.

Shortly thereafter, I got obsessed with seeds and seed politics and people who didn't know about my sketchy drunk punk circus past thought "Scatter" had something to do with seeds.

II.

My mom came home from work one spring evening to find that I was curled up on her kitchen floor, almost catatonic, telling her that I was sorry but I couldn't take it anymore and I was going to kill myself. I was 24 years old. My hands were covered in cuts that I'd let get infected because I was too preoccupied to tend to them. My clothes were dirty and torn. I was getting lost in neighborhoods that I knew like the back of my hand. I couldn't look anyone in the eye when I talked to them.

There was a repeating tape loop in my head telling me what a horrible person I was—that I was a liar and a hypocrite and a coward and I didn't deserve to live. I was obsessed with killing myself. It was exhausting and horrible, and

I was convinced it was never going to end. Strangely, A couple months earlier I'd been on top of the world.

Focused and clear and driven, getting up in front of crowds and giving talks about exciting and revolutionary things, organizing half a dozen projects, I was the model of an activist. But in the middle of it all I just crashed. I stopped being able to get out of bed. All the confidence suddenly disappeared. I stopped being able to focus and started feeling very awkward around even my oldest friends. One by one, my projects fell apart till they were a halo of broken dreams circling above my head as I wandered the city streets alone.

I ended up back in the psych ward and then the same halfway house/rehab program in the suburbs that my mom had put me in as a teenager. I was miserable and lonely. The doctors weren't sure so they diagnosed me with Schizo-affective disorder. They gave me an anti-depressant called Celexa and an atypical anti-psychotic called Zyprexa. I was in group therapy everyday. After a couple weeks they let me volunteer at an organic farm for a few hours each day down the road. I was sowing seeds and potting plants in the greenhouse. Eventually I convinced them to let me move out to the farm and come for outpatient care a couple times each week.

It took a couple months, but I could see that the drugs were working for me. It was more than circumstance—it felt chemical. Slowly the horrible noise and thoughts faded and I started to feel good. I remember watching an early summer sunset over the fields and realizing I was happy for the first time in months. Once I moved onto the farm I would come into the city on the weekends to work the farmer's market and hang out with my friends.

As obvious as it was that they were helping me, I saw the drugs as a temporary solution. They made me gain weight. I had a hard time waking up. My mouth was dry. They were relatively new drugs, and the doctors didn't know the long-term side effects of taking them. How would I talk to my friends about it? What if there was some global economic crisis and instead of running around with my crew torching banks and tearing up the concrete I was going to be withdrawing from some drug I suddenly didn't have access to?

But I didn't worry myself about the long-term. I was happy to have my life back. As the leaves started to change, I was planning my trip back to California. There was a room in a collective house in North Oakland and a job in Berkeley with friends waiting for me.

III.

The police picked me up wandering the streets of Los Angeles on New Years Day, 2002 after I'd been smashing church windows with my bare fists and running through traffic scaring the hell out of people screaming the lyrics to punk songs, convinced that the world had ended. I was quickly given the diagnosis of bipolar disorder again and loaded down with meds. "That's so reductionist, so typical of Western science to isolate everything into such simplistic, bifurcated relationships." I'd tell the overworked white-coated psychiatrist staring blankly from the other side of the tiny jail cell as I paced back and forth and he scribbled notes on a clipboard that said "Risperdal" in big letters at the top. "If anything I'm *multi-polar*, *poly-polar*—I go to poles you'd never even be able to dream up in your imagination-less science. And all those drugs you're shooting me up with. You're all a bunch of fools!" I paced my cell.

Every time you get locked up it gets harder to put the pieces back together. Physiologically, the brain and body take longer to recover. It takes a lot out of someone to go through a mental breakdown. Picture being bipolar like a pendulum swing with suicidally depressed at one end, delusionally psychotic at the other, and with healthy and stable somewhere in the middle. If you swing to one end you're bound to swing back to the other side. After months of sleepless mania your reserves are depleted. It's inevitable that serious depression will follow.

Finally, after the month in jail, a couple weeks in a Kaiser psych ward, and four months in a halfway house for people with severe psychiatric disabilities, I got it together to move into my old collective house in North Oakland. I was taking a mood stabilizing drug called Lithium and an anti-depressant called Welbutrin.

The ground I was walking on was still a little shaky. I was beginning to read after not being able to focus for months. I got a full time job for the first time in my life, started going to therapy, and took really good care of my body. I made it through my one year anniversary of getting locked up and felt so blessed that I had made it that far.

IV.

After they found Sera dead, floating in the Susquehanna River, and I had to grapple with the meaning of her suicide, I started doing the research I'd been putting off for so long. I started to pick up the books and began the internal and external dialogue about my condition and put the puzzle together. I talked to friends openly and used my *Slug and Lettuce* column to talk about madness and manic-depression. I started coming to terms with the paradox that however much contempt I feel towards the pharmaceutical industry for making a profit off of our misery and however much I aspire to be living outside the system, the drugs help keep me alive and in the end I'm so thankful for them.

According to the August 19, 2002 issue of *Time* magazine, 2.3 million Americans have been diagnosed with bipolar disorder. Of course, mental disorders are more confusing than so many other illnesses, more based on cultural definitions that we'd like to admit. Diagnoses that people get stuck with for life are determined by a set of questions in an official book rather than any kind of concrete blood or piss tests. Diagnoses come in and out of style like fashion trends, it used to be "in" for doctors to diagnose children with ADHD, and all of a sudden, it's bipolar disorder. It wasn't long ago that homosexuality was considered a disorder, which is enough to make you not want to ever set foot in a psych doctors office. Someone with bipolar disorder one week, might be considered schizophrenic the next, then schizo-affective the week after that. Plus, drugs work so differently for different people—that's why there are dozens of different anti-depressants.

We have yet to create a reasonable language to talk about it all so those of us who do talk about it end up with all of these sterile and clinical words in our mouths that feel uncomfortable and never get to the heart of things and very often skirt around the issues. When it comes down to it, as a culture we don't understand mental illness so for the most part we don't talk about it and leave the opinions up to the doctors and the drug companies.

In the end what it comes down to for me is that I desperately feel the need to connect with other folks like myself so I can validate my experiences and not feel so damn alone in the world, and pass along the lessons I've learned to help make it easier for other people struggling like myself. By my nature and the way I was raised, I don't trust mainstream medicine or corporate culture, but the fact that I'm sitting here writing this essay right now is proof that their drugs are helping me. And I'm looking for others out there with similar experiences. But I feel so alienated sometimes, even by the language I find coming out of my mouth or by the text I type out on the computer screen. Words like *disorder*, *disease*, and *dysfunction*, just seem so very hollow and crude. I feel like I'm speaking a foreign and clinical language that is useful for navigating my way though the current system, but doesn't translate into my own internal vocabulary where things are so much more fluid and complex. I can only hope that in the near future we will have created better language to talk about all this stuff.

But it's really hard. As a society we seem to remain still in the early stages of the dialogue where you're either for or against the mental health system. Like, either you swallow the anti-depressant ads on daytime television as modern day gospel and start giving your dog Prozac, or you're convinced we're living in *Brave New World* and all the psych drugs are just part of a big conspiracy to keep us from being self-reliant and realizing our true potential. I think it's really about time that we start carving some more of the middle ground with stories from outside the mainstream and creating a new language for ourselves that reflects all the complexity and brilliance that we hold inside.

Original Icarus Project Mission Statement
(written with Jacks McNamara in a tree in Humboldt County)

As the ancient Greek myth is told, the young boy Icarus and his inventor father Daedalus were imprisoned in a maze on an island and trying to escape. Daedalus was crafty and made them both pairs of wings built carefully out of wax and feathers, but warned Icarus not to fly too close to the blazing sun or his wings would fall to pieces. Icarus, being young and foolish, was so intoxicated with his new ability to fly that he soared too high, the delicate wings melted and burned, and he fell into the ocean and drowned. For countless generations, the story of Icarus' wings has served to remind us that we are humans rather than gods, and that sometimes the most incredible of gifts can also be the most dangerous.

The Icarus Project was created in the beginning of the 21st century by people diagnosed in the contemporary language as Bipolar or Manic-Depressive.

Defining ourselves outside convention, we see our condition as a dangerous gift to be cultivated and taken care of rather than as a disease or disorder needing to be "cured." With this double edged blessing we have the ability to fly to places of great vision and creativity, but like the boy Icarus, we also have the potential to fly dangerously close to the sun—into realms of delusion and psychosis—and crash in a blaze of fire and confusion. At our heights we may find ourselves capable of creating music, art, words, and inventions which touch people's souls and change the course of history. At our depths we may end up alienated and alone, incarcerated in psychiatric institutions, or dead by our own hands.

Despite these risks, we recognize the intertwined threads of madness and creativity as tools of inspiration and hope in this repressed and damaged society. We understand that we are a group that has been misunderstood and persecuted throughout history, but has also been responsible for some of its most brilliant creations. And we are proud. We're all struggling to create full and independent lives for ourselves where the ultimate goal is not just to survive, but to thrive. Despite the effort necessary to stay balanced and grounded we intend to make the world we live on better, more beautiful, and way more interesting.

While many of us use mood-stabilizing drugs like Lithium to regulate and dampen the extremes of our manias and the hopeless depths of our depressions, others among us have learned how to control the mercurial nature of our moods through diet, exercise, and spiritual focus. Many of us make use of non-Western practices such as Chinese medicine, Yoga, and meditation. Often we find that we can handle ourselves better when we channel our tremendous energy into creation, some of us paint murals and write books, some of us convert diesel cars to run on vegetable oil and make gardens that are nourished with the waste water from our showers. In our own ways we're all struggling to create full and independent lives for ourselves

The Icarus Project Website is a place for people struggling with Manic-Depression outside the mainstream to connect and build an alternative support network. We hope to learn from each others' mistakes and victories, stories and art, and create a new culture and language that resonates with our actual experiences of this "disorder" rather than trying to fit our lives into the reductionist framework offered by the current mental health establishment. We would like this site to become a place that helps people like us feel less alienated, and allows us, both as individuals and as a community, to tap into the true potential that lies between brilliance and madness.

Shortly after the Icarus Project website went live in November of 2002, I embarked on a cross-country tour in a beat up 1982 Toyota pickup truck, facilitating workshops in radical community spaces and collective house kitchens. I started with a basic set of questions that evolved into some incredible discussions. Here is text from the original flyer:

Navigating the World of Mental Health as a Radical in the 21st Century

As creative folks skeptical of the conventional social system, what does it mean within our extended community for someone to be "mentally ill" or struggling with traditional labels such as "clinical depression," "bipolar disorder," or "schizophrenia?" How helpful is the modern psychiatric paradigm that revolves around medicine and mental disorders and how much of it is really just a function of powerful pharmaceutical corporations, public funding cuts, and a society that equates productivity with health? Are there other frameworks for understanding what it means to be "crazy"? Are there alternative ways to heal? How do we begin the process?

Chances are pretty high that if you're reading this, you or someone you care about has been grappling with these questions for years. Come join an open discussion and learn more about the Icarus Project, a radical support network by and for people struggling with the dangerous gifts commonly labeled as mental illnesses. the Icarus Project envisions a new culture and language that resonates with our actual experiences rather than trying to fit our lives into a conventional framework. By joining together as individuals and as a community, we hope to create space where the intertwined threads of madness and creativity can inspire hope and transformation in a repressed and damaged world.

It literally felt like we were carving space in the psychic architecture with our words—carving new rules for how to interact with one another and inspiring others to do the same. This was part of a mass email I sent out to my extended friends in the middle of that first tour.

Time Travel and Alternate Realities

To amuse myself on the Northwest drives up and down the coast, I've been writing a science fiction book in my head about time travel and alternate realities. Except it's not fiction—it's a metaphor for living with an extreme case of manic-depression and having an interesting life. In traditional Hopi language, there's no past, present, or future in the grammar structure—different objects and people have different "states of becoming"—another way of conceiving time. Working 40 hours and going back to the same house every night it's hard to get a grasp on that but traveling in the crazy way I have been lately, it becomes obvious that we all don't move at the same speeds.

It's easy to get a sense of this if you don't sleep for awhile, or sleep in a different place every night, or hang around lots of different groups of people all the time—everything has a tendency to speed up. You start taking in more information, juggling different things in your head, existing on some other plane of reality as the folks around you. If I slip out of gear and don't get enough sleep a couple nights in a row, I start moving fast and have to find a quiet place and knock myself out with heavy drugs to get moving at the consensus speed of the people around me. It's no fun being the only person at your speed—especially if you have a tendency to crash and burn.

But amidst my short cycle sleep-dep fiascoes on the road, I have this habit of noticing that time bends a lot and everything seems to repeat itself in these ironic and interesting ways. My life curves like a spiral—I end up in the same places with the same people at different times or I end up in familiar places with different people who look like and are doing the same things. Or I end up with familiar people in new places who are older now and I can't help but notice how we keep getting more badass as the years go on. It's like going in a circle, except the circle is spiraling towards the sky.

I can't help but acknowledge how our realities can shift so easily—especially if you're like me and have volatile brain chemistry. In the imaginary science fiction book I want to employ this slick literary device where I describe scenes from the perspective of someone delusionally psychotic—who thinks that he and his friends are superheroes. Then I want to describe the scenes from the perspective of someone who's suicidally depressed—and thinks that he and his friends are deadbeats and losers. Finally the same scenes are described by someone who's grounded and into being human—but sees glimmers of the magic he knew as a "madman" and blends it all together into some kind of interesting story.

I feel like a fucking superhero sometimes. I feel like a fucking deadbeat at times too. And I know I'm just human. And yet, I feel like I'm shaping the world around me. In a couple years, when I pass through these Northwest towns again, I won't be surprised to see some mark that I passed through before—more than the double circle "never give up" tags that I've been writing on the walls. It's gratifying to have people tell me that they got inspired to start growing food in the abandoned lot near their house after I came through and taught an urban permaculture workshop in their town four years before. Or the zine I wrote in a fit of loneliness and alienation got someone through a time in their life when they felt alone. Or that I inspired someone to go ride freight trains and have big adventures.

It makes me feel lucky to be a part of a thriving sub-culture or depending on how you look at it—a whole network of interconnected subcultures existing outside the mainstream. Ironically, one thing that makes us powerful is how small we are compared to the dominant culture. I imagine for most Americans who get their cultural identity from Hollywood movies and the nightly television it's hard to feel possible to make a difference in the world. The guidance and inspiration are stars—so high up and out of touch they might as well be in the fucking sky. I love feeling like the people who influence my life are within reach. In the past weeks I've crossed paths with more than a dozen of my true heroes and heroines. I love the feeling that we're mutually inspiring each other from our little corners. We send off ripples through the fabric of our friends.

A Handful of Seeds in a World Full of War

At the end of the tour I moved back to the East coast and got a job on an organic farm two hours north of New York City. It was the middle of winter. I had all these seeds from the West Coast, and I was determined to settle down in the Hudson River Valley and farm. Jacks got a job on a farm back in California, and we would check in every week on the phone and send each other excited emails when someone new would post on the Icarus discussion forums. I still wrote my gardening column for *Slug and Lettuce*, and tried to make sense of the stories I carried around in my head while I tended to the animals and worked in the fields. That spring I became proficient at using a hard rake to shape and clear beds. The soil was rocky and I would fill the paths with stones and then fill up 5 gallon buckets with them and then use the buckets to fill in holes in the road. The whole time I was pulling up memories and reworking the narratives, filling in the places that needed work as I went.

•　　　•　　　•

The day after they began dropping the latest bombs on Iraq, I was sitting in the greenhouse, planting flats of broccoli seeds. It was overcast with the sun periodically peeking through the clouds. I was surrounded by flats of baby seedlings. The air smelled like springtime, like rich compost and firewood smoke, like life and freedom.

As I dropped those seeds into the soil and placed trays of seed flats into the metal sink to soak up water from below I ruminated over the idea that so much of what seems to be missing in our modern lives is collective memory. We're so disconnected from our own past. Most of us have no idea what life was like for people in the world a hundred years ago; the stories of our ancestors have been replaced by incredibly whack sitcom plots, and the food we buy is genetically engineered in laboratories. I took the seed flats out of the sink and stuck them on the heating pad to germinate thinking of how easy it is to control people who don't know their own history and have no strong connection to the world around them.

These days the government and corporations seem to be able to program us like computers; they trigger our emotions with slick video clips and rewrite their new versions of the Truth every couple months and feed it to us like those mass produced AOL free minutes disks that show up in the mail. TV looks like some deranged Hollywood war movie I watched when I was a kid. I'm desensitized to the reality that there are bombs being dropped on the other side of the world, and people like me, with flesh and blood and families, are dying horrible deaths.

The Ugly Relationship Between Industrial Agriculture and War

At the end of World War II, American engineers used the technology designed for battle tanks and applied it to building huge farming tractors. The nitrate reserves from building bombs were turned into agricultural fertilizers, and nerve gas stockpiles were used to make industrial pesticides. The factories for making war munitions became the factories for industrial farm equipment and chemicals.

Industrial farms practice monoculture—planting single crops over wide ranges to be harvested uniformly. Monocultures need big machines to plant and harvest them. Monocultures need pesticides and herbicides because they don't have any built-in biological diversity. Bugs and diseases love them. Monocultures need to be tilled in every year, a process that destroys any soil structure, any memory in the land of what came before.

Small, diversified farms are more productive and sustainable. We plant the full range of temperate vegetable crops in the same fields, using companion planting and poly-culture to maximize space. We rotate where crops are placed to confuse pests and give the land rest. Rather than tilling the land every year, we hand weed the beds in the spring and put down straw mulch to keep down weeds and hold in water. Rather than spraying chemical pesticides, we grow flowers and make hedgerows to create habitat for beneficial insect predators who eat pests. We select and breed seeds and adapt them to our agro-ecosystems so we don't have to buy seeds made for chemical agriculture systems. We grow fifty varieties of tomatoes!

We'll be cleaning up the ecological disasters created by the monoculture model long after people realize what a bad idea it was. But monocultures are not about efficiency or progress. Monocultures are about control.

War is not so different. Bombs, like modern agriculture, are not about efficiency or progress, or peacekeeping, or justice. Bombs are about control. Bombs and monoculture allow a small amount of people to dominate the majority. When they finish bombing Iraq and move onto the next "rogue nation," the World Bank and the International Monetary Fund will lend the new government money to "rebuild," and they'll make them sign "structural adjustment" agreements to privatize everything and let American businesses import and export as they please, to build their strip malls where profitable. It's about integration into the market system and control of oil.

Although you may find it hard to believe, a handful of broccoli seeds is more powerful than all those bombs. The bombs destroy cultures, erase history, breed fear and disempowerment. Seeds create culture, bridge history, keep people fed and healthy, empower us to take control of our lives.

Tiny broccoli seeds are living history—they have a collective memory stretching back thousands of years to a Mediterranean coast where their wild relatives grew, passing through millions of farmers hands, culled and co-evolved, selected and reselected to be reincarnated every year in farms across the world. The broccoli seeds have the genetic memory of thousands of years of survival and adaptation through wars and plagues and all kinds of bullshit. My friend Frank Morton, who runs a seed company in Oregon, grew these seeds and passed them onto me as a gift of friendship. Now it's my turn to tend to them—

grow them out and pass them on to my friends like good stories.

The City Boy and the Farmer

The thick layer of snow just finally melted a couple days ago. The moon was ripe in the sky, reflecting off the glimmering puddles, and I was outside breathing in the cool spring air. Suddenly there's a whole other world exposed—all the things that have been lying dormant are stirring and rubbing the sleep out of their eyes. When I wake up in the morning I feel a surge of chlorophyll in the greening grass at my fingertips. The chickweed and dandelions are flowering on the garden beds, and the early pollinators are anxiously sucking up the nectar from the tiny blossoms. Baby lambs are just starting to be born—beautiful angelic looking creatures with black curious eyes. The Chinese cabbage in the greenhouse is going to seed and I've been making bouquets of edible yellow brassica flowers and red Russian kale stalks to give to my friends. There's still love and beauty in times of war.

There's an unending supply of work to do around here. The beds need to prepared for the direct seeded crops like spinach and peas and carrots and beans. We weed the beds and add composted manure from the cows and sheep and chickens. The perennial crops (perennial means they don't die in the winter) need to be pruned like the raspberries and asparagus and apples, the herbs like echinacea and thyme and mint and oregano. There are seeds that need to be sown and tiny seedlings that need to be potted up into larger containers. The two greenhouses are full of little plants that need to be watered and tended to. All the animals are going out to pasture after hanging out in the barn all winter eating hay bales. That means setting up electric fences and filling up water troughs, making sure everyone's happy.

One of the things I love about farm work is that it's really challenging and you have to be pretty sharp to be able to juggle all the dozens of daily tasks, but there is plenty of time in the day when I just get to work with my body and let my mind wander. Stacking hay bales, weeding beds, spreading compost, potting up seedlings, mucking the barn—I'm writing stories in the back of my head all day.

But let me back up a second

Five years ago I moved to an organic farm on a tiny island in British Columbia with my girlfriend. I'd written a story about growing up in the punk scene in New York City and I wanted my old friend Chris Boarts to publish it in her newspaper, so I sent her a floppy disk. As an afterthought I put my journal entries from working on the farm, so that she could get a sense of what was going on in my life.

Suddenly I was getting a pile of mail from teenage punks in the suburbs of North America who wanted to know about sustainable agriculture and farming apprenticeships. Instead of my urban punk rock story, Chris decided to print my journal entries from the farm.

So I start answering mail and writing more, and by the time my eight month apprenticeship was done, my life calling appeared to be merging the seemingly un-mergeable worlds of the city and the country. During the years I've been trying to bridge that chasm between myself, the city kid who thrives off energy of all you freaks and needs to be surrounded by mad culture, creativity, and diversity, and the fact that I'm healthier and happier when I'm living under the stars, growing my own food. I've noticed many others in the same quandary. It's a dilemma in our community—braving the loneliness and whiteness of rural living or braving the chaos and urban alienation of the city. Since then I got wrapped up in the fight to save the NYC community gardens and build up the network of Bay Area seed savers, but I've known this whole time that I've wanted to settle down out in the country near a big city and be a farmer.

Four Winds Farm

I'm two hours away from where I grew up in Manhattan. Close enough for my friends to visit and take a break from the smog and concrete and close enough to get my periodic city fix, dance, and ride my bicycle around and check out all the beautiful people wandering the streets.

I live on a 24-acre piece of land known as Four Winds Farm with Polly and Jay Armour and their two kids, Sara and Josh. I work in the fields everyday with a guy named Juan from Oaxaca, Mexico, and my friend Kevin, who grew up in this neck of the woods. Four acres grow vegetables and the rest is a pasture for cows, sheep, pigs, chickens, turkeys, and ducks. I live in a barn with straw bale walls and a greenhouse attached to the side. There are huge vining overwintered tomato plants right outside my window as I type these words.

Putting the Culture Back in Agriculture

One of the great things about working here is that Four Winds is part of a movement known as Community Supported Agriculture. Rather than selling our produce wholesale to a market, CSA farms have members who buy "shares" in the season's harvest and, in return, receive a box of fresh produce every week. It's a great system. Farmers are guaranteed money at the beginning of the season and the members have a direct connection to the people that grow their food. They can come bring their kids and work in the fields if they want. It's rebuilding the culture that's been lost as people have moved away from the land.

Imaginary Conversations with my Internal Vegan

This place considers itself to be a biodynamic farm—they strive to have a closed circle where nothing needs brought in to keep the farm running. The animals eat the grass, we use the animal manure to build the soil to grow the plants, we eat the animals; everything is intimately connected in a tight circle. Unlike industrial factory farms that separate all the pieces and replace the missing parts with chemicals, our system works naturally and more effectively. The animal manure we use is alive with microorganisms that suppress disease and enhance plant growth, it's high in organic matter that helps hold soil particles together and prevents nutrient loss, and it's loaded with trace minerals and micronutrients.

If I could talk to the self-righteous urbanite militant vegan that was my teenage self, I'd say, "Look, city boy, I want to see you grow all your own "non-animal" protein without huge industrial machinery and enormous reserves of petroleum. Get that genetically engineered plastic wrapped long distanced shipped tofu out of your mouth before you dis my lifestyle, kid. If we don't use animal manures to build up the soil structure and fertility, I'd really like to know where the fertility is going to come from to keep growing our food every year."

Honestly, knowing what I know about how industrial agriculture rapes the earth, there's no question that it's more violent to grow monocrops, process, and package the plants into oils, and ship them all over the country in huge trucks than to raise a dozen happy pigs and slaughter them for their meat and fat. I fry a lot of my food in pig lard these days and I can see the pigs outside playing in the mud from the window of the farmhouse kitchen. It makes sense to me, it's honest and real in a way that the cheap plastic bottle of canola just ain't.

I don't have all the answers and I do question my right to take something's life. I think about this stuff everyday and have a lot to learn. I'm not set in my ways, but, in the end, I've realized that it's not the killing of animals that I'm opposed to—it's factory farming industry that enslaves animals and condemns them to a life in a concentration camp. I'm opposed to the system that keeps people separated from where their food comes from, turns everything into a product, and puts profit before anything else. But it's a scale issue. As my farming partner Polly likes to say, "These animals have a great life everyday except the last one. And dying sucks no matter how it happens."

Resistance is Fertile
So I have this little dream that a couple years from now, my friends and I are going to be trading our vegetable and herb seeds the same way we trade our travel zines full of stories and music from our underground bands. More and more of us are moving out onto land and building the urban/rural connections that are going to take our movement to the next level. I have a feeling the alternative models are going to get more and more badass, and as quickly as the mainstream picks up on them, we'll be out there in the fields creating more. This is how we will survive in the future. I am perpetually inspired by the budding network of East Coast radical farmers I see growing, from the Victory Gardens project up in Maine to Caty Crabb and her crew down in North Carolina. We are the guardians of diversity and life in a world of monoculture and war. And amidst it all, if you haven't noticed, we are growing.

Underneath the Wild Garden Waits to Grow

Willy says, here's a story that you may not comprehend,
But the parking lots will crack and bloom again.
There's a world beneath the pavement that will never end.
Seeds are lying dormant and will never end.
Willy says, if you listen you can hear the sound of birds,
Hear their song above the chaos, hear their words.
Listen to their love songs, it will never end.
If you listen you can hear.
And the old one sits with me above the city
While we watch the madness of the world below.
And she laughs and tells me that it's temporary.
Underneath the wild garden waits to grow.
—"Willy Says" by Dana Lyons

Guerilla Gardening in the Hudson Valley

During these hot Summer nights in the mid-Hudson Valley, my crew wanders around New Paltz planting tomato and squash seedlings wherever we think they'll survive and where we can get away with it. Nestled on the edges of irrigated lawns and University fields, we'll be harvesting fruit and inspiring strangers for the rest of the season. Walking the evening streets with spading forks over our shoulders and dirt covering our hands, garden trowels sticking out of the side loops of our shorts, back pockets full of sunflower and marigold seeds, and flats of seedling plugs under our arms, it's hard not to feel like a total bad asses. The first cherry tomatoes are almost ripe, and we all know guerilla gardening is as much about inspiration as it is about feeding people. It's about reclaiming public space and capturing imaginations, sowing our radical culture of spontaneity and liberation in the face of modern 21st century North American life. As our slogan, "Food Not Lawns," implies it's a healthy mixing of the wild and practical in a world gone psychotically too far over to the structured and useless.

The Secret Life of Open-Pollinated Vegetables

I work on the farm in exchange for a place to stay and food, learning as much as I can and trying to be helpful with the knowledge and experience I've gathered in my studies and time spent on other farms. The people I'm working for have given me the opportunity to tend to the seeds, build the raised beds, and plant a half acre. It's been a wonder watching it come together like magic.

After a wet spring the sun is coming on full force, so the plants are beginning to mature and bear fruit. The sugar-snap peas have made their way up the fences, bloomed in all their sexy white and pink floral glory. I harvested two big buckets of ripe pods today for market. We started pulling juicy, orange carrots and blood red beets out of the ground last week. On my section of the farm I planted seven varieties of carrots, all poking their frilly heads out of the ground in proud, crooked lines. There are two healthy, hundred-foot beds full of sweet and long leaf basil that we've been harvesting in bunches for pesto. There are patches of orange and yellow and red and green stemmed chards. There are fifteen different varieties of lettuce that are growing beside each other in a dazzling display of diversity. I've been making beautiful lettuce salads with mint leaves, bronze fennel, calendula and marigold flowers, fennel, cress, golden pursaline, and whatever looks good in the field. It's a different world from the plastic wrapped iceberg lettuce from California I grew up eating.

The crookneck and paddypan summer squash are just starting to come on and sprawl out into the paths with their large spiny leaves. The folks I work for plant a mix of heirloom varieties as well as a number of more productive sure-shot hybrid varieties that bear a lot more fruit but don't taste so rich because they've been bred for commercial production.

Breaking Down the Fancy Seed Talk

When people talk about "heirloom vegetables" just imagine an heirloom of anything else, something so good it's been passed down through generations, seeds saved and replanted, preserved and cherished. When people talk about "open-pollinated vegetables" they are talking about adaptable plants whose seeds can be saved and replanted the following year. Until recently, farmers saved seeds they adapted to the local soil and weather and pests and diseases. When people talk about "F1 hybrids" they're referring to the offspring of two distinct varieties of open-pollinated plants whose genetic base has been selected and reduced to be so narrow and sparse that, when they're crossed, the resulting mix of genes in the new seeds creates a plant that's incredibly productive and very uniform for one season, but are useless for farmers the next season.

Hybrid technology changed the seed industry. It turned seeds from a natural resource and life cycle into a marketable commodity. When the regional seed companies were bought out by the global petrol-chemical companies and they merged with the pharmaceutical corporations to create the "Life Science Industry," they spent enormous amounts of money to figure out how to suck the life out of vegetables and sell them to us as expensive pills, how to genetically engineer their seeds to be dependent on their chemicals. Next they spent just as much money to convince us that these are products we can't live without. This disaster makes my head spin. Growing open-pollinated and heirloom vegetables and saving their seeds is a way to retain some dignity and self-respect in the face of this mess.

Back at the farm, there are fifteen hundred heirloom tomato plants in the ground just beginning to ripen, three dozen different varieties with names like Cherokee Purple, Striped German, Yellow Brandywine, Green Zebra, Garden Peach, Golden Jubilee, Orange Banana, Fruity Cherry, and Black Krim. All of them carry amazing stories in their genes about how they ended up on our farm from all over the world.

The People's Republic of Kale

Polly jokingly refers to my section of the farm as the "People's Republic of Kale." I'm growing 12 varieties—an incredible display of brassica family diversity—from Black Kale to Purple Peacock Broccoli, Rainbow Lacinato, Walking Stick, Wild Garden Kale, Red Ursa Kale, White Russian, Marrowstem, True Siberian, and Mushroom's Curled Kale Grex. The plants look so different than anything else in the field.

I love this family plants because they thrive on diversity. They have self-incompatibility mechanisms encoded in their design so that they're forced to cross with each other, and each new cross creates a rush of genes that makes healthy, new combinations. I picture the mix of genes in my field like a huge family that ended up populating all over the world and are having a big reunion. Even through there is so much variety in shape and color, they're so genetically similar that when I let them go to seed next season they'll cross with each other and what happens next gets to be my little playground.

Alternative seed companies are like underground record labels or zine distributors, and their material is truly live—an amazing little subculture. My friend and teacher, Frank Morton, sent me some works in progress—little hand-stamped packets of seed. For the first time I am growing them and doing my own selections after spending years reading about it and observing others. One healthy kale plant makes tens of thousands of seeds, so watch out Monsanto!

Wild Sex in the Garden

Here's a quick botany lesson. Plants reproduce sexually through their flowers. They tried to teach me about this on a blackboard in a fluorescent-lit classroom in the Bronx when I was a teenager, and I couldn't have been less interested. Years later, spending time around plants, I realized how magical they are. The male part of the flower is known as the stamen and produces pollen to fertilize the female part, known as the pistil. The pistil has an ovary that develops into a fruit and ovules (egg cells) develop into the new seeds for the next season. This wild sex orgy—going on all around me as I write this—is wrapped up in the story of the bees and other insects, because they're gathering pollen and nectar and cross-pollinating plants with each other. Some plants cross-pollinate through wind blown pollen, but most of them need the insects to help them out. The flowers and the insects actually co-evolved with each other the same way that humans co-evolved with food crops—weeds that we domesticated.

One of us couldn't exist without the other, and, in the end, the lot of us—from the bee gathering nectar in my squash patch to that royal idiot sitting in the White House—are intimately connected. And it's a little scary. But it gets more amazing. Flowering plants can be divided into three categories. Most plants have what are known as perfect flowers, meaning that they have both male and female sex parts in the same flower—interesting language given trends in gender politics dialogue and the social construct of sexual identity. Peas, beans, and tomatoes have perfect flowers. They are self-pollinated plants, meaning they don't need other plants to get their groove on with the universe, but the bees end up crossing a certain number of them up anyway, just for fun and diversity.

Then there are plants that are considered dioecious, which means they have separate male and female plants in a population. A good example is the humble marijuana plant. At a certain stage, any given population of pot plants grown from seed will segregate into male and females. Before the male plants have time to set pollen and fertilize the females, they are usually pulled out, which makes the females produce lots of resin on their buds in a vain attempt to capture any stray pollen which might float by. This keeps the plants from producing seeds and makes their buds grow large and swollen. Spinach is another, less racy example of a dioecious plant.

The third type of flowering plants are the monoecious, which have separate male and female flowers together on the same plant. The whole squash family is monoecious—cucumbers, zucchinis, pumpkins, melons, and winter squash. If you get a chance to check out a flowering squash plant you'll notice the big yellow flowers all look similar except that the females have an ovary at their base that ends up becoming the squash fruit once it is pollinated by traveling insects carrying male pollen.

Do yourself a favor and hang out by some flowers and check out the scene. They won't mind, flowers are exhibitionist in nature. It's part of their evolutionary strategy. Look at all the little parts, try and figure out which are male and female. What kind of insects land on them? Where do the seeds form? How do they disperse themselves? Even if it's just dandelions and plantain and dock and mug wart growing out of the cracks in the cement next to your apartment building, it's happening there for you to experience! Once you realize the brilliant colors and sexy, alluring shapes of flowers are all about attraction and sex, and we wouldn't be here without them, suddenly the world feels less cold. To speed the process along, get some flower seeds, scatter them over your neighborhood, and wait for a little rain.

Meanwhile, in Town

Since being a farm hand isn't proving to be the most lucrative career, I've been making money painting houses with a revolving crew, including the mayor of New Paltz! The mayor's name is Jason West. He's 26 years old and won the election on the Green Party ticket. New Paltz is a university town of about 13,000 people about 2 hours north of NYC, down the road from the farm. Jason is part of the radical activist community and won the election with promises of incorporating clean energy, like solar power and wind energy, into the town plans, creating an artificial wetlands to help the local water treatment filter water without toxic chemicals, and using biodiesel fuel in the Department of Public Works trucks.

Up on ladders, painting in the midday sun, the mayor and I talk about everything from Spanish Civil War history to the future of the global justice movement, and how we're going to turn all the extra lawn space in New Paltz into vegetable gardens. We will then setup programs for local kids to work on them, teaching the next generation. Call it a hunch, but I have a feeling that the next few years are going to be interesting.

Conclusion

Last year I got some cayenne pepper seeds from my friend Dr. Kapular in Oregon. When I arrived at the farm in February, I sowed a flat of them and left it on the heating pad to germinate; they were the first seeds I sowed. About a month later I sat alone in the greenhouse transplanting the little seedlings from their crowded, thickly sown rows into their own individual plugs, as the snow came down in sheets outside. I transplanted them in the field three months later. Yesterday I harvested a big handful of the first cayenne peppers off my plants and cooked them up with dinner, and they were so good. They tasted like history and friendship and the past and the future. Working with plants in our gardens allows us the privilege of witnessing and taking part in the life cycle over the course of the growing season, and now, as I'm beginning to discover, over the course of our lives. Working with plants reminds us about all the important stuff: sex, life, connection, change, death, and the power of creation, learning to keep our history and knowing we have some power to shape it as we go.

Blinking Red Lights and the Souls of Our Friends

I.

Like clockwork, or something more divine, the leaves started cascading down from the sky on the equinox, carpeting the ground in a layer of burnt orange, blood red, and mustard yellow. There's a chill in the air, and word in the Hudson Valley says the first frost is coming any day. The last apples, corn, and pumpkins are harvested and the fields are being put to bed. It's the end of the growing season for the plants that aren't frost hearty. We'll wake up one morning, and the vegetables and herbs we lovingly grew from seed will be frozen and dead. You can feel it in the air—the end is near.

But with the end comes a new beginning. Last week we cut half a dozen heirloom striped German tomatoes in half, horizontally down the middle, their thick, juicy sweet flesh a marbleized swirl of reds and yellows. You won't find tomatoes like these in supermarkets anywhere. The fruits we chose were the largest ones off the most productive and healthy plants. We squeezed the seeds into a glass jar, their gelatinous coats settling into a thick layer of pulp an inch deep. We let the jar sit for three days until it was smelly and moldy, filled it up halfway with water, stirred the whole mess and poured off the rotting gel and pulp along with the infertile, empty seeds, which floated to the top. We poured the remainder of the murky water through a metal strainer until we were left with only the glistening seeds and then spread them on a plate to sit for a few days in an airy place out of the sun. When the seeds were dry enough to snap, instead of bend, we put them in labeled packs, and stored them in the freezer to wait for next spring, for another chance at rebirth and life.

II.

My friend Donny dropped dead last week without warning at the age of 32. The doctors say he had a rare, undiagnosed condition that left him with an enlarged heart. His death is one of the most horrible and confusing things that has ever happened to my community of friends. We're still in shock, trying to make sense of it. It feels unfair, wrong, and somehow meaningless. Donny seemed perfectly healthy and was the proud father of three beautiful children. He always had a big smile and a kind word for those of us who crossed his path. There are a lot of grieving people walking around, feeling the huge loss in their lives that his death has created.

Donny and his partner, Lisa, lived with their kids on the Lower East Side of New York City at 7th Street Squat, a place that felt like a second home to me since I was a teenager. A building full of rebels, artists, and activists, the residents of 209 E. 7th carved a life for themselves in a city less and less hospitable to dissidents and radicals. The physical building is one of many old six-story tenement walkups in the neighborhood that was a burnt out, neglected, and uninhabitable shell when the original homesteaders moved in more than two decades ago. So much has changed on the block, in the city, and in the world since those days, but all these years later and, against the odds, 7th Street's proud walls are filled with families who have beautiful children that go to the local public school together and play down the street in Tompkins Square Park. The building is a solid rock in the community and the epitome of everything I love about my hometown in all its diversity and fighting spirit.

Eight years ago when I stayed at 7th Street with my friend Fly, we would sneak into the abandoned synagogue next door to scavenge bricks for patching up the holes in her walls. The windows of Fly's space were framed by cut up 2 x 10 pieces of stolen blue and white police barricades. The electricity and water were pirated from the city. People kept their windows shaded and the front door was always locked. But it still felt so warm and welcoming inside. That fall there was a constant flurry of activity in the building as a group of dedicated people banded together to get one of the spaces upstairs ready for the birth of Felix, Stefane and Arrow's baby girl. In those days Donny and Lisa lived down the street at Bullet Space, another squat in the neighborhood.

At the time it felt like the Lower East Side squatter subculture coexisted as some mysterious, shadow-like parallel universe amidst the rising tide of real estate, which eventually flooded everything, sending a diaspora of my friends to the outer boroughs. A couple dozen old squatted buildings quietly sat among the new, cheaply built condos as the sound of pile drivers digging foundations for more condos shook the neighborhood. Community gardens and underground art spaces quietly kept their doors open as more cafes, bars, and restaurants full of hip dot-comers made their way down the alphabet streets. A pirate radio station broadcasting radical news, underground hip-hop, and punk rock existed a few blocks away from the site of the enormous new police station. Those were strange days.

But the roots of the squatter community go deeper into the history of the neighborhood, at the intersection of incredible lives and stories. The intense friendships and alliances forged amidst battles with the city—at the community board meetings, at eviction watch meetings, in the courts, and mostly in the streets—brought together an incredible group of people. The Tompkins Square riots of the late '80s were the most visible manifestation of the battle for living space in the Lower East Side. But over the years, and outside of the larger public eye, dozens of buildings were evicted violently and dramatically, leaving hundreds of people angry and homeless. It's a battle that changed the course of many peoples' lives, mine included. Within the past few years the city finally struck a quiet deal with the remaining inhabitants of the squats. After all the fighting in the courts and on the streets, 209 E. 7th, along with a dozen other buildings, finally became legit in the eyes of the city.

Amidst this backdrop, Lisa and Donny were solid members of the community, survivors who had stuck it out without ever knowing what would happen to their home or the homes of their friends. They moved into 209 East 7th after the birth of their son Benjamin. Donny went to school to study computer programming so he could make money to support his family, and they built their little nest. As many others retreated over the bridge into Brooklyn or into the Bronx, they stood their ground in the quiet battle with the city. They had created a life worth fighting for—for themselves and their children. And while they could have chosen an easier path, their high ideals and vision allowed them to see the importance of living a radical life, challenging the system that their kids would eventually have to take on themselves.

III.

The Critical Mass rides in New York City happen the last Friday of every month. We meet at Union Square with our bicycles, and at 7 p.m. everyone pours into traffic and takes over the four-lane street, sidewalk to sidewalk. It's a glorious sight. The Masses grew progressively bigger each month, with a thousand of us on a ride where we took over the upper level of the Manhattan Bridge before being dispersed by the Brooklyn police when we stopped to have a party by the river. Critical Mass is a protest of car culture, part of a larger alternative transportation movement pushing for more bike lanes and better traffic laws in the city. There are Critical Mass rides all over the world. But at its heart, the Mass is a celebration. It's a celebration of community and autonomy from the oil companies and corporate monsters who try to stranglehold our lives. It's a celebration of the simple beauty and freedom of riding a bicycle. It's also where so many of us come to see our friends and feel the power of numbers—the power of The Mass.

Weaving around each other, feeling the joyful unity amongst strangers and familiar faces, Critical Mass is a big roving street party that takes the city by storm every month. We ride a different route every time, but we always end up in Time Square, the center of Manhattan, amidst all its corporate Disneyland, Blade Runner-like madness. We hold our bicycles over our heads and scream at the crazy tourist techno-nightmare that 42nd street has become. We're carving a space for the people of the city, so that the tourists see that New York has become more than just a huge digital billboard advertising the end of the world.

I remember a moment when the Mass rode through the tunnel under Grand Central Terminal, a surreal visual cacophony of off-time red blinking lights, and then emerged and took over Park Avenue in a flurry of hoots and howls. I suddenly felt like I knew these people I was riding with, friends of friends of friends, through many degrees of separation. And it felt incredibly peaceful—the sense of momentarily losing individuality among a friendly mass in a sea of blinking red lights. I thought to myself, "If it exists, this is how I imagine the afterlife—a million wandering souls floating in, around, and through each other—strangers and friends—crossing paths over and over forever."

IV.

When you see a red flashing light at the end of a freight train sitting in a yard, you know that train is taking off soon. When you're trying to get out of town in the middle of the night, sneaking through a train yard with a pack on your back, that flashing red light is the sweetest sight there is. People who ride the rails call those blinking red lights "freddies" which is an anthropomorphic slang-play on the acronym FRED (Flashing Rear End Device). Back at the end of the summer, a crew of train hopping old-time musicians, calling themselves the Blinkin' Freddies, blew through New York City and played a free show in the middle of Tompkins Square Park. They had ridden freight trains together all the way across the country from Portland, Oregon with their fiddles and banjos and guitars. They communicated their whereabouts across the country through a free 800 voicemail line, stopping along the way to play shows, busk on the streets, and hang out with their friends.

I'd known most of that crew for years and was proud to see, as I had suspected and hoped, that many of us are getting cooler as we get older. When I hang out with certain friends I feel like I'm part of a secret culture of freedom and hope and adventure. I have respect for people who aren't afraid to follow their dreams and live the vibrant poetry of the universe in their day-to-day lives. I feel happily bound to these people for as long as we're around and I'll shout it for the world to hear. A bunch of us have the same tattoo on our wrists—two interconnected circles, an old hobo sign that means never give up. I look down at my wrist when I feel myself forgetting.

The night the Blinkin' Freddies played in the park there were 50 dirty punk kids doing a beautiful and ridiculous mix of country and slam dancing. There was something pure and raw about the whole thing, all acoustic and loud. It felt like we were waking up the rebel ghosts of the city with joy, fire, and song. I was one of few people that had been around when Tompkins Square was the last park in the city not to have a curfew. I carry that history with me wherever I go. When I'm standing at the entrance on St. Marks and Avenue A, I see the fancy restaurants and boutiques and people, but super-imposed over it all I see a bonfire in the middle of the intersection and hundreds of people reclaiming the streets from a retreating army of police in riot gear. Then I blink, and it's gone.

The cops kicked the whole dancing, dirty lot of us out of the park the night the Blinkin' Freddies came through town, but we just paraded down to the East River and danced some more to their old-time rebel music. I could feel so many layers of history all around me on that walk to the river, like coats of peeling paint on the old tenement buildings falling on the bloodstained streets; old traditions that connect my friends to something more powerful than our own individual lives. On the way to the river I proudly pointed out 7th Street Squat to a couple of my younger friends. "Some of the most amazing people I know live behind those walls. They're the reason we're still walking down this street."

V.

Back in the springtime, me and some of those younger friends planted a garden at what became Jane Doe, the anarcha-feminist infoshop in Brooklyn. I went back to Jane Doe for the first time since the spring and found a forest of collards and kale growing in the backyard. Most were from seedlings I grew and transplanted at the farm in the Valley and now they were healthy plants thriving in the middle of the city. This is the time of year that collards and kale taste good, because the cold weather stimulates the carbohydrates in their leaves to turn into sugars, and they suddenly become sweet. These are the little things that give me hope. I harvested a big green and purple bunch and brought them to Lisa back at 7th Street.

VI.

We sat *shiva* for Donny at the Squat. There were warm rooms packed full of good people and good food. There were little kids running around everywhere. Even a couple big kids and teenagers. It was a forest of people; the kids were like the understory and mid-story. We were the trees. There were lots of old, familiar characters from my life. We had more lines in our faces, more stories on our skin and tongues. There were long embraces and tears. On Saturday night we sat in a room on the floor and took turns telling stories and grieving, sharing our memories and holding each other up together.

While we sat as a group I kept thinking about all the work that's gone into keeping the building alive all these years—from the battles with the city in the courts and the streets, to the years of sweat and blood equity—all the sheetrock carried up five flights of stairs and every last scavenged brick. I started thinking about how we become like the spaces we inhabit, how we grow together in complexity and beauty. Then I started thinking about how when someone as amazing as Donny dies, it's like they become the mortar that holds the walls of the community together. We're the bricks—all of us people left standing. When someone as amazing as Donny dies, they become the spiritual glue that bonds us together for life, until it becomes our own turn, one by one, to silently play that role.

VII.

t's Monday night and a group of us are sitting outside the building smoking, drinking, and telling stories. There are flickering red, yellow, and green candles on the sidewalk lighting a memorial shrine to our lost friend. His haunting photo compels passersby, strangers, and neighbors, to stop and pay their respects. Lisa's at the center of our crew. Everyone knows this is hardest for Lisa. It's getting cold out; winter is coming. This is the easy part of a tragedy, when everyone gathers to give support. The struggle is in the long haul—raising the kids, paying the bills, finding the vision to move forward when times get hard. We know that Lisa and Donny had dreams of building a house on a piece of land up in Vermont and spending their lives together. We know the weight of lost dreams and responsibility that's been placed on her shoulders would crush many people with a weaker spirit. We also know that if anyone can handle the weight, it's our friend Lisa. She is as strong willed and tough as they come. And when all is said and done, there's a pack that's going to stand by her and grow old with her together. I close my eyes, listening to the sound of my friends' voices in the quiet late night street, and just for a second I see blinking red bicycle lights. I'm momentarily overcome with a sense of calm and a feeling that I'm part of something bigger than myself that I don't really understand. And somehow I know it's going to be alright.

Lisa smiles her beautiful smile by the light of the candles as she holds her sleeping two-year old daughter, Leila, in her strong arms. "See how Leila looks just like her father? Same nose. Same lips. Same eyes. It feels sometimes like I'm holding Donny in my arms. Some people would look at my life right now and feel like giving up, feel like this is the end. But I look at the face of my child and know that, in so many ways, this is just the beginning. This is just the beginning."

How I Started Believing in Ghosts

Sometimes I wander around my hometown all lonely, lovesick, and surrounded by ghosts, stuck with this awful longing in my gut and my broken heart beating out of its chest. There are ghosts everywhere on these streets. They're always there but I see them clearly when I don't get enough sleep and I'm walking the bleed in time between late night and early morning—when everything's creeping under my skin and my eyes are glassy and fragile but the most incredible things make themselves painfully clear. I see ghosts everywhere then, in the buildings, in the flickering subway station lights, in the cracks in the sidewalk, in the names of streets, in the clouds in the sky, in the faces of people walking by me. Layers of ghosts like crystal onions or cracked and peeling paint walls of abandoned apartment buildings telling stories in their colored lead rubble dust.

I started believing in ghosts from watching myself and the way I haunt places from my past, how I'm drawn to places long after I have any reason to still be there. Something brings me back that might not exist anymore, something with its own map of the city carved into its graying eyes. If I'm lucky I can cry but usually it makes me stone-faced and frozen stiff, catapulted through time to another place. In those spaces I coexist in a different reality than the people around me—I'm made from something else. I'm transparent—passing through. I'm haunting old territory but it's not there anymore. And then I think about how many others there are just like me, wandering around in a world constructed, insulated, and sometimes set aflame by old memories.

I don't know what happens when we die, if there's an afterlife or if our individual consciousness lives on in another form. I don't know if there's a collective consciousness that we become a part of or return to. I don't know if we take any of this with us—all these stories, memories, love and friendship. I don't know what happens to all my dead friends—do I get to be reunited with them up in the sky or at another place and time? Have we been meeting each other like this throughout history—amidst wars and revolutions—working in the fields and riding on the freight trains and surviving in the middle of the cities and reconnecting with each other in late night forums on the internet? Who knows? I don't know.

I do know people leave their marks—etched in stone, written page, silver screen, or in the faces of their children, and that energy affects our lives. There is a continuum. We carry the dead in our language and the way we speak it. We carry pieces of people we love in our hearts and our eyes and our tongues, even in our slight limps as we walk down the street or the knots in our backs when we come home from work. We carry the dead in stories and the way we tell them and even who we decide to tell them to. If there are powerful people who played important roles in our lives, they burn impressions into us with their words, actions, and visions, literally leaving *impressions* that we take no matter what situations we find ourselves in and wherever we find ourselves walking down this winding road. This is how brilliant people live on after they actually die.

By the end of his life my father was a dying sun. He was a striking man—a bright red beard and piercing blue eyes and a loud, commanding voice until almost the end. Even from his deathbed he burned red hot with intensity that was too much for people around him. I was so young that most memories of him are washed out, like faded '70s Technicolor film from the perspective of a kid who loved his dad so much and thought he'd be around forever.

The last few years of my dad's life were spent hooked up to a machine to help him breathe, mostly in bed, from home to the hospital, surrounded by newspapers, books, and yellow legal pads full of blue felt tip scrawl. My dad was born with Cystic Fibrosis, an autosomal recessive condition that causes mucus in the lungs and problems with pancreas function and food absorption. He violently coughed and was in pain most of the time. It colored relations with the world around him, giving him the perspective of the perpetual underdog. His face would get purple with rage when he was angry. He had a bad temper but was brilliant. He channeled his rage into newspaper articles and books about corruption in city politics.

Before he died they cut a hole in his throat to stick a tube into his stomach. His voice was gone. I watched his beard go white in a matter of weeks and the fire leave his eyes. The last time I ever saw him was the night of my 13th birthday. He was scared, depressed, and silent, trying not to show how much pain he was in. He died two days later, a week before Christmas, and suddenly there was a void in my life where a dad had been.

That was 17 years ago. I still see his ghost all over this city. And I hate Christmas.

•   •   •

My dad's best friend Jack Newfield suddenly died three days ago. They went to Hunter College together in the 1960s and wrote a book about corruption in New York City politics in the late 1970s. It's part of the complicated legacy I've been trying to make sense of for years. My dad wrote with a manual typewriter years before the internet. I often wonder what he would have thought of the work I do now and the world around us. I wish so badly I could talk to him sometimes. For the past two years since I moved back to New York I've been going over to Jack and Janie's house to talk about politics, history, music, and my dad. I discovered some old writings of his at my step-mother's house that I was so excited to talk to Jack about. And now he's dead. Right before Christmas. I've been wandering the chilly gray streets.

The last Christmas I spent in New York I was a lonely miserable wreck that ended up being checked into the psych ward for catatonic suicidal depression. The old ghosts caught up with me and I wasn't ready. But that was six years ago. I have coping strategies now. I force myself to be around friends.

I take care of the basics like food and sleep and exercise. I have an incredible website community to that can hold my melancholic intensity. But all these years later I still have that familiar painful longing in my gut, my heart is still broken like it was when I was 13 years old, I still see the ghosts of my dead friends everywhere when I don't sleep enough, and that's just how it is and how I think it's always going to be.

Return to the Other Side
I.

Making a sign for hitchhiking is like casting a magic spell. Like so many things in life, the trick is that it's about intent. As you watch cars speed by and fill in the letter lines of your desired destination with black marker strokes, you concentrate on getting a ride with the rapidly increasing beat of your heart, and put all that intent into the sign and the universe. Then you hope someone with space will see you, pick up on that humble desire, and deliver you where you need to go. While you keep your senses sharp for any signs of danger or sketchiness, things are not always what they seem, and it's a rule of the road that you are placing yourself into the hands of fate.

The Spanish language lies dormant in my mouth until it's conjured up by necessity or inspiration. Two of the prettiest words in Spanish that I know are *orgullo* and *vergüenza*, which mean, respectively, "pride" and "shame." Coincidentally, these words are things that you must lay aside to communicate in a language that you have not mastered. The risk of being misunderstood, of misunderstanding, is not unlike hitchhiking; each requiring a vanquishing of traditional notions of what we can control.

Sitting in the shade of the trash dumpster next to the *gasolinera*, at the edge of Ciudad Juárez, under the green and red PEMEX sign, I cast my black sharpie heart beat spell with the name of the city "ZACATECAS" on a piece of scavenged cardboard.

I cross the El Paso/Juárez border by foot on that warm Texas late morning a couple days before Christmas with the intention of getting down south to visit my old friend Juan Carlos, whom I hadn't seen for eight years. The last time I had traveled in Mexico I hadn't relied on the highways because of cheap passenger railroad service and the freight trains, the unofficial fourth class travel for citizens too poor to afford regular service. And I have a long-term love affair with the trains. If you look at a map of Mexican railroads you might notice that all the main lines run north to south, a reflection of being built for U.S. business interests—moving natural resources from the south to the north. After the Mexican Revolution the rail lines were taken out of the hands of the foreign elite, officially nationalized, and used for the good of the common working people. Not unlike the nostalgic relationship many older Americans have with the railroads in the U.S., ever since the revolution the trains played an important part of Mexican culture and history as a symbol of pride and patriotism.

On January 1, 1994 the North American Free Trade Agreement (NAFTA) went into effect. Like all recent international trade agreements, the basic idea was that corporate capital could move freely across the border while workers, communities, and the environment would suffer the consequences caused by unchecked "free trade." "Free trade" means that corporations can build factories in foreign countries and employ its people for a fraction of what it would cost to hire them in their own countries. "Free trade" means that private corporations have the right to buy public utilities and resources like telephone systems and transportation infrastructures and entire water supplies. These "efficiencies" of the economic system don't take into account the livelihoods, happiness, or health of the people.

Around 1998 the Mexican government sold off the last of its railroad lines to corporations from Japan and Canada. The corporations promptly discontinued unprofitable passenger service and instituted a more efficient freight service, watching the trains with armed guards at every station to keep freight from being stolen and illegal passengers from riding on the freight cars. To the swelling ranks of the Mexican underclass this meant that they had been robbed of their only affordable means of national transportation. What it meant for me, a gringo traveler in 2003, standing in the central bus terminal in Ciudad Juárez, was paying 90 bucks to visit my old friend because bus companies had cornered the market and only offered first-class service complete with TV screens blaring horrible Hollywood movies with Spanish overdubs. I shook off my disgust, walked out to the parking lot, and in jagged, rusty Spanish convinced the first guy I saw to give me a ride to the nearest gas station and started making my cardboard sign.

It turned out to be a lot easier than I figured it would be. My Spanish magically reappeared and everyone was trusting and open to letting me into their lives way more than the people in my fear-culture homeland. There were streams of caravans full of families headed south to visit their relatives for Christmas. My final destination was not actually Zacatecas, but the smaller neighboring city of Aguascalientes, and within two days I was knocking on Juan Carlos's door.

II.

It is Christmas Eve. Juan Carlos and I have just returned from climbing *el Cerro del Muerto*, the Mountain of Death, which is at the edge of Aguascalientes. My sweater is covered in spines and desert plant seeds wrapped in burrs. I close my eyes and see cactus—maguey and nopal, the red and purple rocks we cracked open to find quartz crystals buried within. Maria, *la madre*, puts a huge steaming hot plate of tamales in front of me. Lupe, *el papa*, and I sit on the bed in the tiny brick and cement room half lit by flashing Christmas lights. There's a gaggle of children and brothers and sisters all around us. Lupe says to me, "Look at this one—isn't she beautiful! *Que chula! Que guapa! Que hermosa!* All of these little children are so beautiful! Look how lucky we are to be surrounded by such beautiful children! What a miracle!" I nod and smile, feeling the deliciously rich food rejuvenating my tired and sore legs, feeling so grateful and blessed for everything in my charmed life.

Juan Carlos has seven brothers and one sister. He is the second to oldest at 29. The oldest, Guadalupe, is 31 years old and the only brother who doesn't still live at home. José is the youngest at 16. He has to take medication everyday because of epilepsy and he sometimes has seizures. His father and most of the brothers do construction work for a living. His mother sells food on the streets outside one of the local factories. Santos, the 22-year-old, works as a night security guard. Jésus, who's 24, is studying at the university. All the brothers share the upstairs room of the house. At night we all share two beds.

Juan Carlos is the freak of the family. All his friends, and even his family, call him "*el punky*." He's a construction worker like the rest of them, but he hitchhikes all over the country and works with the Zapatistas. He has lots of tattoos on his chest and up and down his arms. He has fire in his eyes, a questioning spirit, and a serious and vocal distrust of authority. He brings home strangers, like me, with funny accents and wild stories from faraway lands. Juan Carlos has friends from all over the world because of the anarchist punk community. I am not the first visitor the family has had from another country. His brother Jésus, the student, stays up late with me one night and tells me how much respect he has for his brother *el punky*. He talks about how kids from all over Mexico will come stay in their room during an anarchist gathering, sometimes 15 guys at a time, from as far away as Monterrey and Oaxaca. He tells me how he wishes he had the nerve to go out and hitchhike around, talk to strangers, and live free like his brother.

The barrio they live in is right at the edge of the city. When he was a boy, Juan Carlos says it was all big fields of grapevines. Now it's a working-class neighborhood with colorful brick and cement houses. There's a *tortillaria* and a *carniceria* down the street, little kids playing ball, cacti growing in the occasional empty lot, a family across the street that sells piñatas. Parked on the streets are older American and Japanese cars, a bunch of Volkswagens, and the occasional new American pickup truck with Texas or Wisconsin plates. Most of the people take the bus into *el centro*, the center of town.

Juan Carlos has a crew of friends that he's been hanging out with since he was a young teenager, and they all still live in the same 'hood. They call themselves *la banda* and hang out in an abandoned lot full of cacti between two houses on the edge of a dairy farm. A rowdy crew of punks, hippies, and freaks, they smoke a lot of weed and drink a fermented drink called *pulky* made from the water of the maguey plant. They have an ongoing war with the local cops and don't walk alone if the cops are around. Everyone here knows *la policía* are just another gang, ready to *chinga* honest people at the first opportunity.

Most of *la banda* have snuck across the border and worked in the U.S., sometimes for six months, sometimes for a year or two. After years of working with illegal Mexicans on farms and urban job sites in the U.S., I'm interested in hearing the perspectives of guys who've made the journey to my side of the world and returned home. Their stories come from the perspective of being treated as a second-class citizen, having to endure ridiculous amounts of racism and danger, sneaking around and trying to avoid the cops and immigration police. Once they realize I'm not the average *guerro* (white boy) they're jumping at the opportunity to get war stories off their chests to someone who's familiar with the territory and knows how fucked up and complicated it is. The flip side of those stories is the perspective from the guys who've never made the journey north, but who see their friends come back forever changed—with new trucks and big egos to match, the men who left their families behind to search after the American Dream and return wrapped up in the fantasy, *el sueño americano*.

Juan Carlos and I took the bus into *el centro* to hang out with the anarchist punks. The punk scene in Mexico has some of the same roots as the punk scene where I grew up, but the tree branched off in different places. There are a ton of great political punk bands; from Massacre 68 and Sediccon, to Disobediencia Civil and Fallas del Sistema. A lot of the Mexican bands have been influenced by older groups from Spain: Eskorbuto, Sin Dios, Guerrilla Urbana, La Furia. There are a bunch of Spanish and Basque ska-punk bands influenced by The Clash and British Two-Tone from the late 1970s. The kids in Aguascalientes loved ska-punk. I too have a long-term love affair with ska-punk, pre-dating my aforementioned love affair with trains.

It was intriguing how the world of punk in Mexico seemed to be manifesting itself. We went to an anarchist meeting one night in a rented community space that held a *plática* (talk) about *vegetarianismo* and *veganismo*. It was heated—Mexico has more of a meat-based diet than even the U.S., due to the brutal legacy and cattle culture of the Spaniards. Afterwards, a band played all these classic Spanish and Basque ska-punk songs and everybody sang along and danced with big smiles on their faces. All over the walls there were black and white cut-and-paste posters for protests and *tocadas* (from tocar—"touch," or to play an instrument. Tocada means "show," or in this context, "punk rock show.") Hanging out with a big crew of kids wearing all black with CRASS,

Amebix, and Nausea patches on their clothes, Juan Carlos' friends looked and acted just like me and my friends in the early 1990s in New York City. It was actually a little strange, unnerving, some weird parallel, alternate universe.

But when I asked Juan Carlos about it all, he took the origins of the punk thing even further. One night, over beer and tacos, he spent a lot of time trying to convince me that the seeds of the punk movement in Mexico go further back than the Sex Pistols and The Clash in England, and that the real roots of Punk stem from some group of anarchist artisans in Brazil in the 1920s. And then there's the phenomenon of *El Chopo*, the enormous punk rock/metal market that happens in Mexico City every Saturday since the 1970s. Juan Carlos was telling me it has roots in old Mayan traditions as a barter fair in the communal spirit of the Maya. Whatever the story is, it's an interesting one. There are un *chingo* de punks from Mexico all the way down to Brazil, and because of the harsh social and economic situations they're inevitably more political then the punks in the U.S. It's a thriving subculture south of the border that grows each year and I humbly suggest you start practicing your Spanish and Portuguese.

III.

It's a beautiful late Sunday afternoon in barrio *Loma Bonita*. There are desert flowers in bloom, kids playing in the street, men working on their cars. Women—who inevitably work harder than their husbands because they're responsible for holding down a job and *all* the housework—are sitting around laughing and talking. I'm walking back to Juan Carlos' family's house after going for a long run by myself through the dairy farm and around the edge of the neighborhood. It's been two weeks since I showed up in Aguascalientes. Juan Carlos and I spent a week hitchhiking and having crazy adventures all over Zacatecas and the desert in San Luis Potosi around the New Year. I've been learning all kinds of important lessons that I'm going to be silently taking back with me to the other side. I'm leaving the next day to head home, suddenly seeing everything sharp and magic with my fresh traveler eyes.

In the blink of an eye a black and white police truck pulls up right next to me and two cops, tall and light-skinned, with mirrored sunglasses are suddenly by my side. With their nightsticks waving in my face, they order me to get in the back of their truck. I try to protest—"What did I do? I think you must be mistaking me for someone else!"—but they make it very clear with body language that they'll force me in and make me sorry if I refuse. Suddenly there is no one in the street to see us. I take a deep breath and get in the truck.

As soon as they've locked me in and gotten in the vehicle we've sped down the street in a screech of burning rubber. It occurs to me that the cops are probably drunk. The driver is glaring at me through the reflection in the rearview mirror and firing a barrage of questions as he swerves around streets, "What are you doing here? Do you have a tourist visa? What are the names of the people you are staying with? Do you have a passport?" I answer calmly, "I'm from the United States of America, sir. I have my New York State driver's license. I'm just visiting your city for the holidays. I'm planning on leaving tomorrow." The driver cop screams back, "That's not what I asked you, *puto*! Do you have a tourist visa and a passport?" "I have a U.S. drivers license and I had no idea that in Mexico it was a crime to walk down the street, sir." He's furious, "That's wasn't my question, *puto*! Listen, *pinche pendejo*, we're going to take you out of town right now and beat you so bad you'll be sorry you ever came to Mexico. *Me escuchas, puto*?" I'm scared but playing it cool. "What have I done wrong? I was just walking down the street, sir. If anything happens to me there are going to be a lot of people on both sides of the border who will be very upset." It goes on like this for a while. We drive in circles around the neighborhood three times. The driver cop keeps stalling out, nearly driving on the sidewalk and hitting other cars, catcalling at all the young women we pass on the streets, and telling me what they're going to do to me in a flood of profanity.

After the third lap around the neighborhood we start heading out of town. My hands are shaking. I can see the moon outside the window high up in the sky, the only witness to this whole fucked up scene. I briefly contemplate all the ill shit the moon has had to witness over the years. "I don't know this road, sir. Where are we going right now?" I ask. The cop leers, "Where no one can see what we're going to do to you, *puto*. How do you like that?"
Deep breath. "I still don't know what I have done wrong, sir. Like I said, there are going to be a lot of upset people on both sides of the border if anything happens to me." Silence from the cops. My heart is beating out of my chest.

We pull over on a dead end road just out of town. They're out with their nightclubs and unlock my door. "Get out! Hands against the car!" They frisk me roughly, make me empty my pockets. "How many beers have you drunk today?" They ask.

"Not a single one, sir. I don't drink. I was just going for a run when you picked me up." He's drunk and looking at me crazily, lips curled into a snarl, not saying a word. They're visibly disappointed to find no drugs or weapons and only 50 pesos (not quite 5 dollars) in my wallet. The 50 pesos disappear into the driver's pocket. But after that they keep their hands off me. They tell me to put my stuff away and without another word the cops get in their truck and drive away.

I'm still shaking. Pigs on a power trip, same the world over. I walk back to town slowly. The sun is just setting over *el Cerro del Muerto* and the sky is a wash of purples and pinks. It's the most beautiful thing I've ever seen in my whole life. I have a big smile on my face, thankful for every step, every breath. The moon is keeping watch up above.

The next day I say goodbye to Juan Carlos and get on the bus. I've decided that I've earned the twenty-two hour ride back to Ciudad Juárez with the comfy seats and Hollywood Spanish dubbed movies on little TV screens.

I'm travel weary and ready to catch up on sleep and writing. We're an hour out of town when the bus stops at a military checkpoint. Two soldiers check everyone's ID. They pull two guys off the bus; a young Guatemalan kid who has no papers and me, the dirty gringo. Suddenly five uniformed soldiers with automatic rifles are looking through my pack, grilling me about why I have so much literature from the Zapatistas. They tell the bus driver to continue on, that they are going to hold me for questioning.

On January 1, 1994, the same day that NAFTA went into effect, the Zapatista Army of National Liberation took over a number of small cities in the southern state of Chiapas. The Zapatistas were different than any revolutionary group that had come before them; they used information for more than military strategy, making it very clear to the rest of the world that the path of "free trade" the Mexican government and the multinational corporations had in mind wasn't going to go down without a serious fight. It was the early days of the internet, and the Zapatistas were sophisticated at getting their messages out through email and websites. Their actions inspired thousands of foreigners to travel to the poorest state in Mexico and do solidarity work with the indigenous communities in the jungle under attack from the Mexican military. I still have a group of friends that are living and working in Chiapas to this day. Juan Carlos and I had originally met at the anarchist library in Mexico City. Before I left his house this time he loaded me down with tons of current Zapatista literature.

The soldiers look through every single scrap of it and ask me dozens of ridiculous questions. Do I know how to use guns? Do I know the "leader" of the Zapatista revolution, *Subcomandante* Marcos? Am I a spy? It takes a while to convince them that I haven't come from the tenth anniversary of the uprising celebrations that had just happened in Chiapas. The commanding officer seems to have it in for me. But at some point he tells me to pack up my stuff, that I will be allowed to get on another bus and continue on my way. Thank you, *señor*.

The commanding officer goes off to check another bus, and I'm left with four younger soldiers. As soon as he is gone, one of the uniformed men says to me, "You know what, man? I think the Zapatistas are *chingon*, I think they're fucking cool!" He smiles. My eyes are wide. Another one pipes in, "Me too, brother. It's a just cause, people are hungry and desperate in Chiapas. They're just fighting for what's right." A third one looks over to make sure he's not being watched by his superior, raises his fist and smiles, "Viva Marcos!" They're all smiling at me and laughing. My mouth is agape. I suddenly remember the important rule of the road—things are not always as they seem. It's the early days of 2004, and the year is starting off right. Not quite what I had in mind, but I'm ready for surprises, ready to make the best of this as yet unwritten story. I finish packing my bag and a few minutes later I'm back on another bus, staring out the window at the desert speeding by, heading back north.

Adventures in the Land of Greasecars and Fireflies

"Are you ready?" I asked, glancing nervously over at my friend, Jolie, in the passenger seat as we drove along the curvy, twilight road. She was staring back at me with wide, excited eyes.

"Uh-huh. Do it." I flipped the switch on the dashboard from MAIN to AUX and waited for the little car to lose power with that particular tenseness I hold in my jaw that I've gotten used to when driving sketchy vehicles. We waited. And waited. Nothing changed. If we'd routed the system correctly the car was drawing fuel from the new auxiliary tank in the trunk. "Goddamn—I think it's working! The car's running on straight vegetable oil!" The two of us were suddenly grinning, faces screaming out the windows with excitement. It was like we'd suddenly slipped out of the gasoline war matrix that's managed to grab the whole world by the throat; we were sneaking past the system by feeding its waste right back into itself. A moment later the exhaust pipe went from smelling like diesel to smelling like used fryer grease and the whole thing was so amazing and surreal we just felt high on life and freedom. The two of us were just a couple miles outside New Paltz on highway 44/55, heading over the Shawangunks back home to the wild side of the ridge. It was one of the last days of spring in the Hudson Valley. The sun was setting, there was thick, warm air on our skin, and the fireflies were just beginning to arrive for the season, lighting up the night sky like shooting stars.

Old Time Lessons From the Open Road

Unlike most Americans, I never had much desire to drive a car. Cars scared the hell out of me. They struck me as a good way to get yourself killed or, more likely, to get yourself stuck working a job you hated so you could pay for insurance, gas, and repairs. I saw the trap all around me from a young age and I wanted no part of it. I grew up in a city with good public transportation, in one of the only places in the country where it's common for people to never learn how to drive. I come from a long line of New York City folk who rode the subway and took the bus across town to go to work. My dad died never learning how to drive; to me it always seemed like a family tradition. Bicycles are more practical form in urban areas, and my friends and I all had bikes, so driving never became much of an issue until I decided I didn't want to be a city boy anymore and wanted to live out in the woods. Even after escaping the city, I still managed to avoid driving for years.

Like most of my anarchist traveling friends, learning how to ride freight trains and hitchhike when I was 20 was the equivalent of a mainstream suburban kid getting a driver's license and a family car. It made me feel the freedom to go wherever I wanted and visit places I'd only seen on maps or heard about in stories. But the big difference from having a car was that with this new knowledge of the road came the responsibility of having to acquire a set of other skills—I had to learn how to talk to strangers and find common ground and shared language with folks who grew up in entirely different circumstances than myself. I needed to find my way in strange lands without having a familiar space to retreat to and I had to learn to deal with bizarre situations, be able to think on my toes and live out of a backpack. I needed to learn to make friends quickly and put my trust in kindness. These were important lessons to have and skills to learn, pieces of old time knowledge whispered under train bridges in the middle of the night or in the cabs of semi trucks driving through the desert—lessons learned by hanging amidst the unfamiliar and unknown.

These days, there are few people living that old traveling life. Looking around, it becomes clear that people are scared of each other, and we live in a society so fueled by fear that it allows the wealthy to buy their way out of human interactions altogether. So if you can eat out every meal, stay in a motel every night, and fill up your gas tank whenever it's running low, you have the option of never having to engage with anyone on more than a surface level. Never mind the economic elite who exist in their own reality bubble, away from the rest of us with their own dysfunctional dilemmas. I'm just talking about average middle-class Americans who don't know how to talk to their neighbors, let alone some strangers at a gas station or the people across town.

But it seems to get harder for those of us who aspire to a life of meaningful interactions and soulful connections. Every year it seems like we get closer to a world where self check-out scanning bar code machines, Paypal, Amazon internet shopping, and swiping cards in front of digital displays replace any kind of human contact we once had in the marketplace, out in the streets, or on the road. Travel and vacation are big industries that colonize whole areas of the world and our mass media soaked consciousness. People learn how to interact from Hollywood movies and inane TV talk shows. We learn what the rest of the world is like through the cultural lenses of the people who oppress us, and because of this, ridiculous and twisted stereotypes get burned into our tender brains before we have a chance to even know what's been done to us. These are traps of the modern world, so easy to fall into with our traditional social safety nets cut and our cultural histories washed away in the drowning amnesiac tide of consumer conveniences and corporate monoculture thinking. In a world where we're pitted against each other for the dollar, taught to fear each other in the classrooms and from the newspapers and images we're inundated with, we end up looking only to our wallets or the government for security. Inevitably, tragically, we watch out for the ones closest to us and leave the doors locked and windows rolled up when we're driving through unfamiliar territory.

This is what the world of cars and driving represented to me—a ticket to be like everyone else I didn't want to be like, a ticket straight into the hands of the system. But it's easier to criticize things from the outside, to look with contempt at people driving their little air conditioned boxes while you're sweating on the highway, waiting for the kindness of a stranger to emerge from a blur of speeding multicolored metal and stone cold faces. It's easier to do romantic things, like ride freight trains around the country and be the exciting person passing through town if you don't have anywhere to be or anyone relying on you for anything important. Traveling on the fringes of the system, although it can be full of magic and potential and freedom, has its own world of alienating privileges and strange social pitfalls.

It's such an archetypal punk rock thing if you think about it—being that loner standing on the outside looking in with anger and contempt. It's definitely one of the defining features of a subculture to look at the outside world with fear and distrust. It's a powerful mechanism for maintaining traditions and codes of behavior in the face of cultural homogenization. (Look it up in the sociology books, punk.) Do you remember how scared we were by the internet? The thought of communicating through e-mail seemed alien and cold. I remember the summer of 1998, when Dragonface Dan rode freight trains all over the country and sent me emails about his adventures from public libraries in places like Pocatello, Idaho, and Ogden, Utah. That's when I knew that e-mail was here to stay. No matter how alienating and foreign, eventually, if we're clever, we learn to make the system work for us. Even train-hopping-traveler kids I meet either use those free 888 voicemail lines or have cell phones to stay in touch with each other. Almost everyone uses the internet for something, if they don't have their own web pages and blogs. Times change, people adapt, the world moves on, and creates whole new riddles and lessons for us.

The Era of the Punk Rock Chingers

Not so many years ago my friends and I used to drop 25 bucks at Radio Shack for these little electronic tone dialers that we could reprogram to simulate the sound of quarters going into a payphone. Before cell phones and the internet, this is how we communicated with one another. Tone dialers were created in the '80s when telephones were switching between the rotary system and touchtone. People needed to access new-fangled, tone-operated answering machines from rotary phones. I suppose some people continued to use them to program their phone numbers, and they were just one more piece of electronic garbage made in Chinese factories and sold at identical strip malls around Our Great Nation, destined for obsolescence. The dialers were about the size of a cell phone, tiny black boxes that fit in your pocket. We would buy them, open up the back with a little screwdriver, use a soldering iron to replace one of the microprocessor crystals responsible for making a specific tone with a similarly shaped but different tone crystal, and put the whole thing back together, carefully. We called them "chingers," thus named for the "ching" sound they made when you held them up to a payphone receiver and pushed the button. Five consecutive programmed chings tricked the phone into thinking a quarter was being deposited. A chinger had an infinite supply of chings. This is how we outsmarted the system and talked to our friends without having to pay. In a world where the System is so monolithic and brutal, where the phone company has direct ties to the nuclear arms industry, where their corporate insignias look straight out of the Death Star from *Star Wars*, and where we obviously all wanted to work as little as possible so we could concentrate on being Anarchist Revolutionaries, it was a pretty cool trick. It was like finding a loophole in the communication grid, a clever way to slip through the cracks and use their infrastructure for our needs.

By the time I started using my chinger, only certain payphones worked on the old tone system, but those of us with chingers in our pockets knew where they were in all the major cities, just like we knew where the good dumpsters behind the stores were to feed ourselves. Some of those chinger phone spots became like space/time portals to me—I'd spend long nights on the phone with my friends out west, pumping fake tones into the machine every couple minutes. When I was 19, the first tour of my band was booked from an old telephone on the corner of 8th Street and Avenue C with the use of a chinger and a list of venue contacts. But that was long ago. I hardly even recognize that block anymore. Around the millennium the phone companies switched over to a system that didn't recognize the old tones, and the era of traveling punks with the chingers in their pockets got relegated to a piece of obscure history you now read about in books.

Welcome Back to the Year 2004

For the last 20 years there's been a system of wars going on in the Middle East, and they are primarily about oil and the money being made off of oil. They are about building pipelines through the desert and securing future energy reserves and government ties to big business interests, and corporate contracts to rebuild decimated economies. Those of us with our eyes open know how wrong the whole thing is, but as a society we're addicted to the oil and stuck in the system in place for obtaining it. Fossil fuels are the life-blood of the System. Oil and gas are the backbone of capital-intensive industrial production because they provide the energy for transportation, for industry, and for mechanized agriculture. Our society as we know it would grind to a halt if we suddenly didn't have access to cheap fuel, and there are a small amount of people who control the fuel who are quite skilled at maintaining that control. Everything in the grocery store is there for us to buy because of subsidized oil paid for in blood. The gas we pump at the station is subsidized by the same misery and carnage. We don't want to think about it, so most of us don't. The same disconnect that allows us to live a life where we don't need to talk to our neighbors allows us the ability to shut out logic when it's right in front of our eyes, staring us in the face. The politicians on TV might say it's about "Weapons of Mass Destruction" or "protecting freedom and democracy," but we all know that it's just about keeping the system running. Lo and behold—the system runs on cheap oil.

History is capable of making twists and turns—the hyper-petroleum dependent world was not always so inevitable. The diesel engine, which is still used today for long hauling because of its superiority in strength and reliability to the gasoline engine, was first exhibited at the 1900 World Exhibition in Paris—Dr. Rudolf Diesel had it running on straight peanut oil!

It was a powerful engine that used compressed air and oil without a spark to create an ignition. Dr. Diesel, 34 years old at the time, designed his engine to run on various oils, all of which could be grown by regional farmers. However, the auto and petroleum industries were quick to turn the diesel engine into an opportunity to maximize use of the crude oil they used to make petroleum gasoline. Because the diesel engine is stronger, it can be run on less refined gasoline, and what we call diesel fuel today is actually a byproduct of the petroleum making process. By offering both fuels at one station and coming from one source, it could maximize profit and keep the ability to power engines out of reach of the people.

We don't hear much about fueling cars on vegetable oil, do we? If we could produce the fuel for our engines from crops that we grew in this country—safflower, soybeans, canola, corn—why would we go across the world and kill people? But the answer is the same old story. They've created a need for something they've got and they want us coming back for more. It's the cursed logic of the marketplace. In order for the system to work, it's necessary to make people need what they don't have. If they can do it themselves, you have to take away their ability to do it themselves. This applies across the board—whether it's farmers in the developing world saving seeds or kids in the suburbs producing music. When it gets to be a threat, the system clamps down. They figure out some way to take away the power, and they sell it back to us. In this modern world, everything comes back to oil.

This can be demoralizing if you have the blessing or curse of being able to connect some of the scary dots. Maybe, like me, you swore you'd never be doing it, but suddenly one day you find yourself filling up at the station with everyone else, eating your morals and choking on fumes. It feels horrible and humiliating, standing at the pump, watching the dial ring up gallon after gallon, spending your hard-earned money to fuel the war machine. It's a matter of time before it's going to blow or collapse in on itself, but it feels like a slow, depressing, bloody, painful catastrophe that you're participating in. But you know there are other ways, and that it's probably time you start working on them.

Strange Twists of Fate and Planted Seeds

I first heard about it one snowy night back in 1995 when this woman showed a video called *Living Off the Fat of the Land* at the anarchist bookstore I hung out at on Avenue B. The video was about a group of women from San Francisco who drove across the country in a diesel van they fueled on used vegetable oil they got from fast food restaurants. They mixed the waste oil with methanol and lye and heated it. A chemical process separated the glycerin molecules from the oil and replaced them with alcohol, thereby making the liquid combustible.

By a twist of fate, that winter I studied Spanish at a school in Guatemala where I met Kaia and Josh Tickell, college students from Sarasota, Florida. One night, over dinner, I was telling them about the video, about the women running their car on vegetable oil and driving across the country. Josh was a bright kid with a lot of vision, and his eyes got big, "What an amazing idea!" The following year, Kaia and Josh bought a big old Winnebago RV, painting it all hippie green and blue and full of sunflowers and calling it the "Veggie Van." As part of their senior thesis they ran the Veggie Van on used grease from fast food restaurants and drove it all across the country. They were slick enough to get corporate sponsorship and a feature on *Good Morning America*. They ended up inspiring a whole lot of folks all over the place.

Since then a thriving movement has arisen of people who are making what they call Biodiesel, fuel for diesel engines from vegetable oil. Josh has been at the forefront of it, making his living running veggievan.com and speaking about the future of sustainable energy. But even in those days, Josh and I would argue about what that future was going to look similar. He was convinced that the only way we could save the planet was to get the big oil companies to invest in sustainable technology. I told him that there was nothing sustainable about convincing everyone that it's okay to drive as much as they want and handing over all the power to corporations, which, by their nature, will never have regard for human life or the health of the planet. The only vision that made sense to me was a localized one, where farms could produce oil crops for fuel cooperatives with an emphasis on public transportation and community control. But that was awhile ago, life has moved on and, needless to say, Josh Tickell makes a lot more money than I do.

Meanwhile, I have friends, from Oregon to Maine, who are making their own biodiesel and running it in their diesel engines. I know folks in Oakland who make biodiesel in their garage and biodiesel fueling stations in northern California. I keep hearing about new cooperatives starting up all the time. These days you can buy a pre-made biodiesel processor from people at Real Goods in California. The idea is filtering into the mainstream. Then, in the middle of last summer, my friend Quinn showed up in New Paltz from North Carolina with a Ford F-250 truck that she had converted to run on straight vegetable oil. She had bought a kit from a company called Greasel in Missouri that altered their truck to be able to burn straight grease without having to add extra chemicals. Shortly thereafter my buddy Kevin drove his friend's old diesel Mercedes—also converted using a Greasel kit—all the way across the country. I started having fantasies about converting my own greasecar.

The Greasecar

The conversion of a diesel car to run on grease isn't that complicated. A regular diesel will run on vegetable oil as long as the oil is hot enough not to clog the fuel injectors. Straight vegetable oil at room temperature will clog the system because it's too thick. So you install a second fuel line with a second fuel tank. The aluminum tank has copper coils running through it. The coolant—liquid that runs through the engine absorbing heat to regulate the temperature—is rerouted under the car after it goes through the engine, and then it runs through the aluminum tank, transmitting heat through the copper coils, heating the vegetable oil. The car is started on regular diesel, fuel hoses are re-routed into an electronic switch, and once the system is heated up, you can flip a switch on the dashboard connected to a switch under the hood, and the fuel source changes from the diesel tank to the veggie oil tank. Before you turn off the car you switch the system back to diesel so the fuel lines don't clog with congealed vegetable oil.

Arteries and Hoses, Hearts and Engines

I always assumed that having a car would be an alienating experience, driving along in my little box not talking to anyone. But as I discovered, with the purchase of my first vehicle, this is only the case for people with new cars who have the money to always bring them into the shop. When I drove cross-country in my 1982 Toyota pick-up truck I discovered that driving an old janky car was not unlike hitchhiking—a daily adventure full of joy and incredible frustration. That winter I learned how to change the oil, replace the spark plugs, clean the carburetor, replace the alternator, replace my water pump, use a screwdriver to hotwire the ignition and a hammer to unfreeze the starter. I met exciting strangers willing to hook my jumper cables up to their battery and impart wisdom to me. The way you learn how to work on cars and get over being intimidated by them is to get one, wait for things to go wrong, get over feeling bad about asking for help, and make sure you have time to screw up and get dirty.

One thing I've come to understand recently, as I've gotten over my fear of working on cars, is that, despite my earlier punk rock hatred of internal combustion, they aren't inherently evil. Cars are machines that people created, people like you and me, and we made them in our own image, however flawed and mortal. Of course, Hummers and SUVs are manifestations of human egos gone awry, but cars, especially old cars, can have a lot of soul. The engine of a car is like a heart; instead of blood flowing through its arteries, its pumps are filled with oil and anti-freeze and gas. Just like a human body, all the internal systems are connected, and when one piece goes, it usually sets off all kinds of chain reactions. Cars need understanding and attention to keep functioning, just like us. And like people, the more we understand them and how they work, the more time we spend with them, the less alien they seem.

Obsessed with Diesels

Last winter, when there was two feet of snow on the ground outside our house in the woods, I met Dave Rosenstraus on the greasecar.com message board. Greasecar is a company out of Western Massachusetts that, like Greasel in Missouri, sells DIY conversion kits for diesel vehicles. On their message board folks post questions and advertise cars. Dave was selling his beat up Ford F-350 ambulance that he'd setup to run on veggie oil. As it turned out, he lived in a punk house in Allentown, Pennsylvania, with a crew of other kids, played drums in a bunch of bands, and, inevitably, we had many mutual connections. Dave taught himself to do grease conversions without any background in mechanics. Even though I decided not to buy that enormous, janky old money-trap ambulance, we stayed in touch.

I did as much research as I could over the winter and decided that the most practical and economical car to invest in would be a Volkswagen Jetta, and I began manically searching for one. I was obsessed while traveling across the country with Jacks on an Icarus Project tour. Every chance I got was spent online looking at used car websites. Jacks would laugh and say, "There you go, looking at your Jetta Porn again…" But it paid off, and I finally found one; a 1990 diesel Jetta for about as much as I could afford to pay in a place that wasn't so hard to get to. When I got back to the Hudson Valley with my little diesel car, I ordered a kit from the Greasecar folks, which set me back another $800. Then we organized a three day workshop/party in New Paltz and put flyers all over town that said, "COME TO A DIY VEGETABLE OIL CONVERSION PARTY IN THE AGE OF CORPORATE OIL WARS."

Dave drove in from Allentown to oversee the process, and for the next three days we made a big spectacle in a parking lot behind Main Street, with tools, car parts, coolant hoses, and hose clamps everywhere. Folks showed up to check it out and make things happen. People played music and cooked food.

The mayor came by to say hello. After three days and inevitable screw ups, the car was running, the smell of fryer grease was in the air, and my friend and I were driving off into the sunset, which is, if you recall, how this whole story began.

The Mind Blowing Machine

A month later when I drive by the gas stations and look at the prices they're charging, it feels like the old days when we scammed phone lines to call our friends on the other side of the country. When we pull up and ask permission to hit the dumpsters behind the Chinese restaurants and our exhaust smells like grease, everyone around us is amazed. It's a great way to start conversations with strangers. No one wants to pay $3 a gallon for gas, and seeing other options creates an opening to think about larger change in the world. It's being a threat by example. As Jacks is fond of saying, "It's like we're driving around a Mind Blowing Machine."

At the moment, it seems we've found a loophole in the system we hate, but there's only so long they'll let us use it. Business interests will figure out some way of bringing us into the fold. In a couple years they'll start making us pay for used grease; they'll start taxing or ticketing us. Inevitably, they'll make their own biodiesel from waste grease and sell it to us. Will it be a Josh Tickell teamed up with BP and Chevron to create the Sustainable Shining Path to the Future with computer chips in our brains and genetically engineered oil mono-crops sucking the land dry? Will our badass friends have localized permaculture fuel farms and biodiesel cooperatives in the free states and autonomous zones scattered around the dying nation? Time will tell.

Meanwhile, new technologies are on the horizon—hybrid cars are on the road and hydrogen fuel cells are on the way. The greasecar is inevitably going to go the way of the chinger, an obsolete piece of technology for an out of date system. And, in the end, the whole individualist car culture that we live in is going to change dramatically if there's hope for the planet. The interstate system was built for war, to transport arms and soldiers, and there's still the imprint of the origins imbedded into the design. Our culture is sick and demented and the last thing we need is more highways and roads. But it's the same as when a big, old tree in the forest dies—younger trees come along and utilize the root system that the old tree spent years carving. Why make a new system if you can take advantage of a structure that's already in place?

Conclusion

Jacks and I are pulling out of the parking lot of the High Falls Food Co-op one day when we catch wind of the familiar used fryer grease smell and look up to see a small VW pickup truck pulling in, painted the color of a John Deere tractor. There's a huge sticker on the back that states in bold letters, "This Car Runs on Used Vegetable Oil" The guy driving is Eddy, who proudly tells us with a shy smile that he's driven 25,000 miles in his greasecar.

We make a date to go out and collect grease; supposedly he's perfected the grease dumpster hand pumping system, and I'm anxious to check out his seasoned technique. This is our own little subculture—somewhere between *Back to the Future* and *The Road Warrior*, set on the backdrop of the Hudson Valley in the early 21st Century with corporate oil wars raging across the world. Even though the greedy bastards have made their permanent marks in the land and in our heads, the future is surely not going to look the way they've planned it. The future is unwritten, and if we're crafty enough we'll find a way to build our new world with the broken pieces of all their monuments to power and oil. There's definitely chaos ahead but meanwhile, we're out here dumpstering our fuel, growing our food, breaking the rules, and making as many friends as we can along the way.

Dangerous Gifts

While all of this countercultural action and adventure was going down, Jacks and I were busy trying to get our Icarus Project work funded and into mainstream institutions. Our website was growing daily, and our language was slipping into the dialogue of the radical activist community. In the meantime, I kept writing stories, keeping a record of visions and actions, trying to make sense of my experience and the lives of the beautiful freaks around me. I used the Icarus Project discussion forums as a lifeline and posted on them nearly every day. The following piece of writing was an attempt to merge the superhero comic book mythology I was raised on, my pride at being different, and my real life desperate desire for mentorship and healing.

•   •   •

Writing, for me, has always been a pretty desperate attempt at fighting off loneliness. It's never been something that flows easily out of me. My writing has always been a bit of a dangerous gift, something that allows me to communicate with the outside world while simultaneously threatening to keep me shackled to the computer screen, all alone and feeling like a desperate animal.

When I was a kid I watched a lot of TV and read a lot of comic books, my favorite being *The X-Men*. It was about a group of mutant teenagers being trained by their mentor Professor X to use their superpowers to fight the forces of evil. I always wished I had superpowers. When I got older, I started reading about shamans and medicine people in indigenous cultures—people born sensitive that had endured transformative, traumatic events that gave them special abilities. In these stories, there were always mentors and guides to train them and set them on their paths as warriors and healers, just like in the comic books.

Years later, I started realizing that all the most amazing people in my life—the wildest ones, the ones walking the edges and pushing the social boundaries and making all the connections most normal folks were too afraid to make—all of them were people who had never really fit in when they were young, had been through their share of rough times, and had somehow figured out their own ways of blazing through the world. All the people I knew who had been considered "mentally ill" and "mad" were like the mutants in the comic books, the misfits who had to carve their own paths or else be eaten by the world around them. The mutant teenagers were me and my friends. But most of us never had mentors and guides to lead us through to the other side and teach us how to be superheroes. We just had each other.

Those who are born mutants have it rough. The modern world wasn't made for the likes of us. Modern institutions and industrial standardization feel cold and heartless because our spirits are wild. We see the end of the world in flashing billboards and clear-cut forests. We feel the pain of others like it's our own. We can't hold regular jobs or make regular friends. We're told we're sick and need to be medicated for our entire lives, or else horrible things will happen. There is no place for us except in institutions or out on the street. We're outcasts. And we gravitate towards other outcasts.

People like us need community more. If we don't find strong communities we'll spend our lives feeling out of place, with a gnawing sensation that something is missing. If we're lucky, we find others like ourselves and manage to build our lives on the fringes of the mainstream. But even in our rebel communities, we don't know how to take care of each other. No one taught us to get along with one another. There is so much hidden knowledge that would make life easier, but we have no way to access it.

But that's where our dangerous gifts come in. One important lesson I learn over and over is that the people who can help me when I'm struggling with my madness are the ones who have had the same problems and made it through themselves. Being damaged and traumatized can be a powerful gift if you figure out how to use it to help others come to terms with their own powers.

I got locked up when I was a teenager because I didn't understand that I was different than most kids around me, that I had to take extra special care of myself to cultivate my powers and stay out of trouble. I wish someone had been there to offer guidance—someone who had been through it before and understood what I was going through.

Our culture's version of guidance is to diagnose people as mentally ill, stick them on anti-psychotic meds and lock them up in the hospital. There are so many kids being locked up and given drugs because they don't fit the narrow roles that the System lays out for them. And there's only so much time before the way our culture thinks about mental illness is dramatically discredited and melts into something new. What's it going to look like when it happens?

I read stories from indigenous cultures and imagine a different way.

Shamans stay shamans by *shamanizing*—healing people with their powers, their dangerous gifts. They have to pass on the knowledge. That keeps them healthy. That's why I do the work that I do. It keeps *me* healthy. If I want to survive I don't have another choice; I have to figure out how to help other people who've been through what I've been through. I have to help weave, with words and ideas, the safety net to catch people who fly too high, because it's going to be the same net that's going to catch me when I fall.

Never Never Land and the First Big Icarus Visioning Meeting

It felt historic to me and I don't think it was just because I'd slept so little the night before.

The first Icarus Project Visioning Meeting was an incredible gathering in a warm room on a cold winter's day in New York City. It was the kind of meeting that leaves you tired and satisfied and excited for the future and overwhelmed by all the possibilities that have suddenly opened up. It leaves you hoping that the energy can be carried out into the world and make the changes everyone envisioned together. There were more than 25 folks that showed up over the course of the day, and most of us stuck around talking and brainstorming until six that evening.

We sat in a circle in an office of the Silvia Rivera Law Project, a radical law collective setup to support low-income, transgender people of color. Like the Icarus Project, they're a young nonprofit that's figuring out the tricky transition from being the vision of a couple people to becoming a larger organization that doesn't mimic the top-down corporate structure that destroys other projects. This is an important time of vision and growth for everyone who cares about the future of the Icarus Project and that feeling was in the air.

At 24 years old, I had sat in a therapist's office after my latest suicidal episode. She asked me to tell her about my life. I told her stories about sitting on Earth First! Road blockades in the forest of Oregon and riding freight trains in the summer with friends and living in big collective houses and cooking Food Not Bombs in community centers and the squats on the Lower East Side. I told her about my superhero friends and the things we did together to change the world. She cut me off in mid-sentence, "It's time for you to grow up." I was "obviously delusional and dysfunctional and had been living in some kind of Never Never Land." Who did I think I was, Peter Pan? She told me I needed to get my life together and stop living in a dream world that didn't exist except in my fantasies.

I sat there in her little office, squinting under the fluorescent lights, feeling skinny and weak and vulnerable, trying to figure out if I was crazy and delusional. Did I make up those stories in my mind? Was it all a dream? My whole history felt so far away, and I felt so horribly alone.

•   •   •

Going over the email list from the meeting, looking at all the names, thinking about the people in a room talking about the future, my heart swells up with joy and pride and this powerful sense of belonging. I feel so lucky to have made it this far in my life, to a place where I will never doubt myself like that again. The mix of people came from the Freedom Center, and the Icarus Project support group. They came from the students from NYU and the New School and Sarah Lawrence and Hampshire College. They are all the characters that are in my community, the radical librarian zine makers with self-diagnosed PTSD and magical smiles, the community organizing schizoaffective shamans who walk between the straight and freaky worlds, the visionary punk rock cellists with fire coming out of their eyes, the Fountain House Youth Group dancers/dreamers trying to make their way in this world, the quiet Food Not Bombs orchestrators who play loud music and study neuroscience, the comic book artists with mad superpowers sketching quietly in the corner, the community gardeners and yoga instructors and labyrinth builders, the Visual Resistance/ABC No Rio artist crews, the bespeckled mischievous guerilla theater culture jamming propagandists, the Floridian radical cheerleader originator who didn't say a word the whole meeting, but I saw smiling in the corner, the mad manifesto reading dreadlocked teenage instigators, the Brooklyn Autonomous Space proclaimers, the artists and art therapists who came from far away and who's superpowers are empathy and understanding, the freight train riding former/reemerging activist Hellerwork practitioners, all of these amazing people. We are so lucky to have each other. This community is large and vibrant and growing. The Beehive Collective sent an email to be read about how they want to join forces with Icarus and they might be buying a former nursing home, that they can turn it into an artists' co-op and activist retreat center!

I have all kinds of notes and plans we sketched and different ways that that Fountain House and the Icarus Project and the Freedom Center can work together in the near future. It looks like the NYU kids and the Icarus Support Group are going to join forces and start meeting on the NYU campus. Jacks and I spent yesterday talking about our nonprofit status and how we're going to transition the Icarus Project into something that's run by two people into something that is collectively created and carried by a network of committees and crazy creatures. A little chaos and disaster has to be factored in, but I have no doubt that we're going to take the world by storm and I'll tell you with joy and pride and a sparkle in my eyes—that old cracker therapist at the behavior modification program who told me I was living in Never Never Land can kiss my bipolar ass!

•   •   •

The Icarus Project kept growing. We collectivized our structure. There was a whole amazing cast of characters working with us and we revised our mission and vision statements to reflect more thought-out political and social analysis. We received a grant to do organizing on college campuses and the Fountain House gave us an office in their midtown Manhattan building. Half of our collective went to New Orleans in the aftermath of Hurricane Katrina to help develop mental health support structures for the local community. Icarus members were making and sharing powerful art on the website. Thousands of members were registered from all over the world on the discussion forums, posting about the complex worlds inside their minds. Our local support group in New York City was vibrant and growing. Having a physical location meant we could bring guests and have workshops open to the public. People from different parts of my life were interested in being involved in a radical mental health project, and I felt like a conduit and a bridge builder in the most amazing of ways. I moved to Brooklyn so I could be closer to the Icarus Project action. But even with all the action and seeming support, it was still lonely in the city.

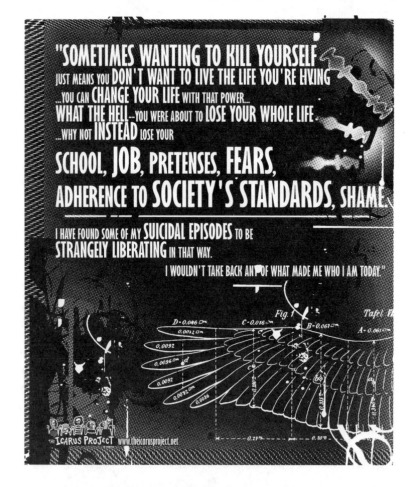

"SOMETIMES WANTING TO KILL YOURSELF JUST MEANS YOU DON'T WANT TO LIVE THE LIFE YOU'RE LIVING ...YOU CAN CHANGE YOUR LIFE WITH THAT POWER... WHAT THE HELL--YOU WERE ABOUT TO LOSE YOUR WHOLE LIFE ...WHY NOT INSTEAD LOSE YOUR

SCHOOL, JOB, PRETENSES, FEARS, ADHERENCE TO SOCIETY'S STANDARDS, SHAME.

I HAVE FOUND SOME OF MY SUICIDAL EPISODES TO BE STRANGELY LIBERATING IN THAT WAY.

I WOULDN'T TAKE BACK ANY OF WHAT MADE ME WHO I AM TODAY."

THE ICARUS PROJECT www.theicarusproject.net

Friday Night Suicide Hotline

My phone rang at 1 in the morning. My friend on the other end was hysterically crying and screaming that she *couldn't take it anymore and she wanted to die that she's had enough and please don't call the doctors and get me locked up I'm SO lonely SO alone in a little apartment on the other side of town.*

I sat on my bed watching the rain pour down. The streetlights reflected orange in the puddles of my front yard. I told her to "be quiet and breathe with me, just deep breaths, come on—I'll do it with you because it'll be good for me too."

"I can't," she said, *my body won't stop shaking. I'm just a huge ball of tension.* "Just one deep breath—come on—you can do it, it's all about the breathing and you know this already, I'm just reminding you. Just be quiet for a minute. Don't hang up on me. Take a few deep breaths."

Alright. She sounded a little more calm but was screaming and crying again in no time—lost in the evil thought loops—*I've been like this my whole life. I've never ever been happy. I'm damaged and I'm never getting better. No one is ever going to love me the way I need to be loved. I'm trapped in this body and I want to get out.*

"Come on, breathe. Your mind is playing tricks on you ol' friend. I talked to you a month ago and you told me you were happy—we talked about how sweet it is to get through this madness to the other side. Everyone loves you. Don't you know that? We all think you're amazing. You're one of the craziest most awesome people I've ever met in my whole life and we have a lot of work to do here."

We talked for an hour but it was no use and eventually she screamed that she couldn't take it anymore and wanted to kill herself and was sorry and hung up on me.

I laid there in my bed with my heart beating fast, all alone, eyes full of tears. I stared at my phone, I looked up at the ceiling, I listened to the sound of the 2 AM rain beating down on the street feeling so helpless. I called her back and cried into her answering machine about how fucking lonely I was, how fucking all alone I was in my room and how fucked up it was to leave me hanging like that.

She picked up the phone and was still screaming and crying and I was screaming and crying back at her, tears pouring down my face, heart beating out of my chest. *What do you mean, you're alone?* she asked. *I thought you had a girlfriend.*

"I don't have a girlfriend, lady. What the hell are you talking about? I don't let anyone get close enough to me cause I'm just as crazy as you. I'm fucking terribly miserably horribly, *Alone. Alone. Alone.* Why the fuck do you think it's 2 AM on a Saturday morning and I'm lying here talking to you?!?"

Long silence. *You said the magic words,* she said.

We laughed.

I can't stand it when I think someone doesn't know what I'm going through. Somehow knowing you're lonely on the other side of town makes me feel better.

"So that's the trick, huh? Come on, let's both try to get some sleep. I'll call you tomorrow to check in."

Plan For Not Going Too Crazy

Will Hall from the Freedom Center introduced me and Jacks to the idea of writing down what you want before you lose the ability to communicate it. He turned us on to the writings of Mary Ellen Copeland who's been championing folks struggling with mental health issues filling out Advanced Directive documents to share with doctors and their community in the event that they end up in a hospital. We were really inspired. Icarus started running with this idea of creating reminder documents for ourselves and the people around us about our warning signs and the kind of self-care we wanted; identifying both our wellness goals and the people we could trust to look out for our best interests. We started calling them our "wellness maps" or "mad maps."

The most exciting part of these maps is that they aren't just for "sick" people—writing down our strategies for health and signs of struggle can help any group of people learn how to be better friends and supporters. By articulating our needs, we can share them with others, our maps can be the glue to building peer-based support structures. The act of figuring out what it means personally to be healthy is about learning to leave a trail back to how we want to be. The clearer we articulate it, the easier it is to get back there.

In the event of a crisis, our maps can help our friends form teams, make sure the basics are covered, help develop sanctuaries, and make it a lot less likely that we will end up in the hospital. I found trying to figure out who would be there for me if I needed them a hard and painful process, but ultimately rewarding. Most friends that I love and love me back aren't necessarily going to be there for me if I'm having a psychotic breakdown, fucking up my life, and scaring the people around me.

The list is fluid—the people closest to me change depending on what's going on with my life, but there's a stable core. Real friendship is a lot of work. Crisis tears people apart or brings them closer. If we can articulate this stuff before it happens and make a list of people we trust, we are that much closer to building sustainable radical mental health support networks. If you try to make a list and realize that your true support people don't exist yet, that's a good place to start; figuring out how to get tight with your friends or make new friends you can be tight with.

Sascha's Plan For Not Going Too Crazy

I, Sascha Altman DuBrul, do not want to get so crazy that it shipwrecks my life again and causes major damage to my self and my relationships. Therefore, when I become aware of the early warning signs of mania, depression, or potentially scary states, I will use the strategies in this document to take care of myself and articulate my needs to my community.

Everyday Wellness (What I'm cultivating and working towards)

-My head is clear with no nagging negative thoughts, not foggy, nor agitated
-Being present and taking pleasure in the simple act of breathing/feeling my feet on the ground
-Well rested and comfortable in my body
-Organized: not procrastinating or scattered
-Routine: I have one and I'm sticking to it
-Checking in with friends and asking how I'm doing (and listening)
-Being present with the people in my life

What can I do when I feel myself slipping out of wellness:

-Look over *Daily Maintenance Plan/Wellness Toolbox*
-Do things to make me breathe/vigorous exercise in which I can't hold my breath: ride my bike up a hill, go running, spontaneous dance parties in living room
-Call a friend (see *Supporters*)

Daily Maintenance Plan /Wellness Toolbox

-Daily Journaling: writing down dreams, recording awake and asleep times
-Routine: clear and delineated hours for work/study/play (when on deadline turn off internet)
-Food: designated time for meals, remember not to run out of food (carry food with you at all times—dried bananas, sunflower seeds, beef jerky)
-Sleep: strive for eight hours, seven is good, six is not enough, five and you should think about canceling appointments, five or less for more than two nights in a row and it's time to drug yourself with Melatonin, Atavan, or 25mg of Seroquil (or even half of 25mg is extremely helpful if you've slipped off your sleeping schedule)
-Exercise: yoga practice/qi gong practice/swimming/weight training
-Community: check in at regular intervals with friends—weekly/bimonthly phone calls/hang out sessions
-Friends and food: cooking food with friends
-Meds: you take 1200mg of Lithium Carbonate before bed.

What it looks like when I'm not well:

-Overwhelmed: feeling so disorganized with so many projects started at once, unable to work on any of them
-Feeling of time running out and tunnel vision, like I work too slow and can never accomplish what is needed
-Holiday blues: deep aching loneliness, seeing ghosts metaphorically, or actually

Early Warning Signs Pointing Towards Mania...

-Waking up early multiple days in a row
-Forecasting dreams and ESP (knowing who's on the phone, what someone is going to say, etc)
-Cutting people off and not listening well
-Other people seem to be in slow motion
-Taking on too much responsibility
-Recruit more people into my life, promise to hang out with everybody, and much easier to make friends
-Black and white thinking
-Thinking more about helping others more than taking care of my own basic needs
-Sense of the world "crawling under my skin" or the freeway "pumping through my blood"
-Sense of porous membranes to other people/energy

Advanced Warning Signs!

-The sense that I'm a character in a story rather than a real person (There's a difference between an ability to access this feeling rather than being stuck in it and not knowing the difference. It increases my feeling of agency and self-importance and increases my lack of connection to others.)
-Brain completely overloaded with multiple layers of music/racing thoughts/out of control observations and metaphysical connections.

Early Warning Signs Pointing to Depression:

-My intuition is off and misjudge people's intentions, have lots of bad hunches
-Assume everyone's thinking about me and noticing how awful I am
-I have low energy or wretched agitated energy, I feel an intense need to withdraw from things
-I feel useless and trapped in unchangeable patterns and start feeling really awkward and weak in my body
-It seems like it requires so much energy to take care of practical things like cleaning room, paying bills, doing dishes, and spending.
-Too much time on internet

Advanced Warning Signs!

-Seems unreasonably hard to get out of bed or out of the house
-Unbearably slow thoughts.
-Doing anything that involves multiple tasks seems so incredibly complicated (requires way too much energy)
-Canceling all my appointments with people
-Start doubting my relationships

Question's For My Friends to Ask Me:

Practical questions like:

-How is my sleep? Am I waking too early? If so, am I able to fall back asleep? Do I try? Am I having trouble falling asleep? Usually, when I start getting manic, the first thing that happens is that I start waking up too early. If things progress, I have a lot of trouble falling asleep as well. If things progress further, I want to be up until 2 or 3 AM, writing and reading, and then I still wake up really early. I often seem to have way too much energy for the amount of sleep I'm getting. Periodically I will complain of being "so tired but I can't sleep."

-How regularly am I eating? Am I eating enough protein and grounding things? Am I eating too much sugar and chocolate? I can quickly be thrown off by not eating well. I can also easily end up using sugar and chocolate as a substitute for healthier forms of energy. (This can throw off my sleeping schedule.)

-Am I meditating? Am I exercising? It's helpful to remind me how much more calm and focused I am when I'm regularly meditating. If I haven't been doing it, remind me to go to the Y or ride my bike in the hills. I need to exercise *every day*.

-How many hours am I spending in front of the computer a day? If more than four then I better have a damn good reason. Remind me to take frequent breaks and not get sucked into the internet. Remind me to turn off web access when I have to spend a lot of time writing.

-When was the last time that I left the city or went for a hike or bike ride in the hills? Leaving the city is essential for my state of mind to stay healthy. Remind me that it's not a luxury, it's a necessity.

I'm exhibiting signs of manic behavior if I answer:

-That I have been having sleeping troubles for more than two days (not able to get at least seven hours of sleep a night)

-That I am having problems with my appetite or remembering to eat

-That I am having trouble sitting still/remembering to meditate

-That I'm spending too much time in front of the computer

I need to start taking steps to slow down. Please insist that I:

-Don't use the computer after 9 PM

-Have a pre-bed slowing down ritual: make sleepy tea, put on candles instead of bright lights, read something of a calming nature instead of using the computer, maybe do my centering exercises

-Get more exercise during the day to wear me out

-Drink more liquids and eat more grounding meals, with people if necessary

-Go sleep in my girlfriend's bed

-Strongly consider taking Seroquel (25mg) for a few days

If this does not work, or things are more advanced— if by the time you are asking these questions:

-I give my designated support people permission to confer about how I'm doing and what should be said to me. Intervene, and sit me down, and make me look at this list. Watch me closely and check in with me very frequently. Insist that I take my meds, go see my psychiatrist, and stop going out and doing a million things.

-I also need to start taking crisis-prevention steps to not get dangerously manic and/or psychotic.

Please insist that I:
-Cut back on my appointments/schedule
-Take 50-75mg of Seroquel for several nights
-Increase my Lithium level back to 1200mg (if it's not already)
-Cut computer time down to a very minimal amount or none at all

If I continue to get worse, regardless of these measures, and three of my support people agree that I am out of control to the point of being dangerous, I give them permission to arrange to take me to somewhere outside the city where I can rest and have a daily routine.

GERMANTOWN COMMUNITY FARM

Then this funny thing happened one weekend towards the end of the summer. I heard my old freight train riding friend Okra P. Dingle was staying up on a piece of land in the Hudson Valley and I really wanted to see him. I also desperately needed a break from the city. I got there and it was a crazy scene— all these drunk circus punks and a bunch of semi-neglected farm animals and acres of abandoned apple orchards. There was also this very earnest crew of hardworking young homesteaders who were living on a piece of land about 40 minutes away, trying their best to hold down the farm responsibilities. The circus punks, including my buddy Dingle, were all getting ready to leave on tour, and the farm desperately needed people to come and take care of it. Somehow, within a couple weeks I'd moved out of my depressing little room in Brooklyn and I found myself fixing up a space in the old farmhouse. By Thanksgiving, the house was filled with people and we were getting ready for the winter, chopping wood, planning a CSA farm for the spring, and developing a collective mission statement:

The Germantown Community Farm is a budding organic farm, a node in a network of rural activists, sharing our land and visions with travelers, family, friends, and neighbors. We aim to foster a cross-pollination between urban and rural living and create a physical space and a forum for community sustainability. Our vision is to be a part of creating a new agriculture in the Hudson Valley based on diversity of culture and biology rather than corporate mono-cropping our minds and fields. We strive for the cultural diversity of the cities mixed with the biological diversity of wild gardens and forests, and we're committed to feeding and teaching people and taking care of each other in the process.

We have 60 acres, a large house and barn, a pond, a forest and a stream in the back. We are caring for three grown goats and three baby goats, baby turkeys and chicks, chickens, roosters, ducks, geese, a large house garden, and ten acres of neglected apple orchards. We are planting a field, and cleaning out the barn for a healing space. We have a deer fence to build, lots of planting to do, as well as a greenhouse to fill. We've got our business license and we're applying to accept food stamps for vegetables. We're starting a CSA for low-income families in collaboration with a community center in nearby Hudson and actively trying to raise the money within our social network to do so. We are working hard and smiling as we follow our dreams! If you can't come for one of our work parties, consider signing up as one of our week-long guests over the spring or summer, or sending a donation.

Growing Together at the Roots With My Friends

Monday morning in Germantown, NY. I woke up to my housemate Kaya asking me to help move the farm truck. I stumbled out of bed, pulling on my soil-stained pants, big snow boots, someone's jacket from the pile by the door. We are always wearing each other's clothes these days. There were half a dozen folks at the bottom of the hill by the barn, blowing steam out of their mouths and noses, getting ready to push the 1994 Ford F-350 orange diesel out of the mud. Kaya put it into gear and revved the engine—wheels spinning, mud everywhere. We piled heavy metal from the scrap pile in the back, old carpet underneath the tires, but she still wouldn't budge. Finally, Erika hooked up her truck and pulled it out triumphantly, up the hill and out onto the road.

I came back inside as Bobby and Patrick started making french toast and omelets in the kitchen with dumpstered veggies, bread from Erika's dad's bakery, and eggs from our chickens. I can hear Ashley working on the goat feeding schedule and people working on various projects, our stealthy cats darting in and out of the doors, a flurry of activity all over the house. I feel lucky on mornings like this, the taste of maple syrup in my mouth, sun shining on my face. This isn't the life on TV shows or in glossy magazines, but I can't imagine what I'd rather be doing than living with friends, working on our collective farm.

We're about to put up a greenhouse, grow seedlings, and in the early spring we're going to till up an acre behind our pond and grow a whole lot of healthy food. We have two beautiful, pregnant goats who are going to give birth and we've been getting ready for the babies. We're having work parties and tree-pruning workshops every weekend to reclaim the ten acre neglected apple orchard. But the most important thing is learning to trust each other, to support each other, and to work together and watch each other's backs in a world where trust and friendship seems harder and harder to come by. I can't believe we're doing it sometimes. I was losing my mind being a city boy living in a dark room down the street from the Brooklyn/Queens Expressway and working in midtown Manhattan. I had a few sad tomato plants in pots on my windowsill and I could barely relate to my housemates. Four months later I'm in this intense relationship with a pack of people, most of whom I didn't know four months ago and we're living our collective dreams, making it up as we go along. It's like it was meant to be.

It feels natural, like how pioneer species grow after a clear-cut. It's a spontaneous process but there is a greater order to it. There's a similar process happening in our relationships to each other and the physical environment. Our friend Asa bought this neglected farm with the dream of hosting a community like ours. We don't know about the long run, but we know it's not going to get taken away from us anytime soon—we can put our love and sweat into it and it won't just disappear into some stranger's greedy hands.

The land has had its share of problems since Asa bought it five years ago: The neglect of irresponsible college kid tenants, frozen pipes, holes in the barn roof, and a healthy dose of drunken circus chaos. We didn't know if this place would ever be a place for healthy and vibrant community. But the right series of pioneers and successions arrived—a small crew of people with vision and drive, a cast of quirky characters with crazy dreams, some old biodiesel vehicles, a pond to swim in, work parties, a 5 gallon bucket of compost tea, folks with carpentry skills, a lost sheep fiasco, a broken stair and a bag of quick drying cement, some rowdy anarchists, a slapped-together outhouse, an impressive greywater system, a bed of healthy brussel sprouts and a ton of cherry tomatoes, a pile of old travel zines, some bee boxes, a couple of bottles of homebrewed wine, three large pigs, and friends visiting friends from the city—you can paint the picture.

You can see dramatic success when the furnace gets fixed and the house is habitable for winter. People gather around fire and heat. The people who stuck around turned out to be committed to seeing this place flourish into a functioning, awesome community. We figured out cleaning systems, hashed out guest policies, made real time for group emotional process, worked out collective money and financial situations, tried to figure out our decision-making process and who we think we are in this world. Meanwhile we make sure all the people and animals are fed, build better relationships with our neighbors, grapple with our reliance on oil, deal with drama in our lives. We bicker about food and dishes. Sometimes we argue about larger questions and don't always end up in happy agreement. We try not to step on each other's toes too much but inevitably end up doing it anyway. We come from different places and backgrounds, and have different relationships to food, work, and money. Living in community is not something we're taught how to do. But we're braving it, taking risks, and getting close. Winter helps. We cook a lot of hot food by the wood stove in the kitchen. We stay up late telling stories about trauma and drama from our childhoods. We're a community of folks who don't fit so well in the normal world, so that's probably why we're passionate about creating something new.

Jay showed up and was teaching how to ice fish out of the pond. Tiger was baking apple crisp and playing fiddle all over the house. Tucker came over and helped me build a platform for my bed. Jolie came over and played guitar and sang freshly written songs. Alecia gave amazing backrubs and cooked good food. Lailye taught yoga. Rene and Moose, refugees from New Orleans, painted the big upstairs bedroom. The entire Beehive Collective camped out in our living room for a week, making art and strategizing the revolution. Our friends in New York City from the More Gardens! Coalition, the Curious George Brigade, and the Bluestocking Collective have come up to work on projects with us and eat lots of food. We know that once the warm weather hits we're going to have friends visiting and working out in the fields together, daily yoga classes in the living room, cooking huge meals with fresh produce, teaching and hosting skillshares, and having dance parties in the barn. There's nothing more exciting than working and playing with your favorite people.

We're also not afraid to ask for help from the older folks. On Thanksgiving our house was packed full of friends and relatives—five different people's families showed up, meeting each other for the first time. Bobby's mom came from New Hampshire and taught everyone circle dancing. Courtney's mom spent hours in the kitchen with us baking pies. My mom and her boyfriend came and brought me a down comforter. The intentional community runs deep. Kaya and Dylan were raised on a big commune in Tennessee. They have thoughts about what worked and didn't. And so do their parents. Kaya's dad showed up with a GPS tool and a chainsaw. The two of them spent the day mapping the entire farm and cutting down dead apple trees for firewood. Their dad continued to visit over the season and had us working together—felling, bucking, hauling, splitting, and stacking—getting our wood pile ready for the winter and giving us lots of hard-earned advice. A 77-year-old local woman named June Munson has been teaching, crocheting, and telling stories.

I'm so excited to be working on such an amazing collective vision. There are these totally magical moments when we're all working together outside or in the barn or in the kitchen. These moments when we're having large group discussions and meals and people are really present with one another. These moments when we're all dancing together at a show that we've all worked so hard to make happen and the music sounds so sweet and everyone looks so alive. These are moments when everyone realizes how important this all is and we're all looking at each other with wonder and appreciation. It's really a sight to behold. No matter how this all turns out in the end it's going to be worth it. We're building the path that we're walking on, making friendships that are going to last our lifetimes.

These days I wouldn't trade anything in the world for standing by the Hudson River in the middle of winter with my friends, just down the road from our crazy house, the sun setting over the Catskill Mountains and reflecting pink and orange and red and yellow in the chunks of ice floating in the water, watching this amazing group of people I call my community taking care of each other and playing around in the snow. It makes me feel lucky and proud, humbled and free to just be myself and know I have a crew that really has my back and will look out for me if I go through hard times. And we have packs of friends doing stuff like this all over the country—from the Albany Free School folks just north of us to Short Mountain Sanctuary in Tennessee to the Rhizome Collective in Austin to the Linnaea Farm up in British Columbia to the Victory Gardens crew in Maine. We're all just getting wiser and more interesting as we get older, our stories more intertwined and more outlandish and more solid—really the adventure's just begun. It's not even springtime yet.

•   •   •

That spring I spent a lot of time jumping back and forth between the country and the city. On multiple occasions I found myself waking up in the peaceful early morning to milk the goats, drive an hour to the train station in Poughkeepsie, and show up in Manhattan just in time for an 11am meeting with a university counseling center or a group of funders. I left my bicycle locked up outside Grand Central Station with two huge chains, and jumped into midtown traffic like a fish in the ocean, back in my urban element. Between the mental health workshops and art shows at Fountain House during the week and the weekend work parties at the farm, my life was all about channeling the energy and excitement of people and building bridges for people to walk across. I saw myself as embodying the kind of change I wanted to see in the world. I felt so much pride being a part of a collective farm, my back strong and hands hard from working in the fields. We were attempting to grow a new kind of agriculture, one that was both ecologically sustainable and culturally sophisticated. I felt like an emissary from a new culture that I was helping to build and it was incredible.

We Are Our Own Safety Nets, We Weave Together

Sometimes when I close my eyes I can see it, like intersecting tree branches in the forest, or the outlines through the chlorophyll on a mature maple leaf when you hold it up to the sun. It's the safety net my friends and I are weaving to take care of each other in this crazy world, and it's as real and strong as the energy, passion, and hard-earned skills we put into it. Sometimes I feel it viscerally, like when we are working in the fields or eating a meal that we've all prepared. Sometimes I feel it all alone or surrounded by strangers in unfamiliar territory— the knowledge that my people are out there and have my back when times get hard. Our net is physical: our house, our barn, our tools, our cars, the fields and the woods. But the net extends beyond our farm with the trust and friendship between people—our crew, our loved ones, and the loved ones of their loved ones—spreading like branches in a network that reaches across the world. The safety net is a force we create, woven in spirit.

I used to travel all over the country meeting new people wherever I went. Part of me always figured that if I made enough friends, I'd never get into too much trouble because I'd have folks to look after me through the rough times—a big anarchist family of freaks and rebels. But too many times I learned that things don't work like that. Hundreds of phone numbers and email addresses in your Slingshot Organizer or faces on your Facebook account will still leave you alone and helpless if you ever really need a friend to be there for you. There are lessons on the road but not so many about stability and continuity. And the internet is great for lots of things, but there's no substitute for another person running their hands through your hair and rubbing your shoulders and holding you when you need to be held. It's taken me awhile to figure out that the way to make friends I can trust to have my back is by working together on intense projects and sticking around to see things through hard times.

But building the kinds of safety nets I'm talking about takes more than just working together on projects. It's about finding language to talk about internal worlds, learning each other's stories and histories, talking honestly about our issues and our triggers, and what we've learned to do about them. Do we stand guard over each other and know what's in each other's best interests when times are rough? Do we know each other's warning signs and know what to do when they appear? Do we make sure that the people in our community are taking care of the basics; getting enough sleep? Eating enough good, healthy food? Exercising everyday? Keeping a routine that works for them? Doing things that they love and feel passionate about? Do we know how to talk about past traumas in a way that feels safe? Do we create regular spaces and times to talk about the hard stuff? Do we respect the people in our communities who've made it through hard times and have lessons to share? There's so much to learn from each other. What does it take to feel comfortable asking for help if you need it? And when you ask, do we know how to respond? What issues can we deal with and when does it make sense to explore healing modalities from herbalism to acupuncture to homeopathy to western psych drugs, if that's what it takes? Can we respect the different personal decisions we make to take care of ourselves?

I've been crossing paths with folks taking an active role in organizing inspiring mental health support in their communities, weaving safety nets out of hard-earned lessons and singed wings. I quietly watched dozens of people on the Icarus Project website talk about forming mutual aid support groups in their local communities. In New York City there's a thriving little scene who come to meetings that mix support and community organizing. We're starting Mental Health Skillshares—folks share personal coping strategies with open forums. We're doing another art show. We're organizing student support groups on college campuses. We have people doing support group organizing as far away as New Orleans, Louisiana; Portland, Oregon; and Northampton, Massachusetts. This is how we hold each other up through the long haul. This is how we weave our own safety nets together.

In Memory of Brad Will: Old Friend, Mad Revolutionary, Taunter of Death

The memories poured out of my head like a flood all day. They overpowered my dreams and spilled all over the sheets. I can't be present with the people around me. My head keeps slipping into that ethereal place between life and death, memory carrying me back more then a decade and then flashing to photos on Indymedia. Photos of Brad Will with a bullet in his chest, lying dead on the dusty street with strangers standing over his body. I have to write this down so I can come back to life and figure out what the hell to do next.

It's so strange when our friends die, how they get frozen in time while the rest of us keep moving and getting older. For the rest of my life, Brad is always going to be that scruffy-faced, fire-breathing rebel taunting the cops on the streets of the Lower East Side; that madman on the roof of 5th Street Squat getting in the way of the wrecking ball on a cold February morning cause he was determined to keep them from demolishing his home; that badass motherfucker who wasn't scared to be right on the front lines and scream in the face of authority. Brad was always tempting fate and putting himself in the line of fire, in a way where it was never clear if he was heroically brave, a raving lunatic, or some complex interplay between the two.

I met Brad Will at Dreamtime Village outside Madison, Wisconsin, during the summer of 1995. He was loud and obnoxious and full of himself and had an explosive, mischievous laugh and told great stories. He had been traveling around with a group of guys, performing guerilla theater in the streets, inspired by the idea of creating Temporary Autonomous Zones and conjuring up spaces to shake up modern capitalist notions of normality and productivity. We reveled in the power of our freaky friends, the magic of the nomadic traveling circus, and the beauty of our underground anarchist culture.

We crossed paths again shortly thereafter at Blackout Books, the infoshop on Avenue B where our people hung out. He'd gotten a space on the second floor of 5th Street Squat and was getting it ready for winter, excited about joining the Lower East Side squatter community, sheet rock dust in his hair and a grin on his face. We were both in New York that late fall when Steal This Radio, the squatter pirate radio station, went live for the first time at ABC No Rio. And we were both there for those roving Friday night parties when the station broadcasted its signal from a different squat every week to evade the FCC. It was the place to be, the best party in town, a radical talent show and celebration. I have warm memories of it being cold outside and Brad Will wailing on his guitar in rooms full of people.

I went down to Central America that winter to do solidarity work in Guatemala and Chiapas and ran into him the following summer in Chicago during Active Resistance, the anarchist gathering organized to protest the Democratic National Convention in 1996. I have this memory of sitting around a small fire on the outskirts of the city and our friends were singing "Angel from Montgomery." I remember Brad rubbing my travel-weary shoulders. He had strong hands, and when I complimented his strength he flexed the tendons in his forearms and laughed that crazy laugh of his, squinting through his spectacles. It's etched into my memory cause that was his freaky style.

We were both riding freight trains but he knew more about the history of the railroads and hobo culture in the U.S. One day on a street corner in Chicago he schooled me about the Dust Bowl and the Depression, migrant farm workers and the Wobblies, incredulous that I didn't know my own history. He busted out his guitar right there and belted out a string of Woody Guthrie songs, looking straight into my eyes as he sang the words:

I worked in your orchards of peaches and prunes
I slept on the ground in the light of the moon
On the edge of the city you'll see us and then
We come with the dust and we go with the wind
California, Arizona, I harvest your crops
Well its north up to Oregon to gather your hops
Dig the beets from your ground,
Cut the grapes from your vine
To set on your table your light sparkling wine

After Active Resistance he gave me the key to his room at 5th Street Squat, and I kept it tucked away in the pocket of my filthy black Carhartts. I showed up at his squat covered in diesel grease in the middle of the night off a Chicago train. I stayed in his room for a month before I left town to head west.

The next time I saw Brad Will, it was the following winter and his image was on a screen from the video of the 5th Street Squat eviction that Seth from C-Squat had sent to my house in Oakland. There had been a sketchy electrical fire in late February, the police forcefully evicted everyone, and then they used the fire as an excuse to demolish the building without giving anyone a chance to get their possessions out.

But they never got Brad out of the building. In the video that crazy motherfucker was on the roof trying to keep the wrecking ball from slamming into the building, waving his arms frantically or triumphantly. It was hard to tell. The footage was grainy but made it more dramatic. They pulled him out and brought him to jail but he burst out as a man on fire. He did a one-man tour talking to groups about the demolition of his building, gentrification, and corruption of the city. He was enraged and desperately wanted the world to know what had happened.

We organized a talk for him at Epicenter in San Francisco. It was the same era as Prisoners Literature Project, when local activists and traveler kids would show up to fill book requests to prisoners from a donated library. Brad was shaking as he told the story and everyone in the room was visibly moved.

Earlier that day Brad had showed up in town at my girlfriend's house with a big crate of fresh asparagus because his family in Stockton were asparagus farmers. Even in his rage and anger, I remember Brad Will as generous and bearing gifts.

A couple years later Brad lived at Dos Blockos Squat on 9th Street. It was the early days of the More Gardens Coalition being organized out of Aresh's tiny apartment on Clinton St. The city was evicting community gardens all over the city, and we were doing direct action street theater by City Hall on a regular basis. There were benefit shows almost every week at Dos Blockos, full of freaks, outlaws, junkies, and hoodlums that called that place home. During the eviction our friends bolted big metal spikes onto the roof of the Dos Blockos so the city couldn't land a helicopter and storm the building. It was a crazy time.

The following fall the People's Global Action Caravan showed up in New York from all over the world to protest the World Trade Organization and Brad was with us in the streets outside of the public relations firm Burson Marsteller, protesting their corporate whitewashing. Brad and I were wearing suits with red paint on our hands asking visibly sketched out employees if they could "help us get the blood off our hands."

On the Halloween Critical Mass Ride, hundreds of costumed freaks shut down Times Square for the first time ever—a crowd of bikes held high in the air, cheering and laughing. I remember Brad Will creating a spectacle blowing huge fireballs from his mouth and a cop grabbed his bicycle from the ground next to him. I'm not sure how, but Brad was slick enough to drop his torch, grab the bike out of the bewildered cops hands, and speed off into the crowd. Later, we were riding down Broadway and Brad biked by, grinning and laughing that crazy laugh of his, and disappearing into the mass.

I don't remember the next time I saw Brad Will. After the WTO protests, he made his way around the world to organize in anti-globalization protests in DC, Quebec, Genoa, Miami, and Cancun. He loved being in the streets. He had a strong sense of right and wrong. And he loved fighting the good fight.

I remember Brad Will on fire in the streets during the DNC in Los Angeles in 2000. There had been a police riot earlier and we were getting shot up with rubber bullets and tear gas, making our way back to the convergence space beaten and weary. Looking down from the second floor I saw Brad Will amidst a sea of people in the courtyard, singing a Desert Rat song, fiercely, loudly, proudly:

So I called upon you brother, and you asked what I would do,
And I told the truth dear sister when I spoke these words to you,
I will stand beside your shoulder, when the tear gas fills the sky,
If a National Guardsman shoots me down I'll be looking him in the eye,

I will wash their pepper from your face and go with you to jail,
And if you don't make it through this fight I swear I'll tell your tale.
I will stay with you in the prison cell in solidarity
And I will not leave that cursed room 'til you walk out with me
For we the people fight for freedom, while the cops just fight for pay,
And as long as the truth is in our hearts we're sure to win someday.
I will not falter when that iron fist comes out of the velvet glove,
I will stand beside your shoulder to defend this land we love.

Shortly thereafter he got passionate about documenting revolutionary movements in Latin America and got involved in the Indymedia scene. He made good money doing stage setup in New York. He would work long hours for travel money and to buy video equipment, spending large chunks of time in South America documenting multiple revolutions. I remember sleeping with a cast of motley characters at the Indymedia office in midtown Manhattan; it was often two AM as we sat below fluorescents and with coffee and deadlines, and Brad and his partner Dyan saving up money to head down south. At some point they lived at that warehouse on Walker Street where I crashed on their couch a couple times. Then later Brad had a cheap little apartment in Brooklyn that he shared with a couple activist friends who were also in and out of town. He'd always offer me his place to crash at when we'd run into each other.

The night they arrested Daniel McGowan[5], and our friends gathered at Bluestockings to figure out what to do, I spent a long time walking around the neighborhood with Brad Will. We were scared for our friend, who was suddenly looking at a life sentence for being a "terrorist" but had never hurt a soul. We talked about the terrifying political situation in the early 21st century, and how it was getting worse. Brad talked about his past clashes with the law catching up with him, how he made enemies in high places, how it was only a matter of time before they would try to pin something on him. The wind was blowing hard on Allen Street that night, the cold settling in for the winter.

We spent hours on Brooke Lehman's roof his last summer, just the two of us, looking over the city. We talked about the revolutions in Brazil, Argentina, Bolivia, Venezuela, and Mexico, how brutal the global political situation was, and how it was inevitably going to explode and spill over into the streets of this country. We talked about the mental health support work I'd been doing. With our radical asses in universities and hospitals, it wouldn't be so easy for them to pull us out when the fight comes. We expressed our mutual love and respect for each other and the paths we'd taken.

I saw Brad Will a month before he died. He showed up at an Icarus mental health skillshare at the Judson Memorial Church. Daniel McGowan was there too, fresh off house arrest. The sun was shining and good things were

5   As a result of multiple arsons against lumber company property motivated by activism, McGowan was forced to accept a plea bargain under "enhanced" charges of eco-terrorism. He was recently released from prison and sent me an email right before this book went to press. It put a huge grin on my face!

afoot. Old friends were teaching workshops amidst the younger crowd. Brad was getting ready to head to Mexico. I asked if he was going to Chiapas, and he replied in that incredulous, obnoxious voice of his, "What are you kidding, man? I'm going to Oaxaca. Haven't you been reading the news? There's a revolution going on in the streets down there!"

•   •   •

I can still hear his voice saying the words. And he still feels so alive to me. I've been hearing his voice talking to me constantly like a running dialogue. And I know from experience that memories fade, that voices fade, that the only way we can keep our people alive is by telling their stories.

It's almost one AM on Monday morning, and I spent the night with all these old friends, and we're all heading into the streets early to the Mexican consulate to shake shit up, Brad Will style. We're still all in shock and don't know what the fuck to say to each other, but we have each other, and we are so strong and beautiful.

So I swear I'll keep telling your tale, old friend, you'll be there in the streets with us wherever we're fighting for justice.

Breathing New Pathways Into My Head and Heart

I was first introduced to spiritual practice from a woman who lived down the road from the farm. Her world views were way out my comfort zone, but I was desperate for change, and I think there's an important lesson there in itself about how change often happens. Although I didn't continue with this particular spiritual practice, it was an important door that led me into realms I'd never truly imaged existed outside of my dreams. And it gave me a taste of the kind of practice that would end up becoming a daily part of my life before too long.

•　　　•　　　•

Sometime around the beginning of February, when the days were dark and the edge of spring seemed a long way off, I paid a visit to Sky. Sky is a woman in her mid-50's who has spent many years of her life immersed in spiritual practice and the healing arts. She lived as a Buddhist monk for seven years— Zen and Tibetan, trained as a body-centered, somatic therapist and studied Peruvian shamanic practices. She's also had a really crazy, interesting life, and is a very good listener and storyteller. Last season I had seen her regularly as kind of a shamanic therapist/life coach for a couple months until I stopped having the money to pay her and started feeling uncomfortable with what felt like an awkward financial relationship. I always end up feeling like that with therapists. But she was the first healer person I ever worked with who had the ability to give me practical frameworks for thinking about the complex things I struggle with that the mainstream psych world only knows to call "psychosis."

By acknowledging that I had "inner voices" that not only talk to me but talk amongst each other, Sky allowed a huge and incredibly helpful awareness shift to take place in my consciousness. I've always had a lot of respect for the power of my dreams, but never had the tools to delve into my subconscious and pull helpful pieces out and try to make sense of them. Sky introduced me to a whole new fascinating vocabulary full of things like "tracking and journeying through dimensions," "traveling between worlds safely" and the performing of "soul retrievals." I'm always been skeptical by nature, especially about stuff that rubs me as self-serving New Age, culturally-appropriative hippy bullshit, but everything I was learning from Sky was actually very practical healing techniques and ways of dealing with fundamental issues of trauma and safety and spiritual groundedness. And it was also really fascinating.

Anyway, this past February I showed up at her house disheveled and exhausted. I'd gotten lost on the way to her house even though I'd been there a dozen times before. My head was just somewhere else. I was in the sad process of breaking up with my girlfriend, I'd been traveling and my sleeping schedule was totally off, my house was cold and empty, I didn't feel at home in the city or the country. I felt extremely rootless and had no structure to my days, living off of savings after taking a month off from Icarus work. So much of what gives my life meaning is my ability to be helpful to other people, but I was having a hard enough time taking care of myself. I felt really desperate.

I was also smoking way too much weed for my fragile freaky bipolar chemistry. I have a complex love/hate relationship with marijuana that goes back a bunch of years, and I always end up with singed wings if I get too close to the flames and don't treat the plant with the respect it deserves. But the flipside of my pot smoking was that I was writing some of the best stories of my life, working on the structure of my dream book, the book that's been burning inside of me for years and is now screaming to get out. Smoking weed opens up these parts of my brain I only know how to access when I'm stoned—whole other sets of memories and perspectives. It's become a pretty essential part of my creative process in recent years. And I come to feel so comfortable in it; it becomes hard to cope without it once I'm in the rhythm. But it's like I'm a whole different person who's not as reliable or trustable but has crazy superpowers. It's like bottled mania for me—so tempting when it's around. So for months I was spending a lot of time stoned and spacey but really tapped into what for me is an important frequency—the *hallucination station*, the out-there brilliant edge space—spending hours every day in a trance-like state, time traveling with my eyes closed and transcribing everything I found swimming around my head into little scribbled parables and clues that connected together into my own psych meta-map of consciousness. But that shit can only last so long and I was coming unraveled and knew it more than anyone.

That night Sky sat me down and taught me a grounding exercise— envisioning a cord from my body down into the center of the earth. Simple breath work and guided visualization. We talked quietly in a room full of books, shrines, sage, stones, feathers, and photographs of her family and teachers. Then she made me an offer that shook me out of my foggy headspace—she said she could teach me to do the things I was doing with weed without smoking. And with real control.

"First you need to be grounded or I'm not going to teach you anything about really flying." She offered that I become one of her students. She would teach me what she knew about being a shaman, so I could teach others and pass on the knowledge. In exchange I'd work with her, build her a garden, and help her create a spiritual community center in Red Hook. That was a turning point.

So I went off and finished my winter travels and when I returned a few weeks later and we started working together. She gives me meditation exercises. I study the work of her teacher, Alberto Villoldo, on my own, and for the first time in my life I'm immersed in a spiritual practice. And it feels incredible and I'm so grateful for it. I'm also still really skeptical of New Age wooiness, and sometimes it feels like I'm teetering dangerously on the edge of it, but I'm opening myself up to possibilities I never allowed myself to imagine. I'm learning a whole new vocabulary and spiritual anatomy and powers of walking through different dimensions. I actually sit with myself now and meditate and I'm just scratching the surface of realizing the incredible power of focusing my mind and going internal. I have no desire to smoke weed these days at all—I'm going to places in my head that are so out there I feel like I have to have all my senses with me. Which is amazing.

These days I meditate and keep my journal next to me to transcribe my dreams. It's amazing what I can do if I just let myself breath and be present with my breath, open up and let myself visualize and talk to the voices that are always there. It's better than any movie on the silver screen. It's like lucid dreaming but I'm in control of when it starts and stops.

Gravel Angels and the Social Freak Brigade: The Icarus Project Comes to Virginia Tech

Meanwhile, back in the Icarus Project story, we were thriving. Despite our subcultural backgrounds and unorthodox messages, we were saying things that many people found compelling. We had new Icarus chapters popping up in cities all the time. At one point we had half a dozen interns from New York University writing papers and working out of our Manhattan office. Our web presence was larger and more vibrant than ever and we were getting media recognition for the work we were doing on a whole new level. The Icarus Project vision had tapped into a larger cultural narrative and we were running with it. I wrote this story somewhere between Madison, Wisconsin and Chicago, Illinois while we were making our way West on a national tour.

It's the year 2007 and I'm traveling with a couple carloads of fellow radical mental health activists to Blacksburg to facilitate a discussion about mental health on the Virginia Tech campus. We were all very excited and nervous. We'd been talking about it for days, unsure of the situation we're walking into. Ever since the massacre on April 16th, when 23-year-old English student Seung-Hui Cho murdered 32 people before killing himself in a display of mass media brutality, this campus has become, among other things, a dramatic symbol of everything that's wrong with college mental health services in the U.S. Of course, what happened at Virginia Tech could have happened at any number of universities, and the odds are likely that it will happen again. There are a lot of alienated and disturbed kids who have fallen through the cracks in a fragmented, traumatized society. There are also a lot of guns.

It feels like we're suddenly in the middle of a war. Or a football game. Or both. It feels like the America that's always viscerally terrified me since I was a young child watching patriotic images on television, the America of jocks and coaches and soldiers, the bullies that make the freaks of the world like me cower in the hallways in fear and shame. Can you tell I got picked on in the playground by how I'm talking? Yeah, that's right, I'm one of those kids that just never fit in, even when I wanted to. And it left marks. In a bully culture there are always going to be the alienated ones like me that don't fit in and get pushed around and end up holding grudges. And we live in a bully culture. These days, America is the bully to the rest of the world and America drop its bombs and pushes its culture and language and draws starker and starker lines between anyone who is on Team America and everyone else who's a 'terrorist'. "Are you with us or are you against us?" And while America's foreign policy just breeds more patriots and more terrorists, the culture of our schools breeds more bullies and more alienated kids.

My friends and I find ourselves asking important questions—in a cultural climate this toxic and demented, what does it mean to be considered "mentally ill?" Can we trust the measurements used to determine "health" and "normality?" Does it help anyone but the drug companies to separate the political and social aspects from supposed "rational science?" And where are the voices that get drowned out by the roar of the conformity crowd?

While the issue of gun rights for the "mentally ill" captured the media's gaze in the days after the Virginia Tech massacre, other important narratives need to be woven into this complex drama. A looming crisis is waiting on college campuses across the country. A generation has been raised on potent psych drugs whose mechanisms and side effects are not understood despite billions in research. These substances treat "mental disorders" such as depression and anxiety and ADD, but are increasingly administered to compensate for a profound failure in our educational system. Meanwhile, a lack of imagination in counseling services is intersecting an increasingly influential corporate sponsorship as public money dries up. The only solutions on the agenda are mandatory mental health screenings, more psych labels and more medication.

My friends and I are doing something totally different than the mainstream. We're part of this international network of folks that are attempting to redefine what 'mental health' actually means in our society and we're out in the world building creative mutual support networks to pose alternatives to the current system. We use language that makes sense to us—dangerous gifts as opposed to disorders, diverse-ability as opposed to disability, cultural evolution as opposed to combating stigma, and we have a website community made up of thousands of people from all over the world that are experimenting with this exciting new language. Most of us have been bullied by the psychiatric system firsthand, and that experience informs our awareness and strategy.

Unlike earlier generations of mental health activists in North America, we acknowledge struggling with serious issues that need serious help. But we shift the focus from the medical model to a community capacity model: We cultivate friendships and prioritize interdependence and cooperation. We have a lot in common with "consciousness raising groups" of the '70s feminist movement in that we get people together and tell stories to raise each others' awareness and inspire us to group action. We are a growing movement. The Mad Gifts Tour has been visiting schools, community centers, bookstores, and living rooms, creating space for dialogue and new visions.

We were invited to Virginia Tech by Dr. Bernice Hausman from the English Department. She's interested in our untraditional message—hoping it might spark needed discussion. We posted this flyer on campus and Facebook:

Come join us as we discuss "mental illness" in contemporary culture, emphasizing ways that people who have been affected by the mental health system are organizing alternative support networks & creating safe spaces for marginalized & misunderstood voices to reclaim their stories & learn to use their mad gifts.

On the flyer is an image of a girl with a pen in her hand, leaning to the side and drawing on her own wings, with the words "Community Dialogue/Safe Space/Celebration of Mad Gifts."

Our gracious host Margaret, who runs the fair trade shop Homebody, and her husband Daniel connect us to the Blacksburg activist community. We meet Bernice in her office, and she gives us a tour of the campus. It's late afternoon and overcast as we walk by the imposing stone buildings. The autumn leaves are falling everywhere. There's a military band playing in the distance, cadets marching around in formation, small packs of students with books under their arms and backpacks, heading off to class or to the library.

Our crew is beautiful. Molly came from Asheville, NC, and, although we've been communicating for months, we're meeting her for the first time. I walk side by side with Neil, a large Asian-American male from NYU Icarus with a Mohawk, strutting around campus wearing a This Is What A Feminist Looks Like t-shirt. Gregory, an NPR reporter with a large microphone in hand, keeps us focused. Pearl is snapping photos. There are stares of passing students. It feels like we're foreign agents of change. The social freak brigade in straightlandia.

We walk by Norris Hall, where the shootings took place. It feels chilling and surreal in its normalcy, like a typical college building, but it has been given power by the weight of recent history. When we reach the memorial to the April 16th victims, it looks strangely bare. White gravel and black stones. Bernice tells us that there are usually flowers all over the memorial but now there's a new sign with a phone number saying that if anyone wants to place anything by the stones they have to be cleared by some corporate office. Madigan is crying. She wants to make a gravel angel on the ground like she made snow angels when she was a kid. It's a beautiful idea but she's scared of getting in trouble with security.

A week before our trip to Blacksburg, we were sitting in Professor Brad Lewis' apartment in the NYU dorm on Broome Street. Madigan told a story about how, when she was in 3rd grade, she would take the school bus every morning with this kid who had big ears that the bullies made fun of and beat up. She organized all the freaks to sit together. They kept the boy with the big ears safe.

We pay our respects to the dead and keep walking. Although we know people from the counseling center will be at our event, we don't realize that a third of the people are counselors. Of the 25 people in attendance, one third are students, one third are from the counseling center, and one third are from the religious community. This is not what we expected and not the usual Icarus crowd.

We have our materials: *Navigating the Space Between Brilliance and Madness: A Reader and Roadmap of Bipolar Worlds*, *Friends Make the Best Medicine: A Guide to Creating Community Mental Health Support*, *The Harm*

Reduction Guide to Coming Off Psychiatric Drugs, as well as posters, postcards, pamphlets, and stickers.

Neil welcomes everyone. We watch Ken Paul Rosenthal's new video, *Crooked Beauty*—10 minutes of Carey and Jacks' voices talking about their experiences with madness as a montage of their art and images from the city and the woods tease out the revolutionary messages. Madigan plays haunting cello behind it. The lights come on and we ask everyone to form their chairs into a circle. Madigan is the facilitator, and she reads our agreements:

The Icarus Project envisions a new culture and language that resonates with our actual experiences of "mental illness" rather than trying to fit our lives into a conventional framework. We see our madness as a dangerous gift to be cultivated and taken care of, rather than as a disease or disorder needing to be "cured" or "overcome." This is a space to come together and learn from each others' views and experiences of madness. People who take psychiatric drugs are welcome here, as are people who don't take psychiatric drugs. People who use diagnosis categories to describe themselves are welcome, as are people who define themselves differently. The Icarus Project values self-determination and mutual support.

We take turns telling stories, each for a couple minutes—our relationships to the psych system, our diagnosis and psych drugs, therapy, our coping strategies, the society around us and the Icarus community, the complexities, and seeming paradoxes. We've been doing this for a long time and we're getting good at it. Neil is the last to talk. He tells the story about working as an intern for the Icarus Project at NYU. There have been half a dozen interns that have worked for Icarus in the last two years, organizing events on campus and having meetings with the administration and the counseling center. He talks about how the administration was terrified of students getting together on campus and talking about their mental health because of legal liability, about the string of suicides, and how the administration went to great lengths to keep public discussion from happening for fear that suicide would spread like some social contagion. He thinks it's important that people talk about the scary things; it's the only way we're going to grow and heal together. And with that, he opens up the discussion. The first person to respond is Maggie, a senior who is part of a group of students that are starting an infoshop in town. She says, "Everywhere you go in this town it says 'We Will Prevail.' I keep wondering *over what?* Ever since April 16th 'We Will Prevail' has been the loudest voice in our community and I keep wondering what's underneath that tired slogan? I think people are scared and confused, and we need more safe spaces to talk to each other."

After that the room opened up. Students started talking about how painful and confusing it was to have the media flocking to Blacksburg after the massacre. Mass media culture makes our lives simultaneously more complicated and hollow. There was no time to heal and process. We talked about resentment toward tourists. Margaret received menacing messages because she refused to hang the maroon and orange colors in her window. The community was living in a culture of fear and disconnection and there was collective relief to have space to talk. A woman from the counseling center said it saddened her to hear how many students felt like they couldn't talk and hadn't had space to heal. Her experience was different because she had been in the thick of it—someone a lot of the police officers felt like they could talk to, and who had participated in large healing events. An older woman who was visibly perturbed spoke up and said that her sister had recently committed suicide. She was upset that we used the term "dangerous gifts" when talking about our struggles. She thought it was irresponsible, that we were romanticizing something that shouldn't be romanticized. She was voicing something that we've heard a lot over the years, and it raises an important question. Will responded that it seems like folks are polarized between thinking that when we say we have "dangerous gifts" that we're saying that people don't need help. But that's not the message at all. We're saying that people aren't getting the help they need. That there are different ways of thinking about ourselves and different kinds of help. We're trying to be reality makers, not reality prisoners.

I talked about the Icarus myth, the boy with wings who doesn't know how to use them and flies too close too the sun, and about my friend Sera who committed suicide, and how if the Icarus Project existed when she was around that I'm sure she wouldn't have killed herself. The woman from the counseling center responded that she thought it seemed like we were talking about celebrating human diversity. "I bet they're helping a whole lot of people." It felt like reality was shifting in the room. Suddenly there was so much more potential. People were speaking their truth and listening to one another. I think everyone left grateful that they had come.

Now it's a couple days later I can't help the feeling that it wasn't enough. There should have been twice as many people. Three times as many. Four times as many. We never even touched the frats and football culture. After April 16th, everyone from the advocates for Forced Treatment to the Scientologists descended on this place, psychically feeding off the spectacle culture of a mass murder and trying to find strategic converts for their manipulative ideologies. Meanwhile, we mostly stayed on the couple blocks of alternative culture at the edge of the University, at Homebody and the vegetarian restaurant, and the back alleys with the spray paint stencils like "Your Medication Scares Me" and "Up the Struggle." They felt like home. But what is it going to take to raise the level of dialogue? What is it going to take to change the culture? What is our role in it as the Icarus Project?

As unlikely as it many seem to the outside world, it seems pretty clear to me that our future depends on listening to the freaks and the weirdos, the ones who don't fit in because they can't fit into this crazy world. And we can't be stopped; the culture is going to have to evolve or just implode. So here we find ourselves at the turn of the century, organizing all the kids who get bullied everywhere, and together we're going to rewrite the rules of the playground and the school bus.

After our workshop, Madigan went to the memorial site and, hidden by the darkness of the night, laid down amidst the stones, waving her arms and legs 33 times, one for every death, including Cho's, leaving the shadow image of a gravel angel on the ground.

The Unraveling

Meanwhile, underneath all the success and excitement of our growing movement, I was unraveling. By the time the winter rolled around, I desperately needed a break from the intensity of my action packed life. The Icarus Project had become such a huge part of my identity and, despite our collective structure, my big personality was taking up more than its share of space. Meanwhile, I was spending so little time at the farm that the other collective members were resenting me while they pulled the extra weight. As it turned out, my exciting stories were great for inspiring and bringing people together, but when I got so wrapped up in all my ideas, I often had a hard time working side by side with others. Some part of me always saw myself as an outsider, even in a group of other outsiders.

I was also grappling with having more social power in my life than I had ever imaged that I would grow up to have. I had always thought of myself as an underdog, fighting from the bottom, and suddenly there were a bunch of people who were treating me as an economically privileged white man who had the social and economic capital to threaten their livelihood and identities. And I didn't know how to handle it.

Meanwhile, all the conversations and internal conflicts in the Icarus Project were public. We had a philosophy, summed up by the classic feminist adage "the personal is political," that we should have nothing to hide. We went to great length to prevent ourselves from abusing our power. We strove for public accountability. All of our collective meeting notes and every last penny of our budget was posted online. We held ourselves personally accountable as representatives of the movement.

But after awhile it felt like every single action I took was in the public arena, like there was no division between my public and private life. Hadn't I asked for this? Didn't I want all of this attention? It was like my delusional teenage fantasies of being broadcast on television for the world to see, but it was actually kind of happening on the internet. It left me feeling lonelier and more self-involved than ever.

After a national tour, we celebrated our 5th anniversary in the Bay Area with a big party, and I was feeling so burnt out that I just wanted to hide in the corner. I went back East to the farm with the intention of spending the winter working on personal writing and trying to make some sense of the last few years. I stepped back from most of my official Icarus Project responsibilities. And amidst it all I made the fateful mistake of continuing to smoke weed while deciding to taper down off my Lithium. I had a story in my head about how it was all supposed to happen, a heroic narrative about coming off my psych drugs and being a role model for others in my community, but it was one of those stories that just didn't correspond with the reality of the situation. It was not the right time to try and come off of my psych drugs. The results were dramatic, to say the least. For a little while I burned spectacularly with the fire of visionary madness. And then it all came crashing down around me.

Mad Pride at Virginia Tech

NOVEMBER 10, 2007, WEEKEND AMERICA

There's black pride and gay pride. And if 32-year old Sascha DuBrul has his way, "mad pride" will become equally ubiquitous. That's mad, as in mentally ill. DuBrul's Icarus Project believes that part of the problem with mental illness is the words we use to describe it. Diagnosed bipolar when he was 18, DuBrul says he could have dealt better with his diagnosis if it had been framed differently, not in clinical terms but as a "dangerous gift." Now Sascha and others are going across the country giving workshops to change the language around mental illness.

"Mad Pride" Fights a Stigma

MAY 11, 2008, THE NEW YORK TIMES

Just as gay-rights activists reclaimed the word queer as a badge of honor rather than a slur, these advocates proudly call themselves mad; they say their conditions do not preclude them from productive lives.

The Icarus Project, a New York-based online forum and support network, says it attracts 5,000 unique visitors a month to its Web site, and it has inspired autonomous local chapters in Portland, Ore., St. Louis and Richmond, Va. Participants write and distribute publications, stage community talks, trade strategies for staying well and often share duties like cooking or shopping.

The Icarus Project says its participants are "navigating the space between brilliance and madness." It began six years ago, after one of its founders, Sascha Altman DuBrul, now 33, wrote about his bipolar disorder in The San Francisco Bay Guardian, a weekly newspaper. Mr. DuBrul, who is known as Sascha Scatter, received an overwhelming response from readers who had experienced similar ordeals, but who felt they had no one to discuss them with.

"We wanted to create a new language that resonated with our actual experiences," Mr. DuBrul said in a telephone interview.

Some Icarus Project members argue that their conditions are

not illnesses, but rather, "dangerous gifts" that require attention, care and vigilance to contain. "I take drugs to control my superpowers," Mr. DuBrul said.

My Faith in the Mad Ones

I've been obsessed with that Martin Luther King quote, *"Human salvation lies in the hands of the creatively maladjusted."* There's something in those words that's like a shining light in the dark to me, reframing the conversation in this brilliant and visionary way. And it was MLK talking in the late 1960s. It's like that permaculture principle "the problem is the solution." It's staring straight at our fears, something about cultural evolution, about wounded healers, something that circumvents the "combating stigma" dialogue in the current "mental health" arena and puts it smack in center stage.

I like the language of the *mad ones*.

As in, I have *faith in the power of the mad ones* because they're the only ones crazy enough to think they can change the world and have the outlandish visions and drive to be able to do it. I've been thinking about what a large coalition of diverse groups uniting in an effective and long term way might look like. I keep reading books about the '60s political movements and they're simultaneously inspiring and miserably depressing because there was *so much* potential. We're trying to recreate that energy 40 years later. It was crushed so hard that most of us don't know our own history.

I don't know about you all, but I want to be a part of a movement that has language to talk about power and class and race and gender without devolving into fragmenting identity politics, a movement that is full of love and actually prioritizes supporting the people in it, a movement that can collectively learn from its mistakes, a movement that knows its history and tells the stories publicly and loudly and beautifully, a movement that prioritizes community health and community support in ways that capture people's imaginations and in ways the state and corporations will never be able to, and a movement that has mad respect for wild dreams and true diversity and the ones who—by their very nature—don't fit into neat boxes and never will under any system.

A movement of the people that respects the freaks and wild ones. I also like the language of *mad ones* because of the double meaning of "mad." It might alienate a mainstream movement, but goddamn there's a lot to be mad about and we better be talking about it with our love and rage. When it comes down to it, we can debate whether there are genetic components to what is now considered "mental illness" but fundamentally our message is that society is driving us mad. Oppression makes people crazy. Maybe some are more predisposed but "mad ones" cuts across race/class/gender lines in a way that has potential to unite different groups.

I have been having this amazing conversation with folks from the Hip-Hop Mental Health Project that's just getting started in New York. As someone coming from the mostly white punk rock world its been really interesting to talk to folks who are part of a people of color led cultural movement. Their analysis of power and privilege is so much clearer than that of me and my white friends struggling to figure out where we fit in to the oppressive system. But part of what I'm realizing is that the punk world offers a rich tradition of celebrating madness. Growing up around punks is how I survived getting repeatedly locked up in psych hospitals without believing that there was actually something wrong with me. Which I think is something to be shared. Thus I feel quite comfortable in referring to my people as the "mad ones." It just kind of flows off my tongue at this point.

On the flipside, last week I caught a Craigslist ride from Oakland to Portland with this young white woman and she was talking about her struggles with depression and how she comes from a really economically privileged background and feels so guilty about all the resources she has that most people never will. *Her class privilege is what has kept her feeling like she has a biological illness* because how could she be depressed if she's so economically fortunate? It was quite a conversation driving up I-5. Because I could relate to her a lot. For years so much of my own shame has had to do with my class privilege and feeling like my problems aren't as serious as everybody else's. It must be brain chemistry, right? But what if we flipped the whole thing around and started talking about the ways that economic privilege makes people sick in the head? That in fact it's the class system itself that makes people sick. Suddenly "mad ones" starts cutting across all kinds of lines. You can be a poor kid or a middle class kid or a rich kid and still be a mad one. Which is really interesting to me as far as movement-building is concerned.

If we're really going to be breaking down stigma we need a term that is going to bring together everyone from the middle-age homeless black man diagnosed with schizophrenic to the rich white girl who's cutting herself because she can't feel anything in her sheltered suburban life. And everyone in between. There are a lot of us out here. And clearly we need to be reframing the conversation to talk about community mental health—not individual mental illness. Somewhere in this vision are beautiful mad maps of many shapes and colors and styles, the excuses for us to talk in groups about the hard stuff, about how we can support one another individually and collectively amidst it all. Somewhere in there is an understanding that some people are really sensitive and good at crossing boundaries and we need spaces to cultivate those skills. Somewhere in there are collectively developed skills and spaces that feel safe to talk about power and privilege and shame that can build the bridges and networks that will hold together a growing movement. Maybe "mad" isn't a term that everyone is going to relate to. But I think it's worth adding to the mix.

One more thing, these days I think a lot about whiteness—about how so much of what's considered "normal" in our culture has to do with European standards of normality which are so invisible when we're raised to be "color blind" and brought up with the ridiculous idea that everyone has "equal opportunity." What if we talked about how "whiteness" is actually this incredible sickness that only exists because all these other cultural roots have been severed and histories drowned in the historical melting pot. It's a sickness that's a bi-product of a sick system. And meanwhile there are so many people out there desperate for connection and community and roots. So many people so desperate for something to belong to and to believe in. What if we started talking about how whiteness and monoculture are the actual diseases. And that the solutions all have to do with respecting diversity and wildness. You may think I'm crazy, but I'm not the only one.

The Edges and In Between Spaces

I've always found the good stuff at the edges and in between spaces, the bleed in time between late night and early morning when the mind runs fast and free and isn't afraid to make connections that might normally seem a little strange; the edge of urban neighborhoods where people from different parts of the world cross paths with each other; the edge between different ecologies like the land and the water, the forest and the grassland, the estuary and the ocean—places where different species learn how to live with each other and create whole new ways of interacting; spaces where strangers meet like bus stops and 24-hour diners and underground parties on the edge of town.

The edge can be a dangerous place to be—there's always the possibility of falling off. I know from my own experience that the part of my mind that is the most creative and fluid can definitely be the most volatile and scary. If I'm respectful and use that part of myself in moderation I can do amazing things. So much of my power is in my dreams, in letting go and not being controlled by the rigid society that raised me—in not being afraid to have grandiose visions and plans. But if I ignore the warnings and let myself fly too high, if I go to that place in my mind for too long—it's hard to come back down. I'm caught on fire. I forget how to sleep. I forget how to take care of my body. The bridge between the conscious rational world which keeps me together and the unconscious irrational world which keeps things interesting opens up and I start losing sight of which is which. The edges all blur—I start dreaming while I'm awake.

•   •   •

First I stopped being able to have conversations with my housemates. They started to get frustrated with me, and then just ignored me. When my closer friends tried to show me the map I had written, all the ways I had left a trail for myself with messages about how to take care in the event I started to get manic, I ignored them. I was seeing signs everywhere and no one else around me could see them. I was convinced I must be different, that I didn't need to tend to my physical body anymore because the material realm was an illusion.

I would walk in the woods and have long conversations with my dead friends and family and it felt like they were right beside me. I felt like I was becoming a ghost, like I was living between realms, and it was scary, but it was exciting to feel the power of immortality! I felt like I had an enormous amount of energy running through me that was coming from the heavens. Some part of me was so desperately trying to hold on to consensus reality but it was like I was a cracked container and the world was pouring through me. I stopped sleeping and my past began erupting into my present everywhere I went. I would see patterns in the clouds, I would speak in riddles, I would hear voices no one else could hear. I slowly pushed everyone away in favor of my lonely brilliant world.

When You're Burning

You connect the dots when you stop sleeping. The spaces between are more porous and full of potential. The souls of the gods whisper like fireflies in your ears. Let me remind you:

When you're burning you can feel people who aren't alive anymore—you can feel them breathing down your neck. You are a conduit between universes. Everything talks to you in its own secret language and you listen with understanding beyond your years.

The silver screen transmits directly to you, the radio is fine-tuned to your stellar frequency. The books in the library close in on you in their intensity. All of those old souls want a piece of your eyes.

When you're burning you can feel Death beside you and you live with the pain that you're going to die before you do a fraction of the things you want to accomplish. You cry in anguish at a cruel trick of mortality—all you've seen and felt will somehow, eventually be gone forever, the memories and experiences lost in time, like tears in rain.

Sometimes people are stronger when they're gone. Sometimes people have that power when they're still alive—they haunt the line between life and death. Their faces on the TV, radio, and the magazines. When you're burning you can reach out and touch them. You talk to them and they talk back. You have a direct line to the heavens.

Then when you're lost in the ocean of your nightmares, your fragile wings charred and torn to pieces—you watch your dreams crumble before your eyes while you lie there, unable to change your miserable fate. You're a fallen angel but now you're just pushing a shopping cart down Market Street, talking to yourself. You're in the Quiet Room in the psych ward on suicide watch, doped up on Haldol to keep from clawing at your skin.

"I have stood here before beneath the pouring rain with the words running circles running round my brain I guess I'm always hoping that you'll end this reign but it's my destiny to be the king of pain..."

That's me! Yo that's me! He's talking about me! I'm the one! I'm the one! It's me!

You are the beginning and the end. The Alpha and the Omega. The words connect back around to somewhere you've been before. You are the connecting link to the entire universe. The answer was there all along, you just needed to squint your eyes right to see it staring you in the face. Somehow you've always known this but it's suddenly like your eyes are clear. Other people crowd around you—you are the new King. You will live forever. You are immortal. The world is flipped completely upside down

• • •

BELLEVUE HOSPITAL CHART
CHART REVIEW PRINT
PATIENT NAME: DuBRUL, SASCHA
PATIENT NUMBER: 1351568
AGE: 33Y SEX: M
HISTORY OF PRESET ILLNESS

PT. IS A 33 Y.O. SINGLE WM DOMICILED WITH 7 FRIENDS WITH WHOM HE IS IN A RELATIONSHIP RESIDING ON A COLLECTIVE FARM IN GERMANTOWN NY, W/ H/O BIPOLAR D/O TYPE I W/PSYCHOTIC FEATURES ON LITHIUM 600MG QHS AND WELLBUTRIN 150MG REQUIRING 3 PRIOR HOSPITALIZATIONS (THE LAST OF WHICH WAS IN 2001), BIB EMS AS EPD ON FRIDAY 7/25 AFTER BEING FOUND ON A ROOF OF A BUILDING ON 34TH STREET, DISHEVELED AND WITHOUT SHIRT OR SHOES, SMASHING A SATELLITE DISH BECAUSE HE THOUGHT IT WAS BROADCASTING ALIEN SIGNALS. PT WAS BROUGHT INTO CREP AND WAS INITIALLY CALM BUT ULTIMATELY BECAME AGITATED, THROWING MEDICAL SUPPLIES, GARBAGE CANS, AND TRAYS OF EMPTY URINE CONTAINERS, AND SMASHED A MIRROR, THUS REQUIRING IM (ADIVAN 2, HALDOL 5). THE MOTHER STATES THAT THE POLICE CALLED HIM AND DESCRIBED HIM AS SHOELESS AND SHIRTLESS AND EXHIBITING ODD BEHAVIOR, CLAIMING HE WAS TRYING TO BEAM SIGNALS THROUGH THE SATELLITE DISH.

"I WENT UP ON A ROOF AND SMASHED THE ANTENNA BECAUSE IT WAS BROADCASTING ALIEN SIGNAL SO I STARTED BROADCASTING MY OWN SIGNALS."

MOTHER STATES THAT THE PATIENT HAD GIVEN HIS ROOMMATES A LIST OF SYMPTOMS TO BE WARY OF AND ASK IF THEY CONFRONT THE PATIENT IF HE STARTED TO EXHIBIT THESE SYMPTOMS. PT'S MOTHER HAD BEEN RECEIVING EMAILS AND CALLS FROM PT'S FRIENDS IN GERMANTOWN NY, STATING THAT HIS BEHAVIOR HAD BECOME INCREASINGLY BIZARRE AND HE HAD BEGIN TALKING ABOUT FEELING "SPIRITS." MOTHER NOTES THAT DURING MANIC EPISODES HE SOMETIMES EXHIBITS POWER AND RAGE CHARACTERISTIC OF HIS DECEASED FATHER. EARLY FRIDAY NIGHT, 7/27, PATIENT'S ROOMMATES HAD AN INTERVENTION WITH HIM AND INSISTED HE INCREASE HIS MEDICATION DOSES. PT ELOPED ON FRIDAY NIGHT AND HE WAS FOUND ON SATURDAY IN NYC ON THE ROOF OF THE BUILDING ON 34TH ST AND BROUGHT IN BY EMS AS NOTED ABOVE.

Bipolar Cartography

SPIRAL BOUND

It feels like I've been here before in some other time. It's midnight in a small, dark kitchen in Flatbush, Brooklyn—the rain coming down outside is a relief somehow, my wet biking clothes dripping from the shower rod in the next room. There's an urban coziness to my life these days. It reminds me of childhood after years in the country. My past is wrapped up in these streets here and the lives of the people that walk them. I live and breathe this place of dreams and shadow visions. I am a little mouse listening to the thunder and rain.

My present is slow and depressive. I take 900mg of Lithium Carbonate and 200mg of Seroquil every night and it feels simultaneously like I'm giving myself a mental disability and allowing myself the luxury of sleep after months of manic flightiness up in the stars. The fire inside is cooled and my mind is rebuilding after a psychotic breakdown. I am intentionally chemically grounded. I'll taper off the Seroquil over the next few months. I'm using it in a way it was meant to be taken. I wrote this part of the map the last time round.

When people ask what I'm doing these days, I say I'm reevaluating my entire conception of what it means to be a healthy, productive person in the world. I paid lots of lip and pen service to change before this breakdown but now I have to do it. There's no other choice—everything has crumbled or I've let it go. Most people sit in quiet desperation with their pain and madness; mine seems to spill out all over the place and I have no choice but to deal with it head on.

We all learn coping mechanisms when we were children that eventually stop being effective and appropriate and inevitably get in the way of our personal growth and development. This has been my solid coping mechanism my whole adult life—when things get hard I turn myself into a character in a story for other people to feel.

I step outside of the action and write stories about it—make lessons out of the hardships. When good friends die, I immortalize them. It becomes my self-proclaimed role in the community. I grieve into the words, and when the story is done, a part of me can let go and give to others through my vision. But in that action I'm always asking people to hold little pieces of my soul. What is my responsibility to those people who feel connected to me and my visions?

This is one way of telling how the Icarus Project came to life—it grew out of a story I wrote to heal myself. I was lonely and wanted more mad friends. I was trying to make sense of my crazy life, and I've continued writing that story for the last six years. The story has thousands of people writing it together now. I get to watch. But I have an internal universe that's wrapped up in my own story and the way I tell it. I read my stories over and over to make sense of what's happened to me and how the world will remember us. I weave our collective history into the larger story, especially when I'm having a hard time. My story and the way I tell it ends up taking up a lot of space around me. It's my faithful coping mechanism for feeling like life has meaning. It's my protective shell. It has allowed me to slip into the mythic realm. o you know this mythic realm of which I write? It's full of archetypes and angels, shadows and forms and signs outside the material realm. We create it together somehow or we're a part of it and it's creating us, but the mythic realm is woven into the fabric of this community. It's easy to get lost in the mythic realm if you're a mad one. They say the shaman swims in the waters that the schizophrenic drowns in. But for me the mythic waters have been a great source of refuge in recent years. They've allowed me to dance with the ghosts of history—to feel my place in the cosmos, the connection with the greater spirit. But if I screw up, I can end up in a total spiritual emergency, my ego gets all fucked up and cartoonishly enormous. I stop being able to tell what's me and what's everyone else. I start thinking I'm the entire universe—the center of everything. It's so beautiful and glorious until it turns really ugly.

I get obnoxious and loud and I stop listening to the people I love who are so worried about me. I check out of consensus reality and start living in the dreamtime—except it's really MY dreamtime. I become a raving narcissist that no one wants to deal with, all my subconscious hopes and fears pour out for the world to see. Eventually I pull some totally dramatic, attention-seeking chaos move and end up in the hospital, strapped to a bed and forcefully medicated.

I really, really, need a new story.

Being in a public leadership position has been full of lessons and challenges. I get so much personal criticism that I don't know how to deal with it—criticism that seeps in when I'm slowed down enough to be present. In the spring of 2008, I started getting numerous criticisms from people whose opinions I valued. A group of women got together to talk about the gender dynamics in the Icarus Project and I ended up with angry fingers pointing at me. I got criticism about my lack of personal and professional boundaries. I got criticism about how my past intimate relationships with women had undermined the power dynamics in the organization. I was told by people I loved that my actions made them feel like "glorified secretaries." I got criticism of my inability to be present with the people closest to me—that a part of me was cold, cruel, and hurtful in a typically male way.

I dealt with the criticism in my old faithful way, to step back and write about what was happening—to be a mythic character in a story in my mind. But I was being criticized for taking up too much space with my story—for eclipsing other's stories. Amidst it all I short-circuited. Instead of being present with the criticisms—sitting with the pain of it and growing in new ways, I kept unconsciously trying to make myself the center of an adventure story—a crucified martyr in a way that wasn't appropriate at all.

The coping mechanism finally hit a big wall and cracked, it was called out and asked to change. Suddenly I got glimmers that I'd been using the excuse of *building a radical mental health support network* as a way to not get too close to anyone in my life. I was doing the classic activist thing—putting the Cause before the personal relationships, and it all unraveled.

So now it's suddenly Fall and I don't live on a farm in the valley anymore. I'm back home where I have to face my demons. The rain outside feels good, cleansing. I'm not sure what I'm supposed to be doing with my life but that's okay for now. When I was in the hospital all these friends just wanted me back on the ground, wanted me to be with them, and I couldn't do it. I was so far away. Now here I am, back in the material realm, sleeping hard and dreaming every night, waking up slow and trying to be gentle with myself. Trying to give myself space to grow.

Whenever I'm about to finish a little piece of writing like this it always feels like I'm leaving myself a strand of golden thread in the labyrinth, something to make sense of later, when I'm looking down from another part of this crazy spiral of my life.

Mad Adventures and the Imagined Communities of Icarus

In Benedict Anderson's history of nationalism, he lays out the following definition of a nation:

> "It is an imagined political community—and imagined as both inherently limited and sovereign. It is imagined because the members of even the smallest nation will never know most of their fellow-members, meet them, or even hear of them, yet in the minds of each lives the image of their communion…It is imagined as sovereign because the concept was born in an age in which Enlightenment and Revolution were destroying the legitimacy of the divinely-ordained, hierarchical dynastic realm…."

I find this whole idea—and the layers that build up to it—incredibly interesting and applicable to questions I have about community, history, and collective identity.

A month before my life dramatically fell apart, I was giving a lecture to a room full of psychiatrists at Bellevue Hospital on the Icarus philosophy. A month later the police picked me up stark raving mad, wandering the streets of midtown Manhattan in my underwear, ending up right back at the same psychiatric hospital for treatment.

When I got out of the hospital a week later, humbled and confused, I had no idea what to do with myself. The people in my collective house were scared of me moving back in, my organization was telling me I needed to step back to let it grow and evolve without me, and I had pissed off and alienated a bunch of people in the months building up to my grandiose explosion. I had to figure out the basics of taking care of myself and it wasn't going to happen in New York City. Upon the suggestion of my good friend, and with nothing in my way, I did something that would have been unthinkable a few months earlier, I moved to a yoga ashram in the Bahamas, where I lived on the beach in a tent. I woke up at 5am every morning to meditate and chant in Sanskrit, do two hours of yoga asanas, eat breakfast, work all day in the kitchen or garden, meditate and chant more, go to sleep, and do it again the next day.

I lived in the ashram for a year before I was ready to go back into the world. The people lived on a small island and followed some form of ancient Hindu traditions passed down through an Indian guru in the 1950s who had sent his young disciples to the west to spread the knowledge of yogic scriptures and practice. Somehow that turned into white folks walking around in orange and yellow robes, keeping a monastic schedule. Because of my semi-broken state, I welcomed the discipline. It was a relief to have people tell me what to do. I had never been in a place where people talked about God all day.

Despite a lot of strangeness, the strangest part—hands down—was that the ashram was filled with Israelis who had done their military service, gone to India and discovered that the disciplined world of yoga was a peaceful alternative to their lives filled with war. I had never spent time around Israelis. They fascinated and horrified me. There was something familiar about them— they were loud and opinionated, felt the world was out to get them, and spoke a language seemingly the same as the one I had chanted for my bar mitzvah in temple as a child in New York City.

I was raised a secular Jew in a place with a lot of Jews, so many that I took aspects of our culture for granted. Like many Jews in my neighborhood, our culture was more about progressive leftist politics than religion, and I never spent enough time thinking about history to understand the dynamics and intricacies of how they became so entangled and estranged. Like people from many backgrounds, I was raised in a whitewash of American culture—McDonalds, Coca-Cola, and MTV were my culture more than the Old Country. I never even thought about the fact that my descendants came from an Old Country on the other side of the world. As a child I learned to chant Hebrew the same way we were chanting Sanskrit in the ashram temple—transliterated with English letters with no context of the deeper meanings.

So when I wanted to understand the culture of the Israelis, I came up against an uncomfortable realization that I didn't know any world history. As soon as I looked into the history of Israel, I had to study World War II, and then World War I, and it became clear that the *whole idea* of nation state as we know it wasn't more than 200 years old. To understand the context I had to study the European Enlightenment, the French Revolution, the Protestant Reformation, and then make my way back to Ancient Greece, Rome, and the Hebrew Bible. As interesting as all the talk about God was at the ashram, it left me wanting to go back to school and be around people using their critical thinking skills to put the talk of God in some kind of context.

So when I got out of the ashram I went to college and spent some time—sponge-like—catching up on my history. Actually, much of that history I learned from podcasts and audio books from the library. While working as a gardener I listened to them and grew this burning desire to travel overseas and see for myself some of these places I was learning about.

Since I was 14 years old I'd been keeping the company of people who called themselves anarchists. My political education happened amidst burning police barricades and smashed windows in the riots in Tompkins Square Park in 1989, and the social and political movements that revolved around those historical events. It was the same year that the Berlin Wall fell and the geopolitical structure of the world began to be rearranged without the force of Communism.

For my friends and I, anarchism was a philosophy channeled through punk records and semi-mystical veiled history about places in Spain and Russia and Haymarket Chicago. For years, anarchism and punk was my *imagined community*—people who saw themselves connected to each other through a larger purpose. But it was also a *real community* engaged in struggles across the world, not bound by allegiance to nation or state or political party, tied by threads of community and resistance to global capitalism and oppression.

For however dysfunctional my community was, it was an actual community of real people who were alienated by the dominant culture, and saw themselves as building a new world outside of it. It helped to give my life meaning.

While reading Anderson's account of the rise of what he calls "print-capitalism" and the printing press, I was struck by the potential power of a bunch of people reading about themselves. How national identity was formed hand in hand with the invention of the daily newspaper. Then I think about our Icarus website, and the people who feel allegiance to the Icarus Project, and feel part of something larger than themselves. I think about social networking sites in our lives like how Facebook and Twitter and blogging sites play a role in our emerging collective consciousness.

I see how wonderful it is to have a crew of folks that have your back, I also see the pitfalls of defining oneself in relation to others, and especially in contrast to others. Having enemies is a great way to build solidarity, but without loving practices of acceptance of one another, the polarization always has the possibility of turning sour. In the world of the ashram, one thing that fascinated me about the Israelis, and was uncomfortably familiar, was that they saw themselves as separate and different. It eerily reminded me of my friends, the punks and anarchists. When my friend, Tristan Anderson, got shot in the head by an Israeli soldier while protesting in the Occupied Territories, I was in the Bahamas wearing white and chanting in Sanskrit in a temple full of ex-IDF soldiers. It was a mind-fuck and it was part of why I got passionate about understanding Jewish history.

So it's all tied together for me—the radical mental health work, the revolutionary movements of the 18th and 19th centuries, anarchism, understanding the rise of the nation state, and collective identity formation. With these pieces I'm learning useful lessons for effective community and movement building. And amidst that, I'm enjoying the fuck out of reveling in the riddles of history and existence, making a place for it with my friends and loved ones.

Ashram Dreams

The ashram was dreamlike. I wore a white uniform everyday. I left all but a few possessions in New York. The first couple months I was depressed and hardly talked to others. Everything out of my mouth seemed like wasted breath, tired old stories that needed to die. No one knew me or had any context about my life back home. I was plagued with self-defeating thoughts, comparing myself to everyone else around me in the most childish ways. The daily routine was comforting and I understood what was asked of me and could complete the tasks. I worked out in the garden laying irrigation or chopping vegetables in the kitchen, moving furniture and carrying luggage for guests. I chanted in satsung (temple services) and slowly learned how to meditate. I listened to the daily talks. I went to sleep every night in a tent to the sound of the ocean lapping against the shore. I was open to new ideas because my sense of self was so shaky. And new ideas were plenty. I wanted to find inner peace—what the ashram specialized in. The inner peace came—along with waves of unresolved questions from my last break with reality. I was trying to make sense of my mad visions, and the ashram had answers. I let their stories become part of my reality, but it wasn't clear if those stories were helping me or making me crazier. Eventually I had to leave the ashram to make sense of it all, to decide which pieces I wanted to hold and which pieces to let go. But the experience taught me valuable lessons that forever changed the nature of my spiritual map.

•　　　•　　　•

Etymology of the word *Attention*: to tend to; to watch over; to care for.

At first, sitting down to meditate for 30 minutes was excruciating. My head was so filled with noise—critical voices, self-defeating thoughts, old punk songs about nuclear war, psychic noise from the depths of my consciousness. Trying to be present with myself just made me feel crazier. The instructions they gave us were simple, "The best way to keep the mind in the present moment is to focus on the breath. Attempt to stay with the sensations of each breath by counting each inhalation and exhalation. Try and make it to 10 and then start from the beginning. Bring your awareness to your heart chakra at the center of your chest. Keep bringing it back. When you realize you've gotten distracted, bring the awareness back to your breath and your heart."

I felt trapped in the room and wanted to run out.

Eventually, I had brief moments of clarity, like a veil lifting. I began to witness my thoughts and emotions as they were arising, and rather than identifying with them, getting caught in them, I could see them disappear, like clouds. It was as if I was watching as a witness, and I felt wonderfully calm and focused. Then, periodically one of the swamis, or a guest speaker, would say something that would hit me powerfully, and I would take the feeling into my meditation practice. I would have a sense of all of us as being sparks of the eternal flame, or drops in the divine ocean, or have a tangible feeling that the secret to peace was hidden inside the human heart. I had one yoga instructor, a hilarious man, who would get us to breathe deeply into these deep, hard to hold yoga poses, and then tell us to find the joy in our physical sensations. He would tell us that joy was a key ingredient of being present, and that if we could follow our joy, it could unlock the gates of our consciousness. Something about that teaching really worked for me. I could feel it tangibly, in my body. That advice took my yoga and meditation practice to a whole other level. A few months later I was teaching the yoga classes every day and using my newfound connection to joy and presence to raise the awareness of the room.

One day after teaching a class I went for a walk on the beach and had a realization that had been building for months. I was thinking about my life back home, my friends, and the community of the Icarus Project, and I concluded I was done with the language of "Mad Pride." Neither "madness" nor "pride" were things I was interested in cultivating. I wanted to be a part of a mental health movement that could help raise the level of consciousness of the world and bring people together, not just fight on the ground with the same old identity games. "Madness," by definition, was about not being in control. Spiritual discipline was working a lot better for me, and I had a hunch that the same would be true for many of the folks who were drawn to the Icarus Project. I longed to figure out how to bring the spiritual connection of the ashram together with the politics of my community back home.

Serendipitously, a few days later this young woman showed up at the ashram reading a book called *Esalen: America and the Religion of No Religion.* It was a detailed history of a place in California that called itself a "Human Growth Center" and in the '60s and '70s lay at the fruitful intersection of recently imported Eastern spiritual practices and Western psychotherapy. I would sneak off from my staff responsibilities to devour as much of the book as I could. It described an amazing cast of characters, from Aldous Huxley to Joseph Campbell to Abraham Maslow to Alan Watts to Fritz Perls—people who influenced the "Human Potential Movement." I liked the sounds of that much more than a "Mad Pride Movement." I learned about these pieces that weren't part of my Icarus Project radical mental health education—Encounter Groups, Humanistic and Transpersonal Psychology, Gestalt Therapy, and the Spiritual Emergency Network of the 1980s. There were people who had already been thinking about the relationship between mental health and spiritual practice and group work. And I wanted to find them.

•　　　•　　　•

We Are Cursed to Live in Interesting Times

By the time I got out of the yoga ashram, Facebook had exploded everywhere. It seemed like everyone I knew was suddenly on the internet all the time. I had been using the Icarus forums for years to communicate with people all over the world, but this was a whole different kind of communication. As the technology quickly got so slick with live-stream videos, the comment/"like" system, and constant access to long lost friends and photos of their kids, it changed the whole way me and so many of people were relating to each other. It was like the future had finally caught up with us and was integrating us all into a new level of cyber reality. It reminded me of my teenage visions of the world ending while we all lived on on television. But I loved it. By late spring I just kept Facebook open on my laptop all the time and would scan the updates to see what friends were doing around the world. I would often find myself thinking about clever things to post about my life instead of actually *living* my life.

And then it got even weirder; I'd be hanging out with real people, and I would secretly be itching to get home because it was strangely *more stimulating* to sit in front of the computer with access to so much information pouring into my eyes. There was something incredible about it. I felt connected to the entire world in whole new ways that I never could have imagined possible. But my eyes hurt, and my neck was stiff, and my ashram-honed attention span was rapidly diminishing. More importantly, I was just acting really strange. My addiction to social networking was clearly becoming anti-social.

Ironically, at this same time, I was going back to Prescott College and studying all kinds of exciting ideas about human interaction and communication. By an unexpected twist of fate, my friend Dr. Brad Lewis, who I had worked with for years in New York City on campus organizing around mental health issues, invited me to co-teach a month-long seminar at the Esalen Institute itself. In many ways it was a dream come true. We developed a curriculum about the history of the Human Potential Movement and lessons that might be drawn from the 60s and 70s for future movements attempting to evolve the culture. So I took a break from Facebook for a while.

In the meantime I did a lot of reading and stumbled upon the teachings of the Existentialists, including Martin Buber, who wrote an essay entitled *I and Thou* where he says famously that "modern developments have expunged almost every trace of a life in which human beings confront each other and have meaningful relationships."

A key Existentialist idea is that inauthentic living leads to emptiness and guilt. Martin Buber had this idea that a person has meaning only in relation to another person, either in a genuine encounter (an I/Thou relationship) or in a manipulative transaction (an I/it relationship.) I was determined to get closer to this idea of authenticity in social relationships, and learn practices to bring groups of people closer to the experience of genuine encounters. It felt particularly critical in these times when so many of us were unwittingly finding ourselves spending hours every day alone in front of computer screens, communicating with one another on cold computer screens.

Here are some of the paths I walked to make sense of these ideas of authenticity and human connection and spirit:

Gestalt Awareness Practice

I learned so much the month I taught at Esalen. I talked to as many old timers as I could find. I read a lot of books, watched a lot of videos, did a lot of meditating by the ocean. I came to understand that much of the Human Potential Movement that had so excited me on paper had ended up in reality being channeled into a watered-down and capitalist-friendly New Age Movement that forgot any kind of grounding it might have had once in social justice. The most practical knowledge and wisdom I came across was studying with Christine Price. Chris had been married to Richard Price, a founder of Esalen who died unexpectedly in the 1980s. His vision for Esalen was informed by being locked up in psych hospitals and given shock treatments in the 1960s. He was passionate about wanting to create a space where people could heal from the effects of the psychiatric system and use their "madness" to evolve the consciousness of society. He had ties to the Psychiatric Survivors Movement of the 1970s and would regularly bring up members for retreats. Richard and Chris developed a mix of Gestalt Therapy and Buddhist practice that they called Gestalt Awareness Practice.

Gestalt Awareness Practice is, according to Chris Price, not a therapy, but a form of peer education, a "congregational model for exploring." She describes her workshops as "going to the awareness gym." I participated in a weekend-long workshop with 15 people, and here are some of the things I learned to articulate from the words of Chris Price—*Seeing is not the same thing as making up stories of what we see. They are two different steps and it is a skill to learn how to separate them. In our practice we are looking for the noticer inside of us that has playfulness and friendliness and shifting our view from the normal 'I'.*

We split into pairs to practice dyad exercises, then came back to the group to share. We stopped and breathed and were present with one another. We did dream work, acting out pieces of our internal lives. Chris's work incorporated elements from my life at the ashram, but with the aim of building group solidarity and learning how to access parts of ourselves that we normally kept hidden, even from ourselves.

I returned to the Bay Area determined to find other teachers from whom to learn group encounter techniques.

Drama Therapy and the Theology of Encounter

As I got back from Esalen I discovered Drama Therapy through a friend who had been taking classes at a place called the Living Arts Counseling Center. The director, a striking looking, white-bearded man named Armand Volkas, was offering a semester-long weekly "Drama Therapy Training Group for Psychotherapists, Interns, and Facilitators." I incorporated the class into my studies at Prescott College, and through Armand's teaching was introduced to the basics of improvisation, acting techniques, Playback Theatre and creative ritual.

Through my work with Armand I was also introduced to the philosophy of Psychodrama. Jacob Moreno, the brilliant and eccentric founder of Psychodrama and Sociometry, had articulated what he called a "Theology of Encounter" inspired by the European Existentialist philosophers' same critique of modern society as alienating. He developed different techniques to bring people together to teach them to get along. It's a beautiful vision and the concept of a "Theology of Encounter" has become one of my personal touchstones, something I aspire to cultivate in my work.

Our weekly group would gather, check in with playful warm-up exercises, then slowly build up to acting out situations from each other's lives, and taking turns in the different roles. We became each other's witnesses, and learned skills to step into one another's stories and mirror back the important parts. We created a container with our support that allowed the group to build a kind of solidarity and trust that was missing in a lot of my other group interactions.

It occurred to me that many tools of Drama Therapy are useful, cleaned-up tools from the more messy Encounter Movement of the 1960s and 70s that suffered from a lot of boundary issues and creepy guru figures. At its heart, "Encounter," which as an idea disappeared from the popular consciousness by the 1980s—was the act of bringing together groups of people to talk about hard, personal issues. In a poorly facilitated encounter group, boundaries can easily be crossed, causing distrust and personal harm. Issues of oppression—such as race, class, gender—make this work particularly tricky in groups of mixed backgrounds. While there is more emphasis on the ideas of creating "safe space" than there was in the 1970s, that doesn't mean it's easy to create spaces that actually feel safe for everyone involved. I kept searching for more tools and ideas.

Generative Somatics

Finally, I had the opportunity to take an eight month course, Somatics and Trauma, developed by Staci Haines and her organization Generative Somatics.

The course was geared towards teaching social justice activists and politicized healers how to use body-based awareness practices to transform their own trauma and be more effective in their work. The Generative Somatics theories and practices are an amalgam of the martial art Aikido, the somatic based work of people like Wilhelm Reich and Ida Rolf, the meditation practices of Chogyam Trungpa Rinpoche, the Gestalt Therapy practices of Fritz Perls, and a number of other threads in the healing arts, language coaching, and contemporary neurobiological research. They speak of their practice as a living lineage.

Generative Somatics takes a trauma-informed analysis of why people struggle in the world and looks at trauma as not only the things covered in the DSM, like being an ex-soldier or a rape survivor, but also social oppression like racism, classism, ableism, and gender oppression. Somatics is not a pathologizing model, it does not focus on what is broken in people. It looks at how the coping mechanisms we've evolved are smart, adaptive responses to the world we've lived in. To transform we need to honor the experiences we've had and the strategies we've come up with to get through the hard times.

In class we would split up into pairs and/or small groups to practice exercises that increase awareness and build skills like how to consciously consent, how to say no, and how to be in allyship with another. We were taught to use an Aikido weapon called a jo in a sequence of movements that help us practice centered power. All of these experiences helped me learn to be more in my body and be in a different kind of relationship to people.

A key lesson I learned with the Somatics crew was the importance of developing *intentional* practices in order to transform the way I show up in the world. We are always practicing something—in our political work and in our personal lives. We become what we practice. What we practice becomes embodied and we act out of it automatically. To make sustainable shifts in our behavior and ways of thinking, we have to "embody" new behaviors.

The path to achieving that embodiment is established through recurrent practices of mind, emotions, language, and body. This embodiment is integrated by building new interpretations of meaning and future possibilities. Embodiment allows for new action. We were asked to come up with specific commitments—personal and movement commitments—that we could articulate in basic phrases and work towards. The questions we were asked were:

"What matters to me?"

"What do I care about?"

"What am I committed to?"

The personal commitment I developed was: *I am a commitment to embodying love and trust for myself so it reflects on the other people around me.*

The movement commitment I developed was: *I am a commitment to laying the foundations for a movement at the intersections of radical mental health, social justice, and spirituality.*

I would wake up every morning, go up on my roof, repeat my commitments aloud and practice with the jo. I found the class really challenging. One of the lessons I kept being taught over and over again during the S&T sessions came in the form of instructors correcting my posture. When we would break up into pairs I would often lean forward towards others and forget that I have a back. There's something about losing myself in another person that feels safe to me. And there's something about always leaning towards others that can be perceived as aggressive and doesn't always build safety and trust. Having folks mirror my body language back to me gave me a profound opportunity to understand how I was impacting others in a way that I had never realized. It also gave me the opportunity to begin practicing something different.

All of these philosophies and practices made their way into my head and heart, and continue to inspire and propel me into some future that is as yet unwritten. But somatics doesn't address psychiatry, and I was still figuring out how to sharpen my analysis of the ways that capitalism and psychiatry have distorted the human experience.

Unraveling the Bio-psychiatric Knot: the Future History of the Radical Mental Health Movement

All of these philosophies and practices made their way into my head and heart, and continue to inspire and propel me into some future that is as yet unwritten. But gestalt and drama therapy and somatics don't address psychiatry, and I was still figuring out how to sharpen my analysis of the ways that capitalism and psychiatry have distorted the human experience. This was a paper I wrote for school which which helped me articulate how we have arrived at a time in history where drug companies play such a powerful role in our understandings of ourselves and our relationships to one another. (or something like that)

"There are few things as powerful as identifying the manufacturer's mark on what we have perceived as our personal demons."
—Aurora Levins Morales

The biomedical model of psychiatry, or "bio-psychiatry," rests on the belief that mental health issues are the result of chemical imbalances in the brain. This is a new idea that quickly became regarded as common sense all over the world. The belief that our dissatisfaction and disease is a result of individual "brain chemistry" has desensitized many from the idea that our feelings and experiences have roots in social and political issues. We find ourselves with medicalized language in our mouths about neurotransmitters and serotonin that doesn't get to the heart of the problems around us. Powerful political and economic forces, which I refer to as neo-liberalism, began in the 1980s, and played a huge role in the paradigm shift in mental health care towards what today is known as bio-psychiatry.

1980 Was the Year

In 1980, the American Psychiatric Association published the third edition of its Diagnostic and Statistical Manual (DSM-III). The DSM, although it was intentionally written in a style that makes it sound scientifically objective, was a creation of one particular school of psychiatrists at a particular point in history with a particular world-view slanted towards the biomedical model.[6] The 1970s were a socially volatile time, the discipline of psychiatry was under attack for both being oppressive and "unscientific." Its makers packaged the DSM as scientific and neutral, reframing the concept of diagnosis from a loose and vague set of descriptions based on Freudian psychoanalysis to a detailed symptom checklist. Today, with the massive support of the pharmaceutical industry, it is accepted as the "Bible" of psychiatry and used as a diagnostic tool all over the world.[7]

In 1980 Ronald Reagan was elected President of the U.S., ushering in the "neo-liberal revolution." The older "liberalism" has roots in the 19th century philosophy that emphasized minimal state intervention and free trade. The horrors of the Depression, the specter of fascism in Europe, and a strong labor movement made the idea of unrestrained free market capitalism less attractive in the 1930s. From the 1930s to the 1970s, a philosophy rose for welfare states in the U.S. and U.K., a philosophy that prioritized social security, public education, and welfare. The 1980s saw the liberalization of trade, business, and industry, massive transfer of wealth from public to private, enormous growth in power of multinational corporations, and the triumph of consumer culture.[8]

One example of biopsychiatry and neo-liberalism uniting to affect our lives was the shifting understanding of "depression." Western cultures and increasingly the rest of the world, are coming to relate human sadness and distress to an individual's brain chemistry without scientific proof that this is the case[9]. The bio-psychiatric world view helps enable big business to maintain power and fuels the needs of the market-based economy.

The Birth of the DSM: How Sadness Became a "Brain Disease"

Modern psychiatry has its roots at the beginning of the industrial revolution and can be seen as a response to the massive reorganization of society along market principles, undermining traditional ways of caring for the sick and older

6   Lewis, Bradley. *Moving Beyond Prozac, DSM, and the New Psychiatry: The Birth of Post-Psychiatry* Ann Arbor: University of Michigan Press, 2006.

7   Watters, Ethan. *Crazy Like Us: The Globalization of the American Psyche*. New York: Free Press, 2010. Print

8   Giroux, Henry A. *Beyond the Bio-politics of Disposability: Rethinking Neo-liberalism in the New Gilded Age, Social Identities* Vol. 14, No. 5 (2008) 587-620

9   Fabrega, Horacio Jr. *On the Postmodern Critique and Reformation of Psychiatry"* Rev. of *Moving Beyond Prozac, DSM, and the New Psychiatry*. Psychiatry 71(2) Summer 2008: 183-196.

support networks.[10] At the end of World War II psychoanalysis dominated the field of mental health, providing leading explanations of mental illness and their treatments.[11] The 1960s were full of social and political upheaval that reshaped ideas of self and what health and wellness looked like.[12] By the 1970s, psychoanalytic theoretical schools and different clinicians had different ideas about the fundamental nature, causes, and treatment of mental disorders. A growing anti-psychiatry movement accused psychiatry of using medical treatment in the interests of social control.[13] There were highly publicized experiments showing the complete lack of reliability of diagnosis made in mental hospitals.[14] Psychiatry's legitimacy was in jeopardy. So the DSM-III was developed.

The DSM-III attempted to create a universal guidebook for psychiatric diagnosis. It was written by a school of psychiatrists who saw their mission to rid psychiatry of prejudice and superstition, by turning it into an "objective science."[15] Their intention was to be scientifically rigorous and "theory neutral," claiming not to presuppose a particular theory or cause of why a patient was mentally ill. The idea was to define disorders on the basis of symptoms and not causes. "It shifted psychiatric diagnosis from vaguely defined and loosely based psychoanalytic descriptions to detailed symptom checklists—each with precise inclusion and exclusion criteria."[16] But in its attempt to be scientifically neutral, the DSM-III left no room for any ideas of mental distress that were not viewed as "illness" and "disease." Furthermore, the idea of "scientific objectivity" put the power for determining well-being and sanity in the hands of the psychiatrists, using a vocabulary that while sounding "objective," was culturally based in Western scientific practice. The new "objective" diagnostic criteria worked better if there were defined treatments for the "disorders." As it turned out, this was very beneficial for the bottom lines of the pharmaceutical companies, as well as opening the door for a drastic shift in the psychiatric paradigm[17].

In the case of "depression," the DSM diagnostic criteria fails to distinguish adequately between two types of depression, "normal sadness" and "melancholia." These diagnoses share similar symptoms including "sadness, insomnia, social withdrawal, loss of appetite, lack of interest in usual activities."[18] The DSM also fails to distinguish between normal sadness that has an outside

10   Foucault, Michel. *Madness and Civilization* Harper Collins, 1967.

11   "The Engineering of Consent" The Century of the Self By Adam Curtis. BBC 2002 Television.

12   "There is a Policeman Inside All Our Heads: He Must Be Destroyed" The Century of the Self By Adam Curtis. BBC 2002 Television.

13   Horwitz, Allan V. and Wakefield, Jerome C. The Loss of Sadness: How Psychiatry Transformed Normal Sorrow Into Depressive Disorder Oxford University Press, 2007

14   Horwitz, Allan V. and Wakefield, Jerome C. The Loss of Sadness: How Psychiatry Transformed Normal Sorrow Into Depressive Disorder Oxford University Press, 2007

15   Lewis, Bradley. "Madness Studies." *Literature and Medicine* (2010): 152-171.

16   Lewis, Bradley. "Madness Studies." *Literature and Medicine* (2010): 152-171

17   Thomas, Philip and Bracken, Patrick. "Challenging the Globalization of Biomedical Psychiatry." Journal of Public Mental Health. Vol. 4 Issue 3 (2005) 23-32.

18   Horwitz, Allan V. and Wakefield, Jerome C. The Loss of Sadness: How Psychiatry Transformed Normal Sorrow Into Depressive Disorder Oxford University Press, 2007

cause, and a depressive disorder that does not. The unwitting result was a massive pathologization of normal sadness.

The Prozac Revolution

In the 1980s the development of Prozac and the ensuing explosion in popularity of Prozac-like (SSRI) antidepressant drugs dramatically changed the landscape of treatment for depression. Almost one in four people in the U.S. were started on an SSRI between 1988 and 2002[19]. The drugs were marketed and prescribed for depression, but the shifting definition of "depression" left room for many emotional states that once were considered normal to be considered pathological. The diagnosis of Major Depression, which included symptoms such as sadness, lack of energy, or sleeplessness as indicators was well-suited for the massive expansion of the market for antidepressant drugs.

At first, the drugs appeared to have positive benefits. The seeming effectiveness of the drugs was used to "prove" the existence of the "disease" of depression, and blurred the lines between happiness, wellness, and functioning. It became easier and more natural to talk about brain chemicals, rather than social conditions or family issues. The ability to "treat" sadness was a defining feature of the period. Anti-depressants worked their way into the lives of many people. Whether they chose to try it or not, taking an anti-depressant became a potential option to choose.

In 1997 the FDA approved direct-to-consumer drug advertisements, and suddenly television was flooded with "ask your doctor" drug ads.[20] "Prozac was one of the first of the new psycho-pharmaceuticals to sit uncomfortably between a treatment and an enhancement, between a medication and a mental cosmetic," said psychologist Brad Lewis.

The pharmaceutical industry became immensely powerful—not just financially. It became a force in determining how we think about our happiness. The example of depression is important. The influence of the pharmaceutical industry extends deep into patient and family advocacy groups, such as the National Alliance on Mental Illness (NAMI), groups that promote the view that depression is a chemical deficiency that requires the use of their drugs. There are now widespread educational campaigns such as National Depression Awareness Day that offer free screenings for depression in universities and hospitals[21]. The pharmaceutical industry sponsors much of the clinical research on depression. Industry-academic collaborations are becoming an increasing source of funding for universities, academic medical centers, and hospitals. Never before has this "bio-psychiatric" culture, which defines our health and happiness in terms of brain chemistry, been so heavily promoted through

19   Lewis, Bradley. *Moving Beyond Prozac, DSM, and the New Psychiatry: The Birth of Post-Psychiatry* Ann Arbor: University of Michigan Press, 2006.

20   Horwitz, Allan V. and Wakefield, Jerome C. The Loss of Sadness: How Psychiatry Transformed Normal Sorrow Into Depressive Disorder Oxford University Press, 2007

21   Horwitz, Allan V. and Wakefield, Jerome C. The Loss of Sadness: How Psychiatry Transformed Normal Sorrow Into Depressive Disorder Oxford University Press, 2007

the media, become embedded in central institutions, and embraced by policy makers.[22]

Rise of the Neoliberals

Simultaneously, an equally complicated paradigm shift was happening in economics and politics. The 1980s saw mass privatization of public enterprises, the reduction of wages by de-unionizing workers and eliminating workers' rights that had been won over many years of struggle, the elimination of many health and environmental regulations, and the dismantling of social services such as health, education, and welfare.[23] The consequence included massive unemployment, underfunded schools, overcrowded prisons, and shrinkage of our social and economic safety nets. Along with these political and economic changes, has been the transformation of poverty from a social problem to an individual failure.[24]

Similar to the ideology of bio-psychiatry, neo-liberalism uses scientific sounding language that talks about "free trade" and "self-regulation of markets" that sound neutral, but masks an ideology which benefits the powerful and wealthy. The two systems work seamlessly together. The notion of chemical imbalance in our brains plants the seeds of doubt about our own happiness and well-being. A driving force of the market economy is dissatisfaction—the market place would not function without a consumer culture that operates on feelings of inadequacy and lack of personal fulfillment. But what if the society itself—the toxic world-views we inherited—are driving us mad and making us depressed?

"A society that is increasingly socially fragmented and divided, where the gulf between success and failure seems so large, where the only option open to many is highly demanding and low paid work, where the only cheap and simple route to carelessness is through drugs, is likely to make people particularly vulnerable to mental disintegration in its many forms. It has long been known that urban life and social deprivation are associated with high levels of mental disorder. Neoliberal economic policies are likely to further increase their pathogenic effects. By medicalizing these effects, psychiatry helps to obscure their political origin…The social catastrophe produced by neoliberal policies has been washed away and forgotten in the language of individual distress."[25].

Meanwhile, both the bio-psychiatric model and neoliberal economics are global. There is a lot of evidence that, with the help of the DSM and

22   Horwitz, Allan V. and Wakefield, Jerome C. The Loss of Sadness: How Psychiatry Transformed Normal Sorrow Into Depressive Disorder Oxford University Press, 2007
23   Martinez, Elizabeth and Garcia, Arnoldo "What is Neo-liberalism?—A Brief Definition for Activists" Corpwatch.org 1996. Web. 1 April, 2010 . http://www.corpwatch.org/article.php?id=376
24   Brown, Wendy. Neo-liberalism and the End of Liberal Democracy Theory & Event. Volume 7, Issue 1, 2003.
http://muse.jhu.edu/login?uri=/journals/theory_and_event/v007/7.1brown.html
25   Moncrieff, Joanna "Neo-liberalism and bio-psychiatry: a marriage of convenience" Libratory Psychiatry: Philosophy, Politics, and Mental Health. Ed Carl I. Cohen Cambridge University Press, 2008 235-55. Print

the pharmaceutical industry, the bio-psychiatric paradigm is rapidly spreading throughout the world. Joanna Moncrieff in *Neo-liberalism and Bio-psychiatry* says "From Hong Kong to Tanzania to Sri Lanka, Western ideas of mental illnesses—depression, schizophrenia, anorexia, and PTSD are growing, with the resulting loss of traditional forms of knowledge and understanding of health and wellness."[26]

A Growing Movement at the Intersection of Social Justice and Mental Health

The situation is difficult to discuss partly because it lies at the intersection of different fields—from biology to neuroscience, cultural studies, economics, history, and politics. It is challenging to untangle the social, political, and economic hijacking of what is considered mental health and illness, when these are states we tangibly live with and have to navigate on a daily basis. How do the language and diagnostic categories affect our understanding of ourselves?

If we are going to do anything to change the mental health system we need to acknowledge how fundamentally flawed the current model is, how little room it leaves for alternate views of health and wellness, how it privileges the knowledge of scientists and experts, and belittles the resources of local communities, families, and alternative health care practitioners. We need a clearer distinction between the usefulness of modern psychiatric medications, and the reductionist bio-psychiatric paradigm that reduces our emotions and behavior to chemicals and neurotransmitters. We need to talk publicly about the relationship between unhealthy economic policies, the pharmaceutical industry, and our mental health. We need to redefine what it means to be mentally healthy, not just on an individual level, but on a collective level, community and even worldwide. We need to move from the ideology of disease and its treatment, to public health and disease prevention. We need to look closely and critically at the root causes of our mental distress, because it is likely that many of the causes come from the same ideology that offers the current bio-psychiatric solutions.

When I think about solutions, I envision a vibrant social and political movement made up of a coalitions of local community groups and professionals in the field—people who understand the importance of economic justice and global solidarity and the critical need for accepting mental diversity and not falling into the trap of trying to fit into a society that is obviously sick. I envision a movement that has the wisdom and reverence for the human spirit and understands the intertwined complexity of these things we call mental health and wellness. I would love to see focus groups of scholars and activists who can help to make relevant theories and histories easier to penetrate.

Fundamentally, if we are going to shift the current mental health paradigm we are going to need a movement that both has the political savvy

26   Watters, Ethan. *Crazy Like Us: The Globalization of the American Psyche.* New York: Free Press, 2010.

to understand how to fight the system, and the tools to be able to take care of each other as the world gets even crazier. I think some of the answers are going to come from revisiting the useful aspects of countercultural movements that were questioning the mainstream models of mental health in the 1960s and 70s. From humanistic and Jungian psychology to encounter groups and gestalt therapy, from the Feminist consciousness-raising groups, to the more radical aspects of the "human potential movement," there were many powerful ideas that came from the intersection of Eastern spiritual philosophies and Western psychotherapies and that were informed by the political charged atmosphere of the times and in the 21st century seem to have been virtually eliminated from the dominant dialogue in psychiatry and psychology. While clearly there were flaws in those young movements that seemingly got crushed in their tracks or channeled into a watered-down, capitalist-friendly New Age market, I think it would be quite a worthwhile project to identify which of their aspects and tools would be useful to embrace in a contemporary radical mental health movement.

•   •   •

THE OPPOSITE OF BEING DEPRESSED

An interview with Sascha by Al Burian (Berlin, Germany. June, 2011)

Al Burian: (turning on recorder) I think it's working. Cool. But we're both so soft-spoken, it's just going to just be a mumble.

Sascha: I can be soft-spoken, but I can be really loud too. You should have seen me yesterday with all those Germans. It was hard to get them to react. There were about fifty people in the room, and I literally got up out of my chair, stood in the middle of the room, and was waving my arms around, making these huge hand gestures. "Do you all understand me? Say YES!" (laughs) People were very uncomfortable.

A: Well, Germans are pretty reserved.

S: But I got a lot of positive feedback afterwards! (laughs)

A: In Germany, when you're playing a show, the audience just stands there and doesn't react, but then afterwards everyone has a really intelligent commentary.

S: Yeah, that's even more infuriating, actually. Because it's a concert, where you're supposed to be losing your shit.

A: Right, whereas you were…well, what were you doing, exactly?

S: I was facilitating a workshop on radical peer-based mental health support. I was creating a space for people to think about issues that normally are really uncomfortable to talk about. This is kind of the stuff I've been doing for years like getting a room full of leftists, anarchists, radicals, punks—whatever—together, and saying, hey, look, as you might have noticed, people in our community often have a really hard time with their mental health, and don't know what to do when someone's in a crisis. The language we use to talk about mental health stifles us. So I present some new words and ideas to talk about. I don't just make it theoretical. I actually reveal really personal things, talk about getting locked up in a psych hospital, talk about what it was like to be really alienated and suicidal. You know, things that it's normally uncomfortable for people to talk about.

A: Did it seem to you like social circumstances in Germany are different? Were people concerned with the same issues that they are in the U.S.?

S: Well, one very striking difference between the U.S. and Germany that I've been seeing is, in the U.S., psychoanalysis really fell out of fashion in the Eighties. It's very hard, unless you have money, to actually go see a therapist. It's a luxury. Whereas people here still have health insurance. The reason it happened in the States is that the pharmaceutical companies are so powerful there that they just crushed it… But, as far as your question, are people in Germany concerned with the same things? Are the issues the same? The answer is, yeah. Sure. Feeling alienated and lonely, wanting others to understand them, not knowing how to take care of someone in a crisis, needing support, wanting more resources, wanting better language to talk about these things. It was all the same stuff.

A: The social context isn't that different, I guess.

S: One thing that is intriguing to me about the culture where we come from in the US, which can't really be separated from the economics, is the whole ideology behind bio-psychiatry, the idea that our problems reside within our brains, and that there's brain chemistry.

A: That our brains are like car engines that just need more oil.

S: Right. It's incredibly ahistorical. I think we come from a very ahistorical land.

A: It's very American to reinvent yourself.

S: Yeah, but it's spreading—obviously—it's spreading all over the world.

Part of me was conscious of that; I knew I was coming to Berlin, this city with an enormous amount of history. And that I was going to be doing a workshop in a community that was very conscious of that history. So that was interesting. I feel like I'm often doing this work from the belly of the beast, you know? The bio-psychiatric model is really coming out of the U.S. One of the things I feel really good about with the culture of the Icarus Project is that we've created the space to be able to have conversations outside of the bounds of bio-psychiatry, to create a more empowering culture. We've created this system, people call them "mad maps" or "wellness maps." First of all, you figure out what it means to be in a good state of mind—how do I know when I'm well? How does it feel in my body? What kind of stuff do I think about when I'm well? And then, we write it down for ourselves and our friends. Like, if you don't see me come out of my room, then you're allowed to knock on the door and ask, "Hey, what's going on? Have you eaten? Have you slept?"

A: How did you get involved in this kind of work?

S: I was raised by really intense people. I was raised by a man who grew up in the 1950's in Queens, New York—he was a working class Irish Catholic guy who got politicized when he was a teenager and worked for the Civil Rights Movement. He was a radical journalist who went down south in the Freedom Rides. He was a really angry man. He had an enormous temper. And also, he had a disease called cystic fibrosis, so he was dying from the time I was a little kid. So I got to watch this man who was, you know—my dad, die slowly and painfully.

And then, my mom, who was as equally intense—was raised a working class Greek Jew in the South Bronx. She came of age and got politicized working for the John Kennedy campaign. It was that generation. She was more idealistic than my dad, my mom is the classic good liberal. Those are the people that raised me, and probably what had a bigger influence on me as a kid is that they hated each other. (laughs). I grew up between two different houses.

A: They were separated?

S: Yeah. My mom left him, in 1977, when I was three. At the height of when lots of women were leaving their husbands. Actually my first memory is from the NYC blackout of '77, when I was two and a half. The lights were off in the little room I lived in. That's the only memory I have of my parents being together, and I can pinpoint it to that specific moment.

I have a stepmother, too, who was married to my father, who is a Jewish lady that was raised by communists in San Jose, and came of age in the United Farm Workers Union, and was raised around Mexicans. So I come from this very political family.

A: Activism is not something you had to seek out.

S: No, but my way of rebelling when I was a teenager was, I started hanging out with the anarchists.

A: Why was that such a rebellion?

S: I was raised by people who really believed in electoral politics. And were culturally pretty straight. My parents were both a little bit older. When the Sixties were happening, they were... I mean, they listened to the Beatles. But they were definitely not hippies.

My father died the night before my bar mitzvah, when I turned thirteen. I found the anarchists and punks when I was fourteen. As a fourteen-year-old, I ended up smack in the middle of the Tompkins Square Riots. (laughs)

Also, I kissed a girl at camp. She had a Misfits T-shirt and listened to the Sex Pistols. Then, a friend went to Bleeker Bob's, a record store in New York City, and got two tapes: Operation Ivy *Energy*, which had just come out, and *The Day The Country Died* by the Subhumans. We listened to that shit incessantly.

When I was sixteen, my mom wanted to get me out of New York for the summer, because I was getting arrested all the time at demonstrations. I was a pretty angry and rebellious teenager. This is one of the things I always say in the workshops, is that we do the political work that we do because we want to change the world, but underneath that we have our own internal reasons, whatever it is that fuels it. And for me, it was the death of my father. I was just so angry and heartbroken.

Punk was an important part of my life. I was into the scene in New York, and went to Berkeley for the summer to study. That was the summer when all the riots happened in People's Park. That was formative. I fell in love for the first time and was smashing windows on Telegraph Avenue and ended up in Oakland Juvenile Detention Facility.

A: You were talking earlier today about the need to be part of something bigger than yourself...

S: The first time I felt that sense of being greater was being at a punk show on the Lower East Side. Being in a little squatted basement somewhere, pressed up against all these people, knocking into each other. It was like, "oh my god, this is where I belong." Meanwhile, my mom was going to Friday night services over at the synagogue. Which was the most boring thing I could imagine.

A: Perfect thing to rebel against.

S: Well, that's the irony, all these years later I'm a lot more interested in Judaism. I studied Hebrew last summer.

A: So you came around to embrace your Jewish side?

A: Well, it's old. Punk is not so old. That's one thing that's so fascinating about being in Berlin. I mean, what it means to be a Jew here compared to being a Jew in New York City. It's the dominant culture where I come from, in a lot of ways. I was raised to think of myself as another white person. American Jews have historically played an enormous role in the creation of American white identity, and what it means to be a successful American. So many Jews were determined to give up their identity from the Old Country because it was so stigmatized. And America offered the ability to do that. But this idea of whiteness—it's very complex.

A: Maybe this is too big of a jump, but how did you go from punk shows on the Lower East Side to living in a yoga ashram for a year?

S: Do you remember where we first met?

A: Sure, Portland. We were both going to Reed College. We hung out a few times and then you disappeared. That happened once a week at Reed.

S: My senior year of high school, I had all these friends that started shooting dope. My girlfriend started shooting dope. I got really scared. I was going to ride freight trains around the country and have adventures. Instead, I studied really hard, I got good scores on my SAT's, and I got into Reed, which is where my stepmother had gone.

My dad wanted me to go to Harvard. He went to City College. I was raised by this guy who was identified as working class and hating rich people. Yet he wanted his son to go to Harvard. He wanted something better for me, but he also had very traditional ideas of what "better" meant.

Going to Reed was a terrible idea. I left all my friends behind…these days the first thing I do when I'm speaking in college classrooms is ask, "How many of you have a Facebook account?" Everybody raises their hand. "OK, of all those 'friends,' how many people would be there for you in a crisis?" I had friends, but no one who was really close.

When I was eighteen I was locked up for the first time and diagnosed as bipolar. It was the summer of 1993. I spent the whole day walking around, convinced that it was my last day on earth. See, there's this thing that happens when you get manic: It's like the opposite of being depressed. When you're depressed, nothing has any meaning, but when you're manic. . .

A: Everything is loaded with hidden messages and subtexts?

S: Right, exactly. So, that day in New York, I got down in the subway tunnel and started walking along the tracks. I walked through two stations before they pulled me off. It was a Friday night at rush hour. I didn't actually think that I was trying to kill myself, I just thought it was what I was supposed to do.

A: Do you take bipolar medication now?

S: I've been taking Lithium for the last ten years. It seems like there's a lot of people that take Lithium and have a really bad reaction to it. On the other hand, it's the only drug that works for a whole lot of people, including me. I don't plan to be on the stuff forever. But I have a pretty intense personality, you know?

That's how I ended up in the ashram.

For years, what I used to say was that I regulated my brain chemistry through a mixture of Lithium and marijuana. Because they are like opposites to each other. I could stay stable with the Lithium, and then smoking weed is instant mania. Now I've learned that I have to be really careful with it. Three years ago, I lost it again. That's how I ended up in the ashram.

A: What happened?

S: I totally lost interest in other people. I felt connected to larger forces outside of myself. . . . I can't let myself go there too much. For sure, if I'm ever going to get off of Lithium, I'm not going to be able to smoke weed!

A: In that sense, it isn't so ahistorical.

S: What do you mean?

A: The idea that you've got some brain chemistry that you need to regulate. Coming up with some chemicals to level you out—people have been using drugs and alcohol for that purpose for a long time, pretty much for as long as there have been people.

S: Well, you could draw a parallel between Monsanto trying to regulate seeds, and governments telling people, no, you can't use those kinds of drugs, even though you can grow them, you can produce them yourself, you have control of them—you have to do *these* kinds of drugs, that we have control over. But for sure the drugs can be really helpful. Sometimes you just can't think your way out of it.

I think that's really key. I thought about that quite a bit yesterday, interacting with the Germans, who are all clearly so up in their heads. Part of me wanted to just say, "Ok, everybody up, out of your chairs! Let's do some breathing exercises!"

That's what the yoga ashram taught me. I was depressed as fuck when I showed up in that place. And it was regimented, it was almost militaristic in its regimentation—praying, meditating, doing yoga. You make a three-month commitment, and you can go live there. You'd get up at five, at 5:30 you're sitting in the temple meditating, you do that for half an hour, chant in Sanskrit for another half an hour, then you go do two hours of yoga, eat breakfast, and then you work all day.

A: Work on what?

S: Just physical labor, stuff that keeps you occupied. The idea is that you're supposed to think about God all day. It was fascinating to me. I was raised in a very secular environment. But there is something missing from that, you know? And it wasn't that I need to be bowing down to statues of Ganesha or Vishnu. It was the feeling of being around a bunch of people who actually, really *valued* feeling that connection to something higher. I could relate to it. Even though I wasn't raised in a spiritual context, the experiences that I've had with mania have been so spiritual, if I had been raised a Christian I'm sure I would have thought I was Jesus.

A: Instead you're an anarchist.

S: (laughs) I've read my history. I learned about the European Enlightenment, made sense of where the philosophies of the sub-culture I came from drew their historical understanding. Marxism is in some ways very Biblical. There are a lot of things about Buddhist philosophy that are pretty punk. All of these things eventually overlap. I don't think there's any future in de-spiritualized communities, or cultures. You can look at the Left in the U.S., and how much better the religious right is at organizing, because they have God on their side. Compare that to my mom in her apartment in Manhattan, reading The *Nation* magazine, trying to understand everything in these Enlightenment era constructs of Reason.

For myself, it came from having what I didn't realize at the time were spiritual experiences—in the punk scene, with the anarchists. The ashram was so weird, but it was good for me. I had been living there for two months and I one day asked this question to the Swami: what is the relationship between Hinduism and yoga? And he gave me a good answer, which is that every major religion has mystical components to it, the Jews have Kabbalah, Christianity has all these Gnostic sects, Muslims have Sufism, and Yoga is the mystical element of Hinduism. It's more complicated than that, but if you just take that and think about it—all of these mystical philosophies have a lot more in common with each other than the larger religions do. There is a core set of beliefs about Oneness. You can see where the religions come from. They come from these brilliant people who are in touch with stuff that not everyone is in touch with. And then, ideas get formed around them, and at some point it gets really fucking stupid, because it doesn't make any sense when it's so removed from the original context. Because I come from the punk scene, which is very much a sub-cultural community, I have a large appreciation for how subcultures end up affecting the mainstream. But in order for them to continue to do it, they have to stay subcultures, they can't totally become mainstream. The metaphor I started using some time ago is dandelions, check it out; *He walks over to the side of the airstrip, where, in a patch of scraggly grass there are, indeed, dandelions blooming.*

Anytime you see stuff growing, there's the topsoil that it's growing in and then there's the sub-soil below it—that's the heavier stuff that's based on the bedrock that's further below. Most of the action is happening in the topsoil, but then there are certain plants, like dandelions, that have taproots that go down into the sub-soil, and pull up nutrients from the sub-soil that can't be accessed by the other plants. When the dandelions die, that stuff breaks down into the topsoil. So they are a necessary part of the eco-system. You have to have the plants with the deep taproots.

•   •   •

Generative Narratives and the Counterculture Psychiatrists

I went to a conference in Phoenix, AZ called Innovations in Public Service Psychiatry put on by the American Association of Community Psychiatry and an organization called Recovery Innovations. It was interesting stepping into this unfamiliar scene and I made unexpected friends.

Brad Lewis, my cool psychiatrist friend who teaches at NYU, invited me to present with him on Narrative Psychiatry and the Icarus Project. For outsiders critical of mainstream psychiatry, "community psychiatry" is a counterculture within biomedical psychiatry. I don't mean they had flowers in their hair or facial piercings. They were wearing suits in a hotel with carpets that smelled like terrible chemicals. But compared to psychiatrists touting the bio-psych line, these people are radicals, and I am heartened that they are attempting to shift the dominant paradigm.

Community Psychiatry has its origins in the 1963 signing of the Community Mental Health Centers Construction Act, which established more than 750 community mental health centers throughout the U.S. While they were mainstream, these centers emerged during the rise of bio-psychiatry and big pharma in the 1980s. People attracted to community psychiatry aren't doing it for the money—they want to make a difference in people's lives.

Flash forward to 2012 and the main narrative that Community Psychiatry is using in the psychiatric arena is "recovery." To a radical interested in large scale social and political transformation, "recovery" misses the mark, but within the dominant language of "brain disease" and "lifelong mental illness," the narrative of "recovery" has an important role to play and opens up space for dialogue and hope.

Amidst presentations and workshops I heard language like "mental health in not simply a function of biology, genetics, or personal choice—it is also a function of the social conditions in which people are born, grow, live, work, and age"; "well-being must be measured as mental, physical, spiritual, and social"; "medicine should be about health, not disease, prevention, not repair."; "shared decision making—the value of relationship in informing choice"; "understanding the link between coercive, directive practices and inadvertent re-traumatization"; and "recovery is remembering who you are and using your strengths to become all that you were meant to be." These are doctors who see their former patients as experts and teachers and having important wisdom to share.

What impressed and surprised me was that it was full of people who like and feel comfortable around "mad" people, can relate to our kind because they're around us all the time, and don't just see us as people to drug into normality. When I talked about the *Harm Reduction Guide to Coming Off Psych Drugs* and how critical it is that psychiatrists understand that one day their patients will have to come off of them, people clapped! Borrowing from Brad Lewis' language in *Narrative Psychiatry* "No matter how many psych drugs we take or don't take, the fact is that we think in stories. Bio-psychiatry, like Recovery, is a story, and one of them is pathological and one of them is generative."

We desperately need to shift the story.

There are deeply ingrained power dynamics in the discipline of psychiatry, and although the "peers" get to be a part of the dialogue, at the AACP they're not running the show. By definition, reform moments take the steam out of revolutions, the history of the Nonprofit Industrial Complex is about giving jobs to discontents and channeling radical energy into institutions to keep capitalism going. The Icarus Project has been talking about "dangerous gifts" for years, and I'm realizing that the "gift" is not only about sensitivity. It's also a kind of yearning. We know the world can be better and it's our responsibility to make it so.

Mindful Occupation

And then the Occupy movement exploded onto the world stage. It happened so fast, and it captured the imaginations of people all over the globe. From the occupation of a small park in the Wall Street area of lower Manhattan, within a couple months there were more than 1,600 occupations around the country and the world, some big, most small, some no more than one angry soul on the side of the road with a sign that said "We are the 99 percent."

For me it was like watching a thousand Tompkins Square Parks erupt all over the country. I knew there must have been so many young people whose minds were suddenly being blown open by the possibilities of free space and collective practices—turning off the television and getting into the streets. Except now so many of us had smartphones in our hands and were broadcasting videos to each other as it was happening! We actually had become the media! Facebook and Twitter were allowing everyone to network in ways that would have been unimaginable back at the beginning of the millennium, during the WTO protests in Seattle, let alone when I was a teenager in the streets of Manhattan and the police were beating our heads in. In YouTube videos, we watched crowds in New York City use "the people's mic," where one person spoke, and the words were repeated by everyone in shouting distance. And then we started copying the practice in Oakland. Within days people were doing it all over the world.

Suddenly huge groups of people, all over the country, were talking about economic justice and the system's greed and corruption. The enormity of student debt, tuition hikes, foreclosures, unemployment, medical costs, and the other economic afflictions of average Americans suddenly moved to the top of the news. A wave of energy was washing over the world, from the Arab spring uprisings popping up all over the Middle East to the 15M movement a.k.a. Indignados in cities around Spain, to the Occupy movement in America, we were manifesting a massive force of global energy against capitalism. A whole bunch of strangers all over the country were meeting one another and learning group decision making practices that came right out of anarchist practice, waiting underground for just this opportunity. Through occupations of public space, these ideas of direct democracy were being put into practice—horizontally-organized structures like general assemblies and spokes councils, aimed at consensus-based decisions, were being applied by thousands of people, many of whom had no idea what anarchism was.

In Oakland, not far from my house, the Occupation was happening in Oscar Grant Plaza, a park renamed by protesters for a young black man who was murdered by the police. It was smack in the middle of downtown for everyone to see and walk through. Early on the tent city that had been lovingly created was violently evicted at 3am using tanks and a small army of police, and the following night thousands of us were in the streets to take it back. It was a wild and diverse scene. So many young people, and so many old friends, came out of the woodwork. There was food, art, music, there were places to hear lectures, places to read, places for childcare and play, a chillout/crisis intervention space with peer support. There were lots of tents to sleep in. People were calling it the Oakland Commune. And of course it faced repeated violent evictions.

One night, in a confrontation with the police, an Iraq War veteran named Scott Olson was shot in the head with a tear gas canister. The street erupted in police violence when the crowd defiantly refused to disperse in a thick cloud of chemical gas. The next night more than two thousand of us showed up for a General Assembly in the plaza and we spent three hours communicating by people's mic, one phrase at a time, so that every person had a chance to hear. One group made a proposal for a general strike and we broke up into groups of 20 to discuss the proposal. Suddenly I was face to face with a bunch of strangers, surrounded by groups of people all discussing the pros and cons of the same vision. Never in my life had I felt group solidarity on such a large scale. By consensus we decided to call a strike.

A few days later I ended up on International Blvd. in the mostly Latino Fruitvale neighborhood, going store to store asking the owners to post General Strike HUELGA flyers in their windows. I had amazing conversations with folks on the street in my rusty Spanish about the economy, the police, *la migra* and global revolution. I wandered into the Cesar Chavez public library to look for a bathroom and walked right into the seed library, modeled after the one we started in 2000 in Berkeley. I had this sense during those days that all of the little community projects, were rising to the surface, visible and connected, like they'd been waiting for a healthy climate to flourish.

On the day of the general strike there was a giant carnival spilling out from the tent city in Oscar Grant Plaza. Thousands of people took over downtown Oakland. The Teamsters union was serving BBQ, Food Not Bombs was serving veggie food, there was live hip-hop blasting from speakers and tons of people were dancing. There were teach-ins about urban permaculture and radical ecology. There was a place for people to write their stories of economic hardship and display them on a wall. By the mid afternoon there were tens of thousands of us in the streets, and we marched to the Oakland docks, shutting down the port with the solidarity of the dock workers. People were ecstatic. There was a palpable feeling of solidarity across the usual divides of age and race and class. There was a dizzying hope that everything could be different, and then the exhilaration in the moments when it already was.

Amidst all of the social and political ferment, I got invited to be a part of a group called Occupy Manifest, mostly young New Yorkers who had been organizing on the ground at Zuccotti Park from the beginning. It was organized by some old friends from the Watershed Center who think strategically about long-term systemic change. The Manifest group was a really important turning point for me because I had the opportunity to engage with fellow activists on a deep spiritual level in ways I had been dreaming about since my days at the ashram. These were some words I was inspired to write at the time to explain why it felt so important.

Why Occupy Manifest is So Important to the Larger Struggle

There are points in history where the social and political fault-lines rise to the surface and large, previously unimaginable shifts have the potential to happen quickly. If the collective infrastructure is in place, those of us engaged in activism and organizing can do the work of "hospicing" the dying of worldviews and institutions that no longer serve, and "midwifing" the birth of new models and visions into existence. We are living in such exciting and volatile times. Of the projects I have encountered evolving from the Occupy Wall Street movement, Occupy Manifest holds the most potential for raising the consciousness of the participants within the movement and laying the foundations for advancing long-term systemic change.

The Intersection of Social Justice Activism and Spiritual Practice

Ultimately why I think Occupy Manifest is so powerful is that *it lies at the fruitful intersection of social justice activism and spiritual practice.* Manifest aims to transform our routine spaces into transformational spaces. It recognizes the deep power that exists between people and actively fosters that power in a group context. Every participant has a personal "breakthrough initiative" that they work on in relationship to Manifest and to the larger movement. People's Breakthrough Initiatives relate to their areas of passion, from organizing students around the debt crisis to getting corporate money out of politics, through neighborhood teach-ins to building mental health practices into activist security culture. We spend time together in retreat, practicing communication tools, experimenting with new language, cross-pollinating our ideas, and fostering group trust and play. Monica Sharma, the former Director of Leadership and Capacity Development for the United Nations, facilitates the process and there is a lot of experience in the room to channel the collective energy.

Accessing Our "Wisdom Source"

Many of us come to the movement with years of experience working with our minds and emotions, but not knowing how to access our hearts. If we are working from our hearts, we're often not conscious about it. Early in the group process, Monica draws an important distinction between acting from "emotion" and acting from "heart/spirit." She uses the language of *the broken hearted courage*—the ability to access the pain our hearts feel from bearing witness to all the many layers of suffering and tragedy on the planet. This is different—although overlapping—from personal emotions we feel of pain and loss in our lives. This larger *broken hearted courage* gives us access to something transcendent, a connection with forces greater than us, and gives us the ability to step into a space where we're not acting from our egos but from an engaged observer mind. Monica leads the group through a series of exercises to tap into this deeper space where it is possible to access compassion, generosity, and curiosity, and then brings the conversation right back to the practical—how to grow the movement in a sustainable way.

New Tools and Shared Principles

Occupy Manifest begins with the understanding that, if there's not going to be a set hierarchical leadership structure, we have to have a minimum set of collective tools, techniques, and a set of principles that stay constant. We spend lots of time developing these tools through group conversations, and "building the ship while it's sailing." We speak of leadership as the ability to stay grounded in our principles and foster leadership in others. These are some of the new ideas and paradigm shifting questions I've been exposed to in the Occupy Manifest training:

- What are the design principles that lead to changing a system?
- Generative listening: Listening with an intention to shift and grow
- Emotional intelligence: Self-awareness and self-regulation, social awareness, and knowing strengths and limitations
- The importance of noticing gaps in integrity—otherwise they will only get bigger
- The importance of noticing, understanding, and addressing the background conversations
- Drawing a distinction between destructive anger and dignified outrage
- Sensing the commitment behind the complaint
- Focusing on intended impact

The Importance of Retreat

The retreat is an essential component of this transformational process. Having the space to step outside of conditioned roles and come together as a group allows necessary bonding and trust building if a movement is going to have solid foundations. It was only upon returning to the frenetic pace of the city that I realized just what an important gift it was to have the space and time for connection to get to know people.

My Breakthrough Initiative "T-MAPs"

I was invited to participate in Occupy Manifest without having any idea of what I was getting myself into, and how much it would shift my consciousness in relationship to my work. My "breakthough initiative" came early when I showed up at the first retreat. While I had envisioned the idea for the project, it took Monica's coaching to draw the details out of me in front of the group and, more importantly, my actual experience of participating in the Occupy Manifest retreats to realize what my project might look like if it was successful.

I call my project T-MAPs (Transformative Mutual Aid Practices) and at its heart it aims to empower people to take better care of each other. It's a set of interactive workshops and materials that provide tools and resources for building a personal "map" of healthiness and resilience practices which can be shared with others.

Through the Manifest process, I recognized that my own inner capacity of dignity—specifically around the shame regarding mental health issues—was a key factor in being able to do this work. My own inner capacity needed to be reflected in the principles of the project.

When we discussed intended impact, I was struck by Monica's story of combating rape in a small village in India by, among other things, focusing on creating positive male figures in the community. I had never seen so clear an example—in a polarized and traumatizing situation—of "focusing on the positive impact" rather than combating the problem. Similar to my T-MAPs project, we're "fighting mental illness" by not even framing our work in the context of mental illness but of "mental health." I understood that it was important to circumvent the "illness'" language, but now I have a principle and a philosophy to back me up.

Having a room full of people who are engaged in similar projects, being coached by a visionary expert, and then given the space to share and grow together, is a recipe for building a stronger and more effective movement. I feel incredibly grateful to be a part of the emerging process.

•　　　•　　　•

I returned back to Oakland after the first Occupy Manifest retreat and the camp at Oscar Grant Plaza was having a lot of problems. Like many Occupy camps around the country, there were regular internal crises. As we all learned, bringing so many people together in close quarters ended up magnifying many of the social problems we already deal with on a daily basis. The poverty, sexism, racism, addiction, and myriad forms of psychic suffering rampant in our society was reproduced in the Occupy camps. Women and gender variant folks got harassed and assaulted. Many people of color didn't feel comfortable in the white-dominated organizing spaces. There was friction between the homeless and the housed. People who were perceived to have untreated mental health problems were often disruptive and those in positions of leadership were at a loss for how to respond. There was a lot of drinking and chaos that made it hard to sleep at night. On top of that, many folks who came to the camps were already traumatized by the world, and then faced the constant danger of police harassment and brutality.

In response to these needs, I got involved with a group of Icarus Project members and Mad Pride activists from around the country who decided to remotely collaborate on a zine called *Mindful Occupation: Rising Up Without Burning Out*. Its intention was to discuss the importance of self-care, mutual aid, coping skills in times of stress, and also provide material about first aid for emotional trauma, navigating crisis, and healing from and preventing sexual assault. We put it out there with the aim of inspiring teach-ins, skill-shares, and peer-support groups to help sustain the movement over the long term. And hopefully we planted some good seeds.

The Occupy movement brought a lot of people together. Despite a coordinated attack to crush the movement, it's still all over the place and growing with new names and forms. Occupy Homes groups are fighting banks through strategic home takeovers and defending homeowners—often successfully—from being foreclosed on. Through Strike Debt, activists are striving to build a people's movement to break the chains of debt and create new bonds of solidarity. After Hurricane Sandy hit New York & New Jersey, people organized into the disaster relief network called Occupy Sandy, often outperforming FEMA, National Guard, and local police. The list of Action, Issue, Regional, and Project Hubs on InterOccupy.net illustrate many avenues of activism issuing from the Occupy movement. For many, each is a new excuse to see each other out in the streets and active in our communities. Although the initial energy which unified Occupy appears to have dispersed into nothing, it still radiates out into the world, gaining strength as it influences more and more lives. I expect that, whenever it comes back together, we will be stronger than ever.

Radical Mentorship and the Future

I've experienced explosions of organizing activity in social justice arenas—from the anti-gentrification battles on the Lower East Side to the explosion of the Global Justice Movement to the rise and fall of Occupy. I've witnessed and participated in creative activist movements and peer support networks for a significant portion of my life. And I've seen excitement over Icarus and radical approaches to mental health wax and wane and wax again. But how do we sustain these movements over the long-term? How do we, as individuals, sustain ourselves—our physical and emotional and spiritual health—over the long-term? It's clear we need more mentorship and inter-generational solidarity, the kind of support and courage one might find in a loving family. For movements to endure, we need to put lots of energy into relationship building, not just organizing strategy. We need to focus on lasting connections and developing mentorship.

We all come to our movement work traumatized in different ways, trying to heal ourselves as we're healing the world. One of the most important things we can do is learn life skills that work for us, and pass them along to others who need them. To manifest real, sustainable changes, we have to change both ourselves and the institutions that harbor our old belief systems. To really grow and thrive we have to address racism, sexism, ableism, and other prejudices that are internalized in our present movements. We need to collectively practice the values that align us with the world we want to see. I want to see us actually live the values that we want to inspire in other people. I want to see us do the spiritual work necessary to be solid organizers and good mentors.

As I'm turning 38, I'm finding myself stepping into the role of a mentor to younger activists while looking for guides of my own. What would it look like if there was a culture of leaderfulness, rather than leaderlessness, in our movements? To step into a mentor role is one of the hardest things to do in a community that rarely likes to acknowledge the importance of leaders. But what if we thought of leaderfulness as the ability to stay grounded in our principles and foster leadership in others? What if we had a set of shared practices, tools, and values that allowed us to communicate and make decisions without traditional hierarchical leadership? What if we applied the tools of small groups like Occupy Manifest, and gave them the resources to replicate into larger networks while holding onto the tangible love and support that comes from working together to make the world a better place? What if we had more individual and collective maps that reminded us how to take better care of one other?

While the internet has globalized our consciousness and allowed us to communicate in nonhierarchical ways, it has left us without the means for deep connection—the kind of encounter that can't happen sitting alone in front of a computer screen no matter how many millions of people are connected into the network. So many of us have an intense longing for authenticity and the desire not only to be a "part of the solution" but to actively feel the power of group process at work. I want to be a part of a movement where people actually hang out in person: in each other's homes, in the city streets, out on land growing our food. I want to see more takeovers of public space where we take good care of each other. I have a hunch that in the coming years there is going to be a greater desire for face-to-face conversations about making the world a better place. And I'll be doing my part to bring lessons and wisdom from the movements, healing modalities, and spiritual traditions I've crossed paths with that have clues to a brighter future.

•　　•　　•

I've taken a long and winding trail of golden thread, sometimes left by a person other than myself. There have been so many times over the years when I was sure I was stuck in an endless labyrinth of suffering and madness. When I thought that the only way out was by taking my own life. In the dark times, no matter how much I tried to leave a trail for myself with words, I didn't have the skills to bring peace to the warring factions within. If I looked inside myself there was no solid ground. If I looked to society to mirror my life back to me, I was a mentally ill criminal.

If I hadn't been locked up and forcefully medicated when I was 18—if, instead of the psych ward there had been a place I could have gone with caring people who understood what was happening to me and been allowed to go through my "psychotic" process and get to the other side of it—I don't think I ever would have ended up in another psychiatric hospital. I don't think I'd be taking this Lithium Carbonate I've been putting in my blood stream every day for the last 12 years. I don't think I'd have this bipolar disorder label that keeps close-minded people from taking me seriously because they can always just write me off as being crazy. There are understood ways to help people in psychotic processes, especially in the early stages, and our society isn't yet enlightened enough to put the financial resources in to develop trainings and programs to create them.

We desperately need to create sanctuaries for people who are having the kind of spiritual and emotional crises I was having when I was a teenager. The world will be a better place for it. Some of us are just more sensitive than others and that doesn't mean we need to be taking more psych drugs to suppress our symptoms. A breakdown has the potential to be a breakthrough. It's taken me decades to make sense of what happened to me when I was young, and many people in my situation never have that chance. Never underestimate the healing power of individual and collective story telling. There is a small but growing network of alternative institutions in the recovery movement—respites, 24/7 sanctuaries, and runaway houses that reach out to young people who are having their first psychotic episodes and don't want to end up in the mainstream psychiatric system. There are already a bunch of people who are working on developing these kind of institutions. They need support. You can learn more about this growing movement at the theicarusproject.net and madinamerica.com websites.

•　　　•　　　•

When I asked Juan Carlos to write an ending for this book, he sent me this:

Hey my brother! Well, it's been many years since we traveled together. The situation in Mexico is bad these days, there is a lot of violence, the army is on the streets fighting against drug dealers, and many people have died. There are 30 businessmen and corrupt politicians who manage the destinies of this country and what awaits us is surely worse.

We can only keep fighting and resisting, transforming what needs to be changed. My mom died recently and my life took a drastic turn. I still live with my dad and two of my brothers. I work on a ranch in Aguascalientes, building cottages with natural materials in ancient style.

I have traveled a lot and lived in several cities like San Luis, Mexico, Guadalajara, Puerto Vallarta, and Tepic. I'm further away from the punk movement, but I am still connected with many punk friends.

If you come to Mexico, we can go to Oaxaca to eat mushrooms or to San Luis Potosi to the desert to eat peyote. You are always welcome in my home. Take good care of yourself my brother. I will be here waiting for you.

I hope you remember that night in the desert when death visited us. I looked through its left eye and saw it full of nothing, stuffed till the edge of nothing. Death is all I'm waiting for and till it comes, I continue to learn everything in this crazy world. Goodbye my good friend—*el pinche gringo loco* Sascha. *Viva Zapata, El goberno mata.*

Epilogue

One spring morning, two years after I wrote *Sellout Story*, I was walking down Avenue B and ran into my old friend Scott Sturgeon. As teenagers we played together in a punk band called Choking Victim. I was passing through town on my way to the big protests against the World Bank and had been up all night writing press releases about global debt. I hadn't seen Scott in years. When we were teenagers, Choking Victim was part of the soundtrack to the New York City squatter scene. We played music our friends liked to dance to.

Back in those days I had had a double life—during the day I studied anthropology and literature at Columbia University. But at night I played bass and sang in illegal tenement buildings full of drunk, rowdy kids. We played catchy songs that mixed desperate teenage alienation with violent fantasies of retribution against politicians and police, channeling the restless ghosts of defeated political rebellions of earlier eras. I was taking an urban anthropology class and writing a paper called *The Squatter Subculture of the East Village*. It was an ethnography of the people occupying buildings around Tompkins Square Park and the rebel culture they were creating for themselves outside the law and mainstream society. It was a paper about my friends.

I desperately wanted to be a part of the squatter community, but part of me always felt like an outsider. I feared if people actually knew me, deep down they'd know I didn't belong.

Mid-semester I had an identity crisis because I was writing in the third person about things I wanted to be doing. Some part of me was scared of ending up locked up in the hospital again. But a stronger part of me knew that I needed to be an actor in my life, not just an observer of other people. I didn't want to be singing songs about bondage and frustration. I wanted to actually be free.

I dropped out of school and quit the band. I hit the road and started writing the stories in this book. I never again wrote about my life in the third person—from then on it was "I" and "we" and "us." That critical perspective shift changed not only the narrative of my story, but my identity, and eventually, my destiny.

But I hadn't seen Scott in years and he was dragging me back into an old, unfinished story.

"Sascha, didn't you hear? We got signed to Epitaph Records! They owe you money for those songs you wrote, man! Call them up and they'll start sending you royalty checks!" I stared at him, incredulous.

Five years later I was standing on a stage with Scott in front of a thousand kids packed into the center of Tompkins Square Park, singing our old songs. Hundreds of people were singing along and dancing in an enormous circle pit at the front of the stage. Choking Victim had become a legendary New York City punk band. Our narrative was wrapped up in the lore and mystique of the squatted buildings and riots that had defined my teenage years. Since then punk had morphed into something enormous and foreign, Hot Topic spikes, high production values, and well-financed astroturf rebellion—a caricature of itself.

Somehow, amidst it all, my old friend Scott had crossed over into the realm of a genuine rock star. He had maintained his squatter punk credibility but he was adored—or vehemently hated—by thousands of strangers, mostly alienated teenagers. I was impressed and repulsed by the fame in the same way that I had been as a kid.

Except now I was much closer to it. In the ensuing years I had created my own narrative of freight trains, seeds, and visionary madness. Most of the people in my life knew me more from legend than reality, from stories I had told about myself and songs that had been written about me. I had seemingly triumphed—I had written myself into the myth I wanted to be living. I had escaped the stigma of mental illness by writing a better story, a true-life adventure that was admired and respected, but things aren't always what they seem.

In my own mind I was trapped in the role of being a character in other people's stories. I carried around an imaginary audience in my head following me around, watching my epic love story with the universe, while I played the narrator and the main character. Some part of me had believed that if enough people thought I was amazing, that it would make me amazing. That if a whole bunch of people thought that I was free, that it would make me free.

But freedom was waiting in the most unexpected place of all. Freedom wasn't just about writing a new story for myself, it was also about learning how to step out of that story. In order to get *to the other side*, I needed to smash the mirror of my constructed identity and find my ground in something deeper. I needed to find my breath, my connection to spirit, and my home in my body.

Through a consistent meditation practice I've learned to reach the engaged observer inside myself, the part that's not wrapped up in my story, not concerned with how anyone else sees me, or my achievements. This part has compassion for myself and for others. I've learned how to have conversations with the hurt voices in my head, hold them like children. Be a parent to the part of myself that never felt like he belonged.

Through stories spanning multiple decades and borders and continents and adventures, I have made myself a map that helps me get back to the place where I have the *feeling that my body fits well on my soul*. A place where my mind feels calm and centered and open—able to respond in the present moment and not get lost in some old story. A place where I feel connected to something larger than myself. Sometimes it just takes a few words to remind me how to get back there.

This is how I've had the self-awareness and distance to finish this book, hand you my story and tell you that writing the next chapter is your responsibility.

Acknowledgements and Mad Love

It took a freaky village to finish this book. Having an extended community of friends and collaborators is the secret to what keeps me going in this crazy world, and behind the scenes there are so many people that contributed to making this thing happen through their inspiration and support. In particular:

Jacks McNamara, zebra soul mate, partner in crime, behind the scenes wordsmith.

My mom, Anita Altman, for 38 years of being a wonderful mother and looking out for me through some very challenging times.

Joe Biel, who pushed hard to get this book finished and has shown great skill, patience, and haggling prowess as an editor.

Chris Boarts Larson for many years of support and encouragement in the *Slug and Lettuce* years.

Brad Lewis for believing in me and my crazy visions, and opening so many doors I never would have had the institutional legitimacy to walk through on my own.

Aaron Elliott for switching places and truly helping me feel less alone in this world.

Everyone who's been a part of the Icarus Project community over the last decade, especially all the moderators of the website, the facilitators of the support groups, the language and cultural translators, the artists and bloggers and everyone who's figured out creative ways to get our materials into schools and clinics and hospitals.

Jonah Bossewitch for teaching me the ropes of cultural media activism and for years of late night mad revolution brainstorming.

Brooke Lehman for being there to save my ass at all the right times.

Also:

Sarah Quinter, Jeff Conant, Maryse Mitchell-Brody, Todd Chandler, Kathy Rose, Pastrami, Madigan Shive, Liza Hirsh Medina, A.C. Thompson, Agustina Vidal, Mike "Antipathy" Alberts, Citlalic Ozelomaitl Jeffers Peña, Fly, Kehben Grifter, David Solnit, Dyan Neary, Holly Hodge, Jane Lecroy, Kiran Nigam, Will Hall, Kevin Capliki, Faith Rhyne, Wheels Darling, David Martinez, Isabell Moore, Francine Buckner, Cleo Woelfle-Erskine, Avram Drucker, Christopher Shein, Jennifer Bleyer, Erez Gudes, Andy Stern, Felix Chrome, Eric Drooker, Emma Coleman, Ellery Homosex, Juan Carlos Becerra Garcia, Suki Valentine, Dumpy, Jessica Violetta, Moose Jackson, Kat Aaron, Mike Wilcock, Bec Young, Sol Kinnis, David Nishizaki, Ivy Schlegel, Leonie Sherman, Jason Devastation, Neil Robinson, Gregory Warner, Ben Schwartz, Carey Hope, Jen Angel, Barucha "Calamity" Peller, Corin Wenger, Polly Armour, Cristy Road, Leah Lakshmi Piepzna-Samarasinha, Joanne Rendell, Sarah Lombardo, Barbara Robin Lee, my Fort Rad homies, Beck Cowles and the Ecology Center for hosting BASIL for all these years, Bill Times Up and the Museum of Reclaimed Urban Space, RJ Maccani and Challenging Male Supremacy, Bold Jez and the Occupy Archive, Josh MacPhee and the Interference Archives, the Occupy Manifest Crew, Bluestockings, Al Burian, the Runaway House in Berlin, and everyone who's couch or bed I've slept on or in over the last 20 years.

For your mentorship, teaching, leadership and inspiration:

Monica Sharma, Robert Whitaker, Paul Kivel, Mary Ellen Copeland, Armand Volkas, Aurora Levins Morales, Ian Mackaye, Kate Bornstein, Lane Arye, Daniel Tisman, Mary Kate Connor, Arnold Mindell, Oliver Kellhammer, Ruth Ozeki, Michael Cornwall, Christine Price, Joe Davis, Staci Haines, David Treleaven, Rebecca Solnit, Steve Duncombe, Daniel Mackler, Caledonia Curry, Ruth Messinger, Tom Hayden, Deena Aranoff, Naomi Seidman, Ethan Watters, Sandor Katz, Jordan Flaherty, Daniel Hazen, Michael Aanavi, Sabrina Chapadjiev, Joshua Kahn Russell, Clare Bayard, and my grandpa Fred Hirsh.

Also, The mental health support communities of the Hearing Voices Network, Open Dialog, Madness Radio, WRAP, Voices From the Heart, the National Empowerment Center, Mindfreedom International, and our whole Esalen mad movement strategy crew.

I dedicate this book to all my wild and beautiful friends who are out there making the world a more brilliant and just place.

To my friends who have enough love and bravery to be raising children in the 21st Century.

To my friends who are teaching the new generation in the schools, on the streets, in the jails, and in their homes.

To my friends who are doctors and nurses and acupuncturists and herbalists and homeopaths and midwives and doulas and body workers and therapists and coaches and healers of all shapes and stripes.

To my friends who are CSA farmers and backyard gardeners and seed savers and water havesters and land lovers and permaculture teachers and members of the growing Food Justice movement.

To my friends who are community activists and rabble rousers and labor organizers and muck raking cyber journalists.

To my friends who are freaky sex-positive popular educators and anti-oppression trainers.

To my friends who are radical artists and writers and singers and poets and dancers and DJs and street musicians and sculptors and actors and fire breathers and audio/visual visionaries.

To my friends who are grant writers and administrators and executive directors and are behind the scenes laying the logistical foundations of our movements.

To my friends who are plumbers and carpenters and electricians and mechanics who are building and fixing everything as it breaks and needs to repairing and rebuilding.

To my friends making incredible music that we're all singing together as we tear down the old walls and rebuild this world anew.

To my friends who are running community centers and infoshops and cafes and land projects and radical libraries, opening up their doors for community gatherings and strategic retreats.

We are the minerals underground.
We are the dandelion roots pulling them up to the surface.
We are the radical messages filtering into the mainstream.
We are the seeds spreading far and wide.
We are the change we've been waiting for in this very moment.

If there's one lesson that I want you to take with you after reading this book, it's this:

There are so many of us out here actively building a better world, living loud and proud with our dangerous gifts and big dreams and rebel stories, and we're waiting for you to join us.

Some of the stories in this book originally appeared in these zines:

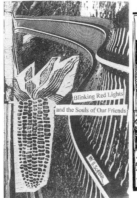